By angels driven
The films of Derek Jarman

cinema voices

Series editor: Matthew Stevens, FLICKS BOOKS
Series consultant: Brian McIlroy, University of British Columbia

This series provides critical assessments of film directors whose work is motivated by social, political or historical concerns, or reveals an opposition to conventional filmmaking systems and structures. The following titles are published or in preparation:

Auteur/provocateur: the films of Denys Arcand
Edited by André Loiselle and Brian McIlroy

Dark alchemy: the films of Jan Švankmajer
Edited by Peter Hames

Queen of the 'B's: Ida Lupino behind the camera
Edited by Annette Kuhn

By angels driven: the films of Derek Jarman
Edited by Chris Lippard

Poet of civic courage: the films of Francesco Rosi
Edited by Carlo Testa

Agent of challenge and defiance: the films of Ken Loach
Edited by George McKnight

A call to action: the films of Ousmane Sembene
Edited by Sheila Petty

By angels driven

The films of Derek Jarman

Edited by
Chris Lippard

cinema voices series

FLICKS BOOKS

A CIP catalogue record for this book is available from the British Library.

ISBN 0-948911-82-4 (Hb)
ISBN 0-948911-87-5 (Pb)

First published in 1996 by

Flicks Books
29 Bradford Road
Trowbridge
Wiltshire BA14 9AN
England
tel   +44 1225 767728
fax +44 1225 760418

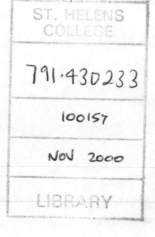
An edition of this book is published in North and South America by Greenwood Press in hardback, and by Praeger Publishers in paperback.

Printed and bound in Great Britain by Bookcraft (Bath) Ltd.

Contents

Acknowledgements   vi

Introduction
Chris Lippard   1

The principle of non-narration in the films of Derek Jarman
Tracy Biga   12

Perverse law: Jarman as gay criminal hero
David Gardner   31

"The rose revived": Derek Jarman and the British tradition
Lawrence Driscoll   65

The process of Jarman's *War Requiem*: personal vision and the
    tradition of fusion of the arts
Joseph A Gomez   84

"The shadow of this time": the Renaissance cinema of Derek Jarman
David Hawkes   103

Opposing "Heterosoc": Jarman's counter hegemonic activism
Martin Quinn-Meyler   117

Language games and aesthetic attitudes: style and ideology in
    Jarman's late films
Richard Porton   135

Interview with Derek Jarman
Chris Lippard   161

Derek Jarman: filmography
Compiled by Chris Lippard   170

Derek Jarman: selected bibliography
Compiled by Chris Lippard   176

Index   193

Notes on contributors   202

Acknowledgements

For their help at various stages in this project, the editor would particularly like to thank Tiffany Rousculp, Tracy Biga, Gill Dunford, Brian McIlroy, Richard Morrison, Lawrence Driscoll, Guy Johnson and David James.

For supplying stills, the publisher would like to thank BFI Stills, Posters and Designs, and the Joel Finler Collection.

Introduction

Chris Lippard

The title of this collection was suggested by Baudelaire's poem, "Love's Wine" (also known as "The Lovers' Wine", in which the lovers are "Like a pair of angels driven/by some implacable fever,/up into morning's blue crystal".[1] These words seem appropriate to Derek Jarman's films for a number of reasons. Angels appear commonly in his films – the character in *Jubilee* (1978); the boy in *Caravaggio* (1986); the men and women who circle his bed on the beach in *The Garden* (1990); perhaps the spirits of *The Tempest* (1979) and *The Angelic Conversation* (1985). The editors of *Afterimage* magazine chose to title their special issue on Jarman published in 1985 "Of Angels and Apocalypse", and the same title served for the exhibition of his films that toured the United States in 1986 and 1987. Jarman's own "implacable fever", the HIV virus, deeply influenced the last six years of his life, but just as implacable was his drive to continue producing paintings, books and films at an astonishing rate. These projects culminated in the large, expressionistic canvases exhibited in two major shows in Manchester, *Queer* (1992) and *Evil Queen* (1994); in the book, *Chroma* (1994), his exploration of colours as experienced by painters and peoples through the ages; and, of course, in *Blue* (1993), perhaps his most successful, human and intimate film, as well as his most formally radical and avant-garde.

Jarman's cinema was always intensely personal. He made his films on shoestring budgets, as artisanal rather than industrial projects, returning often to Super 8 footage. He frequently appears himself and always worked with friends, sometimes incorporating into the film whichever of them might chance by. His own queer identity and the political concerns to which this led him frame most of his projects.[2] He regarded the books that accompany many of his films as further assertions of the personal, writing in *At Your Own Risk* that "[m]y obsession with biography is to find...'I's. The subtext of my films have [sic] been the books, putting myself back into the picture".[3]

Although Jarman was quickly recognised as a powerful and distinctive filmmaker, acclaim came late in a career characterised by controversy. He struggled throughout his artistic life to make the films he wished to make, and, although he usually succeeded eventually,

1

the distribution and screening of the films both in the cinema and on television were often sadly inadequate. He completed his first feature, *Sebastiane* (1976), with a suitcase of cash from an anonymous Italian businessman, and it took him seven years to raise the money to make *Caravaggio*. Rarely did he begin a project with all the required financing secured. Yet, Jarman spent extraordinarily little on his films, pointing out in 1990 that his total output of eight features had cost less than £1 million. He sometimes indicated that he continued to think of himself as a painter who had made some films, and art critics such as Norman Rosenthal, exhibitions secretary of the Royal Academy of Art, have supported this view.[4] But Jarman will be remembered primarily for the variety and power of his cinema, its unflinching engagement with the personal and the political in contemporary Britain, and its forging of a space for queer lives both in the record of the past and in the images of the present.

Born in north London in 1942, Derek Jarman grew up on Air Force bases in England, Pakistan and Italy. His pilot father, Lance, was a New Zealander who made many Super 8 home-movies in which Derek and his sister were the "stars". Indeed, Jarman has suggested that his father might have made a very competent professional cameraman. Two of Derek's greatest loves, for gardening and for painting, developed early, but he made an agreement with his parents by which he would first go to university, as they wished, and then to art school. Thus, having finished a degree in English, history and art history at the University of London, in 1963 he enrolled as a painter at the Slade School of Art, where his slightly older peers included David Hockney and Patrick Procktor. Jarman lived and worked in London, travelled to the United States and Canada, and began to discover a queer sexuality that he had long recognised but had been unable to express.

Having already designed the sets for two of Sir Frederick Ashton's productions at the Royal Ballet, Jarman's first involvement with film was as set designer for Ken Russell's *The Devils* (1970). He created a Loudun of stark white stone walls, a massive sarcophagus, surrounded by desolation and infiltrated by the plague, which Oliver Reed's Grandier tries to defend against Richelieu's centralising authority. He worked with Russell on another film, *Savage Messiah* (1972), and eventually an opera, Stravinsky's *The Rake's Progress*, in Florence in 1982. By this time, however, Jarman had made several of his own features. In 1970, the same year in which he spent so much time working on the big-budget *The Devils*, Jarman picked up a Super 8 camera that an American student, Mark Balet, had brought to his warehouse loft on the south bank of the Thames. Thus began his own smaller-scale, independent cinema: his earliest films are records of his visitors, and they were screened at parties on the walls of the same rooms in which they were shot.

Rather than work with Russell on another film, Jarman began his own. *Sebastiane*, a largely unscripted account of the martyrdom of Saint Sebastian, was shot on a shoestring budget on the beaches of Sardinia with dialogue in Latin. *Sebastiane* played to packed houses at London's Gate Cinema, and remained an important film for Jarman throughout his life because it provided an onscreen vision of queer desire not otherwise accessible to the gay community in Britain. As Jarman later remarked, "even if I couldn't put two pieces of film together they were going to come".[5] In fact, referring to himself as "cine-illiterate", Jarman has often commented on the advantage that his lack of technical filmmaking skills may have given him.[6] Although his own expertise developed over the course of his career, he continued to rely on the skill of his collaborators both behind and in front of the camera, thus drawing out ideas that might otherwise have remained unspoken.[7]

Jarman's next feature, *Jubilee*, provided a scathing account of Britain on the occasion of Elizabeth II's 25th year on the throne. Although he focuses his analysis on the exciting but nihilistic punk subculture of the period, Jarman also draws a comparison with the England of the first Elizabeth, who is conducted on a tour of her country's future by her court astrologer, John Dee. This is the first of many attempts to come to terms with the Renaissance; his next film, a version of *The Tempest*, is another. Most famous for the camp sailors who dance the horn-pipe to Elisabeth Welch's sumptuous rendition of "Stormy Weather", the film also presents a second version of the Renaissance magician-manipulator in Heathcote Williams's Prospero.

Although Jarman had produced three independent features in a short space of time, he still found it hard to obtain financing, and it took him seven more years to raise the necessary funds for his film of the life of Michele Caravaggio. In the meantime he continued to make Super 8 films, experimenting with stop-motion photography and refilming, developing experimental and personal cinema relatively untrammelled by financial stringencies. In his book, *The Last of England*, he recalls that "[t]o keep myself occupied during those years, I took up my Super 8 camera, deciding to develop a parallel cinema based on the home movie which would free me. A space where I could paint my garden".[8] In the early 1980s he produced some of his most interesting avant-garde work, culminating in the feature-length *The Angelic Conversation*, a beautiful and meditative envisioning of the male body in labour and passion, shot on Super 8 and transferred to 35mm. The film is without dialogue or other synchronous sound, but the images are accompanied by the music of Coil and Judi

Dench's reading of fourteen of Shakespeare's Sonnets written to a young man and dedicated to "Mr. W. H.". Jarman's film reminds us that perhaps the most fêted romantic poetry in the language is written by a man to a man.[9]

Jarman finally made *Caravaggio* in 1986. Shot in an empty warehouse at Limehouse on the Isle of Dogs, the film shows Christopher Hobbs, Jarman's regular production designer, at his most skilful, using a very few carefully chosen props and backgrounds to startling effect. Like *Sebastiane*, in which the Roman legion relaxes in the surf with a frisbee, *Caravaggio* avoids the strictly re-creative urge of the historical bio-pic in favour of a postmodern anachronism – we hear and see motor cycles and pocket calculators. *Caravaggio* is also characterised by its restaging of the paintings by which we now know the artist. The set-ups constantly reassemble Caravaggio's canvases and, indeed, imitate other artists, as when Caravaggio's fiercest critic, pummelling away on his typewriter in the bath, relaxes into the pose of David's assassinated Marat.

Jarman had also been directing various music videos throughout the 1980s, an activity for which he claimed to have neither much interest nor much aptitude. His own vision, he felt, became inevitably subsumed by a required look, little different from that of a television commercial. Nevertheless, his three-song package for The Smiths, *The Queen is Dead* (1986), impressively adapts the techniques of his avant-garde work to the faster pacing and better-financed music video, especially in the extraordinary title track, a swirl of stop-motion images and superimpositions filmed in the same decaying urban landscapes that dominate his next feature film, *The Last of England* (1987).

Jarman takes the title for this film from Ford Madox Brown's painting of the emigrants' goodbye to the white cliffs, and presents an uncompromising attack on the state of Thatcher's England.[10] Near the beginning of the film, we see a booted youth stamping fiercely on Caravaggio's "Profane Love" (in fact, Christopher Hobbs's copy of it left over from the previous film). This sets the tone for a series of bleak images: Balaclavered "soldiers" intimidate a forlorn population of refugees from the new England; a naked man chews despairingly on a cauliflower; a mock-wedding is celebrated in a burnt-out building; a soldier/terrorist and a drunken youth struggle passionately but menacingly on a Union Jack bedspread.

At the end of 1986, whilst editing *The Last of England*, Jarman was diagnosed as HIV+ and quickly made this knowledge public; in doing so, he became a still more visible and significant representative of queer rights. Although it was not until his final film, *Blue*, that Jarman directly addressed AIDS, his *War Requiem* (1988) is an examination of war and the death of many young men. Taking his soundtrack as a given – Benjamin Britten's 1962 *War Requiem*, with its incorporation of several of Wilfred Owen's war poems – he compiled a series of accompanying images that emphasise both the ubiquity of war in the 20th century and individual suffering, loss and grief. Despite the predetermined nature of the soundtrack, Jarman felt much less constrained than when working in music video, and achieved a personal vision distinct from those of both Britten and Owen.

Meanwhile, Jarman had adopted a new location in which to pursue his writing and develop another long-cherished project. With money he inherited after his father's death in 1986, he purchased a small fisherman's cottage on the beach at Dungeness in the lee of the nuclear power station.[11] From 1987 he divided his time between his London home in a building off Charing Cross Road and Prospect Cottage. He had John Donne's "The Sun Rising" inscribed on the east wall of the building, but his most striking and important addition to the Kentish landscape was the creation of a garden on the shingle that surrounded his new home. Jarman's interest in gardening had been strong since boyhood, but his new garden, the establishment and flowering of which is lovingly recorded in the diary entries that structure his book, *Modern Nature*, brought him the interest and admiration of an entirely new and more diverse audience.[12] It was featured on the BBC's long-running programme, *Gardener's World*, became the exclusive focus of his last and posthumous book, *derek jarman's garden* (1995), and is still much visited after his death.[13]

The garden also became the inspiration and backdrop for a film of the same name. *The Garden*, which Jarman called "a simple domestic drama",[14] is structured in a similar way to *The Last of England*, as a series of set pieces, but here they are loosely connected by a narrative of the Christian Passion. Jarman's Christ-figure, however, is represented by a pair of gay lovers who are variously humiliated by authority, yet provide the focus for an alternative and loving approach to life that was missing from the earlier film.[15] Jarman wrote in his diary that "I just film my life, I'm a happy megalomaniac",[16] and *The Garden* also includes footage of Jarman at his desk, in his garden, filming with a Super 8 camera, supervising the turmoil of the film-shoot, and in a hospital bed on the beach. These last images remind the viewer of Jarman's condition; in fact, during post-production of the film he fell seriously ill, attacked by AIDS-related infections that left him struggling for breath and sight. Thus, the details of the final ordering of the images were left to a large extent to his collaborators.

As soon as he recovered a modicum of health, Jarman began writing and planning his next projects. In *Edward II* (1991) and *Wittgenstein* (1993) he returns to more narratively driven and thus broadly accessible accounts of queer lives. His version of Marlowe's play is probably his most widely distributed and seen film, both in Britain and worldwide. Once again, Jarman emphasises the struggle between a heterosexist society and queer desire, the explanation for Edward's removal from the throne being clearly linked to his sexuality. Indeed, this is the film in which the rapacity of the villainous straights is perhaps most marked; *Queer Edward II*, the annotated screenplay that Jarman prepared to accompany the film, drives his point home still more forcibly. Although narrative is foregrounded in *Edward II*, Jarman does not hesitate to suspend it both for interpolated OutRage demonstrations and for Annie Lennox's rendition of Cole Porter's song, "Every Time We Say Goodbye". Such musical set pieces are common in Jarman's films – *The Garden*, for example, pauses for a rendition of Roger Edens's "Think Pink" – as Jarman provides the music without the video.

Wittgenstein was commissioned by Channel 4 Television as the first in a series of films about philosophers, a series that was later cancelled. Substantially adapting Terry Eagleton's original script,[17] Jarman sets the philosopher's life in a series of brilliantly coloured rooms to produce a revealing and wittily entertaining comic portrait of a philosopher whose work is often close to poetry. As with his previous two films, *Wittgenstein* was well-received by critics, and Wittgenstein's biographer, Ray Monk, suggested that Jarman's film "almost...achieves the impossible; it shows us how philosophy can be dramatized".[18]

Jarman, approaching the terminal stages of his illness, was once again close to blindness when he made his next film, and just one colour provides the complete image-track of *Blue*. The unchanging blue glow of the screen is, however, accompanied by a soundtrack in which four voices, including Jarman's own, survey many of his experiences with the virus, and provide an account of the eponymous "blue" that seems sometimes a human figure, sometimes a feeling or experience. *Blue* received great critical acclaim, and provides a demanding and exciting cinematic spectacle. It stands as Jarman's final challenge to the constraints of traditional filmmaking, a fitting testimony to his personal vision.[19] It is perhaps appropriate, however, that Jarman produced yet one more film. Released posthumously, *Glitterbug* (1994) is a compilation of many years of his Super 8 footage, reminding us both of so much of his life in film and of film's most basic apparatus, one that Jarman has used more individually and creatively than anyone else.

Tracy Biga's essay which opens this volume begins with Jarman's written texts – mixing present and past experiences, personal and filmic opinions and revelations – that accompany so many of his films.

Biga uses them to trace the relationship between Jarman and his father, and the attitude to the paternal that exists in many of the films. Discussing the full range of Jarman's cinema, Biga considers both thematic and formal qualities in order to show the importance of this relationship to Jarman's work.

David Gardner's essay similarly makes extensive reference to Jarman's writing, as well as offering close readings of the films. He sees Jarman within a tradition of Queer filmmakers – Genet, Pasolini, Cocteau and Eisenstein – who, in striving for a position outside the dominant heterosexual/ist orientation of the cinema, emphasise the criminal in their work.

In contrast, Lawrence Driscoll underscores Jarman's place within a somewhat conservative British tradition. Jarman often portrayed himself as the traditionalist protesting against the new-fangledness of the Tory Right. Drawing on Alan Sinfield's work on the connections between politics and culture in Britain, Driscoll places Jarman firmly in a line of middle-class dissent that often overlaps with a homosexual agenda and situates itself in opposition to mainstream British politics of both the Left and the Right.

Joseph Gomez argues for Jarman's place within another tradition, that of the composed film – in which the images are fitted to a predetermined music track – in relation to perhaps his least discussed film, and one that Jarman himself tended to forget in conversations about his work, *War Requiem*. Indeed, Eisenstein, Powell and Russell – each of whom have influenced Jarman's work in general – have all attempted some kind of composed film. After a brief survey of their work and other attempts, such as Disney's *Fantasia* (1940), Gomez proceeds to a close reading of Jarman's images in conjunction with both Britten's requiem and Owen's poems.

David Hawkes's essay reviews three – perhaps the most important three – of Jarman's forays into and queering of the English Renaissance: *Jubilee*, *The Tempest* and *Edward II*. Hawkes demonstrates how Jarman's Renaissance films both accentuate the homoeroticism implicit in early-modern constructions of gender, and make use of it to oppose contemporary sexual oppression in both cinema and society.

Jarman's position as perhaps the most prominent queer man in Britain over the last decade, and his fight against the hegemonic oppression of "Heterosoc" in the era of AIDS, are the focus of Martin Quinn-Meyler's essay. He sees Jarman as an oppositional figure to British Heterosoc and its film industry well before his diagnosis as HIV+; from that point onwards, however, Jarman became still more clearly the key figure in the gay community's voluble opposition to a hypocritical Thatcher government. Quinn-Meyler offers a reading of

Edward II that sees the film not simply as the updating of a queer story, but as a reading of queer loving and oppression across many centuries. While Biga's essay considers Edward's relation to his father, King Edward I, Quinn-Meyler discusses the film's presentation of the upbringing of Edward's son, the future Edward III.

Finally, Richard Porton uses Wittgenstein's notion of the language game to examine Jarman's "late works" – his last feature-length films, *Wittgenstein* and *Blue*. Porton sees both Wittgenstein and Jarman as practitioners of mixed or "blurred genres",[20] sharing a recognition of the formative power of language.

Although it is *Edward II*, Jarman's most commercially successful and perhaps widely seen film, that receives the most attention, the seven essays in this collection consider all of Jarman's major films to some degree. Most of the essays, particularly the opening accounts by Biga and Gardner, also weave Jarman's written work into their texts. They find his sources in his notion of his family, in the approaches of earlier queer filmmakers and of his most visually compelling English precursors, notably Michael Powell, in the English countryside and tradition of dissenting intellectuals and artists, and in the texts of the Renaissance, both in Britain and Italy.

Several of these issues are raised in the interview that completes this volume. It was conducted in November 1993, before the essays collected here were written. I hoped to talk to Derek again later, but I was aware, of course, that this very likely would not be possible. He was hospitalized once more late in 1993 and died on 19 February 1994, as Parliament voted to lower the age of homosexual consent from 21 to 18, thus reducing but preserving the disparity with the age (16) established for heterosexuals. There can be no doubt that Jarman would have considered this a dishonourable compromise. As Peter Tatchell, his colleague in OutRage, noted, "[t]he only law reform worth having is full legal equality".[21] To the very end of his life, Jarman worked towards this goal, rejecting compromise with an oppressive society and attempting to subvert it in his filmmaking, writing and painting.

Upon Jarman's death the plaudits flooded in, acknowledging his unique place in British cinema. Several commentators considered him Britain's most important filmmaker.[22] Less than five months after his death, on 16 July 1994, Britain's Channel 4 Television – whose power and influence in the financing and screening of contemporary British cinema over the previous ten years had helped many filmmakers, but, Jarman felt, had hindered his own career – screened *A Night with Derek*. Beginning at 9.15 pm with an introductory programme narrated by Clancy Chassay (who had played Wittgenstein as a boy in Jarman's film), the night featured successive showings of *The Tempest*, *The Last of England, Blue* and *Sebastiane*, interspersed with reminiscences from a wide variety of Derek's friends, colleagues and collaborators. *Sebastiane*'s male nudity almost certainly dictated that it went out at 3.30 am. However, no such tribute to the power of his cinema had been seen while Jarman was alive.

In a television interview with Jeremy Isaacs, recorded a year earlier and broadcast on *The Late Show* during the week after he died, Jarman reported that, upon dying, it would be "marvellous to evaporate and to take all my works with me". Yet he usually enjoyed his own films and defended them vigorously, both in themselves and in comparison to the work of contemporaries in the British cinema such as Peter Greenaway and Stephen Frears. Despite the struggles to get his films financed and screened, Jarman commonly got great pleasure out of the process of making them, and he remarked on several occasions that he was "the most fortunate filmmaker of [his] generation [because he'd] only ever done what [he] wanted".[23] By the end of his life he had completed the majority of his most cherished film projects.

Notes

[1]   Charles Baudelaire, *Les Fleurs du Mal*, translated by Richard Howard (Brighton: The Harvester Press, 1982): 117.

[2]   In *At Your Own Risk: A Saint's Testament* (London: Hutchinson, 1992), Jarman complained about the words available to describe his sexuality: "Anti-homosexual morality and ideology, at every level of society, manifest themselves in a special vocabulary for denigrating gay people. There is abuse like 'pansy', 'fairy', 'lesbo' to hurl at men and women who can't or won't fit into stereotyped preconceptions. There are words like 'sick', 'bent' and 'neurotic' for destroying the credence of gay people. But there are no positive words" (65). A few pages earlier, however, he writes that: "For me to use the word 'queer' is a liberation; it was a word that frightened me, but no longer" (27). He used it in the title of *Queer Edward II*, the text that accompanies the film, *Edward II*. The political power of 'queer', taken over from the catalogue of denigrating terms makes it the most appropriate, I think, in most discussions of Jarman and his work. For further comments on the implications of the word "queer", see note 27 to Martin Quinn-Meyler's essay in this volume.

[3]   Ibid: 27.

[4]   Rosenthal is quoted in Ken Butler, "All the Rage", *Vogue* December 1993: 158. Rosenthal contributes a brief essay to the catalogue for *Evil Queen*, the exhibition of Jarman's final seventeen paintings, in which Butler's piece is also reprinted.

[5]   "Face to Face" interview with Jeremy Isaacs broadcast on *The Late Show*

(BBC 2, 22 February 1994).

6   For example, in his *The Late Show* interview with Jeremy Isaacs.

7   Jarman has argued that a greater knowledge of the difficulties involved might have prevented his ever starting several of his films.

8   Derek Jarman, *The Last of England*, edited by David L Hirst (London: Constable, 1987): 90.

9   Even when pessimistic about the importance of film in general and his own in particular, Jarman remained engaged by *The Angelic Conversation*. In an interview in 1990, for example, he remarked: "I'm not certain any of my films are any good at all, or of any consequence, except *The Angelic Conversation*" (Jonathan Hacker and David Price, *Take Ten: Contemporary British Film Directors* [Oxford: Clarendon Press, 1991]: 259).

10   In many ways Jarman is a distinctively English, rather than British, filmmaker. The power of England within the British state often makes it hard to know whether to refer to "Britain" or "England". In this instance, Jarman's title suggests the use of the latter term. In some places I have deemed "Britain" or "British" more appropriate. Most writers in this book lean towards "Britain". Lawrence Driscoll's essay, in particular, draws attention to this issue.

11   In *Know What I Mean?*, the introductory segment to Channel 4 Television's "A Night with Derek", broadcast on 16 July 1994, Jarman compares the nuclear power station to the Emerald City of *The Wizard of Oz*, a film he had seen as a child and which continued to be one of his favourites.

12   In his *The Late Show* interview, Jarman remarks that "a much more varied group of people come down to see the cottage garden than to see the films".

13   During the summer of 1995, the garden was apparently attracting up to 1000 visitors each weekend, a substantial influx to the small town of Dungeness. Keith Collins, Jarman's partner during his last years, concludes his preface to *derek jarman's garden*: "Dungeness is a magical location. When you visit, tread softly, for many choose to live here for the solitude and silence that once attracted Derek, and now holds me." (*derek jarman's garden*, with photographs by Howard Sooley [London: Thames and Hudson, 1995]).

14   Derek Jarman, *Modern Nature: The Journals of Derek Jarman* (London: Century, 1991): 130.

15   Perhaps as a consequence of Jarman's new-found love for Keith Collins. Colin MacCabe, in his obituary for Jarman in *The Independent*, credits this relationship with providing a tenderness in the later films that is missing from the earlier works.

16   Jarman (1991): 131.

[17] *Wittgenstein. The Terry Eagleton Script. The Derek Jarman Film* (London: British Film Institute, 1993).

[18] "Between Earth and Ice", *The Times Literary Supplement* 4694 (19 March 1993): 16.

[19] I last saw *Blue* screened in semi-derelict Hackney Hospital in north London. In its final days before demolition the vast Victorian building was the site for an exhibition, "Care and Control" mounted by the arts organisation, Rear Window, that combined the work of professional artists and the hospital's users or patients. *Blue* shared the X-ray department with Jo Spence's photographic collages of her struggle with cancer and, screened in the silent, dead hospital, Jarman's words and image became still more intensely moving.

[20] The term is from Clifford Geertz, *Local Knowledge* (New York: Basic, 1983).

[21] Letter to *The Independent* 21 February 1994.

[22] See, for example, the obituary by Colin MacCabe in *The Independent*, reprinted in *Genre*, and the comments of Ben Gibson, head of production at the British Film Institute, quoted in *The Guardian*'s obituary.

[23] See Jarman (1991): 131. Jarman uses the same words in making this point during *Know What I Mean?*, "A Night with Derek", 16 July 1994.

The principle of non-narration in the films of Derek Jarman

Tracy Biga

To be an astronaut of the void, leave the comfortable house
that imprisons you with reassurance. Remember,
To be going and to have are not eternal – fight the fear that
engenders the beginning, the middle and the end.[1]

The metaphoric work of eventual totalization determines the
meaning and status of the metonymic work of sequence –
though it must also be claimed that the metonymies of the
middle produced, gave birth to, the final metaphor.[2]

The final metaphor – the end – is (whatever else it might be) a
metaphor of death. Because immortality is so uninteresting, the end
is necessary; only termination confers meaning. At the end of one of
Derek Jarman's last films, his Wittgenstein says: "Don't think I'm afraid
of dying. It's death that gives life its meaning and shape". Within
narrative, this necessary death necessarily arrives at a rigorously
prescribed position – according to the demands of the beginning,
middle and end. Disruptions of this arrangement – which distort the
significance of the end – can be found throughout Jarman's written
and filmed work. These disruptions operate on the levels of both form
and content, details and the overall patterns of texts, and they
continually frustrate the progression of narrative. Jarman's principle of
non-narration can be seen as an element of his artistic style, linked to
a political strategy. In particular, Jarman's art expresses a continual
refusal of patriarchal logic and, with this refusal, a sense of
undifferentiation inconsistent with the gendered law of the father.

In his study of narration, Peter Brooks states that "[t]he telling [of
a life] is always *in terms of* the impending end".[3] Jarman's principle of
non-narration consists of taking the telling of lives out of these terms,
of de-hierarchizing the metaphoric work of "eventual totalization". A
refusal of the end constitutes a refusal of that reproductive logic – the
"gave birth to" and "engenders" – to which both Brooks and Jarman
refer. With this refusal, narrative transmission no longer flows
according to a paternalistic model of father to son. The non-narrative
organisation of Jarman's books and films, like their content and even

12

their mode of production, works continually against patriarchal hierarchy, as well as against other forms of hierarchy and authority.

Jarman disrupts narrative through a variety of formal strategies: the eruption of varied modes, such as the music video or poetry; non-chronological development; use of tableaux; and repetition. A disruption of narrative can be most readily identified in those films which are not adaptations or biographies. These include a number of home-movie, Super 8 films, some of which are gathered in *Glitterbug* (1994); features and shorts shot on Super 8, such as *In the Shadow of the Sun* (1980), *Imagining October* (1984), *The Angelic Conversation* (1985) and parts of *The Last of England* (1987); the 35mm features, *War Requiem* (1988) and *The Garden* (1990); and various music videos, such as *Broken English* (1979), *The Queen is Dead* (1986) and Jarman's segment of *Aria* (1987). These texts are frequently classified by critics as experimental or avant-garde, and as emanating from a "marginal position".[4]

Disruptions of narrative also function significantly in Jarman's more mainstream, commercial or conventional films: *Sebastiane* (1976), *Jubilee* (1978), *The Tempest* (1979), *Caravaggio* (1986), *Edward II* (1991) and *Wittgenstein* (1993). With the exception of *Jubilee* and the adaptation of *The Tempest*, each of these feature-length and more narratively-driven films works as historical biography, making the life-span an important organisational element. Jarman's written texts are similarly based on a life – his own. All his books – *Dancing Ledge* (1984), *Derek Jarman's Caravaggio* (1986), *The Last of England* (1987), *War Requiem* (1989), *Modern Nature: The Journals of Derek Jarman* (1991), *Queer Edward II* (1991), *At Your Own Risk: A Saint's Testament* (1992) and *Blue: Text of a film by Derek Jarman* (1993) – overlap. In them, Jarman continually returns to personal experience, often presenting versions of significant moments which differ from text to text. In some ways they can be thought of as a single text expressing different aspects and emphases of a single subject: Jarman's life and personality.

While I will discuss Jarman's own life and family experiences as described in his autobiographies and as imaged in film, I do not wish to analyze his family as it exists historically, attempting to decipher its relationships or implying that his interpretations remain static across all the texts. My analysis concerns not the lived biography, but what Jarman chooses to represent and, in many cases, what he chooses to repeat. His concerns extend beyond a family dynamic to include a political dimension, as he links his inability to inherit unproblematically in his own family to his inability to function as an equal in English life.

In *At Your Own Risk*, Jarman includes two unusual but related anecdotes. After discussing his friends in the art community and how they "lived together as a generation, not as a family", he recounts:

> Talking of families, one of the strangest encounters that I heard of was from a friend of mine, Gawain, who picked up a young man, who introduced him to his brothers and his father. The father was sleeping with his sons and the sons were sleeping with each other and Gawain and his boyfriend were asked to join in! They shared a holiday and an enormous communal bed.[5]

Later, Jarman tells a similar story – also characterised as "strange" – this time quoting a "miner's son" met on Hampstead Heath: "'I fucked all the boys in my school, every single one of them. They are all married now except for me – my father joined in! Isn't life strange?'".[6]

Jarman presents both stories with little comment and no clear implication that they might describe the transgressive. Of the miner's son, he says nothing, and of Gawain's experience only that "[e]veryone was very happy". Yet, in both of these examples, patriarchal transmission has become a kind of trans-semenism, which must inevitably shift relations of power. Here, as in other Jarman texts, homosexual sex can break down boundaries of authority and subjugation, in this case the boundaries between father and son.

This possibility is raised with the regularity of a motif, and it extends to most realms of public life. Jarman argues that the Army will not admit Queers "because they'd destroy its hierarchy. You couldn't have squaddies fucking with Major-Generals".[7] The film studios in which he worked as a set designer were "hierarchical, and our sexuality was betrayed by the cinema".[8] He similarly critiques his schooling: the boys "obeyed imaginary hierarchies where accidents of origin and the caprice of nature were magnified".[9]

In situations where hierarchy is typical or presumed – as in, for example, teaching – Jarman's ideal is to do away with it. He praises his art teacher, Robin Noscoe, because "he ignored the gulf that separated master and pupil and embraced you as a collaborator and equal".[10] This equality is part of being recognised as an individual. By circumventing hierarchy, sex provokes the best kind of teaching, and teaching becomes the best kind of sex: "That is what teaching is about; it has to have a sexual element".[11] Of the 1960s art scene, Jarman says: "Sex was bonding, pedagogic, a way of learning".[12] He praises the Greeks for their practice of combining teaching and sexual relationships.

Throughout his autobiographies, Jarman laments that he himself was never sexually initiated by an older man. For example: "If only I had met someone who could have helped me through my adolescence".[13] These expressions show a desire to frustrate and confuse patriarchal hierarchies. One passage in *At Your Own Risk* is worth quoting at length, because it both culminates in an unusual and telling lack of clarity and raises the matter of Jarman's own father:

> I wasn't to meet anyone until I was twenty-one who admitted he was Queer and he was as old as my father. I didn't tell him of my feelings – I didn't dare. I was another young man corrupted and co-opted by heterosexuality, my mind still swimming about in the cesspit which is known as family life, subjected to a Christian love whose ugliness would shatter a mirror. I had to destroy my inheritance to face you and love you.[14]

The "him" to whom he does not tell his feelings could be either the older man or his own father. Only the less obvious choice of the father can make sense of the final sentence. Who is the "you" to be faced and loved? Is he the unnamed older man – abstractly representing an initiating lover – or Jarman's father? If these figures become mixed, as they are in the other anecdotes quoted above, the authority of the paternal function dissipates.

The nature of the "inheritance" which must be destroyed is also unclear. By evoking a "cesspit", Jarman confuses waste and property as possible legacies. This confusion can also be seen in his films: in *Edward II* he places the play's opening line – "My father is deceased" – in a cesspit, the sewer of the castle. As this film emphasises, patriarchy involves not only the establishment of rank and levels, but also always the issue of inheritance. For his own part, Jarman – as he depicts himself in his autobiographies – stays outside heterosexual society or "Heterosoc", not only because of sexual practice, but also because of a chosen attitude towards inheritance – of property and obligation.

Across his autobiographies, Jarman develops a portrait of his own father in keeping with his Aunt Moyra's assessment, "[y]our dad really was a strange man".[15] Unlike the "strangeness" of the incestuous fathers, the senior Jarman's strangeness arises from the blurring not of sexual hierarchies, but of those of property. This blurring can be seen in the repeated tale of Jarman's higher education: firstly, English history and art at King's College, London, and then art at the Slade School of Art. Jarman's father agreed to put him through art school if the son first completed university. After Jarman "meticulously fulfilled" this "pact",[16] his father concluded the transaction with an act described in *Modern Nature*:

On my twenty-first birthday my father presented the account, my school report and bills, the cost of an education to make me 'an Englishman.'[17]

And more elaborately in At Your Own Risk:

> Could all of this be conceivably thought 'a normal upbringing'? Everyone seemed to think so and my parents, bless them, paid for it. So much that my father proudly presented me with a complete set of receipts on my twenty-first.[18]

Jarman never clarifies what he considered so notable about the presentation of the bills, and he never suggests that his father intended him to pay them back. Perhaps he considered it odd that his father would so painstakingly record what was seemingly a freely assumed obligation. The incident, so significant that Jarman repeatedly reported it, suggests an inheritance perceived to be turned around or, at the very least, begrudged.

Jarman describes another example of the paternal legacy reversed: his father's kleptomania: "He stole, and stole from his friends and relatives".[19] At the end of the senior Jarman's life, he took "anything that glittered or was loved", including his wife's ashes which he apparently misplaced. Even Jarman's mother, portrayed far more sympathetically than the father, expressed the family's disordered inheritance. In Dancing Ledge, Jarman quotes his mother, Betty, saying, "[i]t's a pity neither you nor your sister inherited our good looks",[20] and he repeats the comment, in almost identical language, in Modern Nature.[21] (As he got older, Jarman felt more at odds with her assessment, eventually deciding that as a young man he had been handsome enough.)

Jarman's accounts of his problematic access to inherit within the family echoes a larger issue: the recognition that as a gay man in England he lived as a "second-class citizen, deprived of equality and human rights".[22] The system compromised him by granting him "no right of inheritance",[23] no right to assume a life. This unequal treatment is not mitigated by the fact that Jarman clearly chose to reject that "straight" life which he described as "a giant vegetable nightmare".[24] In the past, he says, "all the queers got married";[25] his was the "dazed first generation" able to resist that imperative. Yet, even if Jarman refuses the trappings of "Heterosoc", he recognises that no individual can operate completely outside the disposition of property. He concludes Dancing Ledge with a disposition of his own property – an inventory of his personal assets. In At Your Own Risk he describes with a sense of paradox, how – upon learning of his

HIV+ status – he walked to Oxford Street to buy "a daybook for 1987 and a scarlet form to write out a will".[26]

The Jarman family's most potent legacy – their home-movies – suggests a different kind of paradox. In one way, these films represent a kind of patriarchal succession. The footage displays the father's mastery of the family and of filmmaking technology. That he operates the camera and therefore seldom appears in the shots simply reinforces an Oedipal drama dependent on the Father's abstraction and absence.[27] The films also display the mother's beauty which Derek was supposed not to have possessed. Jarman incorporates these home-movies into his own work, most notably in *The Last of England* where they are juxtaposed with apocalyptic scenes of the poverty-stricken, media-saturated, terroristic present. In the vividly coloured home-movie footage dating from the 1940s, the toddler Derek, his mother and sister frolic and pose in a series of gardens. Jarman may be said to have incorporated the family's images as inheritance. In fact, to a large degree, all his films have been influenced by a home-movie sensibility.[28]

Yet the nature of the home-movie itself works against paternal transmission. As a genre, the home-movie is profoundly non-narrative, with no clear beginning, middle or end. The length of shots is often determined less by an artistic choice than by the length of the film reel, or the actors simply leaving the frame. Therefore, although home-movies are shot, they can hardly be said to be authored. Often multiple agents will shoot a single "film"; their identities and contributions may be unknown or quickly forgotten. The films themselves are frequently mislabelled, mixed-up, damaged, lost or destroyed. Jarman's use of home-movie footage in *The Last of England* emphasises its fragmentary nature. The identity of the figures, date of filming and authorship are left unmarked. Jarman himself appears in them as a small, vulnerable child, heir to a legacy of non-narrative. In this film about the current state of England he inserts a low-technology, faded and fragmented image as his artistic inheritance.

A refusal of patriarchal logic can be seen not only in Jarman's autobiographical work, but also throughout his films – where fathers are uncommonly scarce. Only in *The Tempest*, an adaptation, does Jarman depict a biological father. More frequently, he self-consciously erases the paternal figure. At the beginning of *Wittgenstein*, for example, the child Wittgenstein (Clancy Chassay) introduces his large family. A few brothers who committed suicide or died at birth are not shown, but the most significant omission is the father. He never physically appears and his death is not reported; yet, much is made of the family's wealth (described as "filthy rich") and of the fact that young Ludwig gave away a substantial inheritance to his surviving

17

siblings. *Wittgenstein* also represents a countered or refused legacy.

While Jarman's films consistently reject the hierarchical father-son relationship, they often replace it with something else: the gay male couple as the locus of an anti-hierarchy. This shift can be seen perhaps most dramatically in *The Garden*, a highly abstracted life of Christ. The film covers several recognisable episodes from the Gospels, in addition to many images, characters and events that have no obvious relation to the Passion story. Among the latter are a man in SM leathers, a woman lip-synching to "Think Pink" from *Funny Face* (1956), and Jarman himself in a bed positioned in the ocean surf and surrounded by torch-carrying angels.

Significantly, *The Garden* depicts no heavenly father who sacrifices his son. Instead, there are two separate versions of Christ – a traditional robed figure revealing stigmata (Roger Cook), and two similar-looking and similarly dressed men who together form a loving gay couple (Johnny Mills and Kevin Collins). These two versions create a doubled doubleness seemingly incompatible with typical characterisations of Christ which usually emphasise his singleness and unrepeatability. The robed Christ figure wanders through the stark landscape near a nuclear power station and Jarman's own cottage in Dungeness, interacting only with a jogger. Like Elizabeth I in *Jubilee*, who travels through time to visit contemporary England, this Christ wears a baffled expression. In contrast to his isolation and marginalization, the gay couple becomes increasingly prominent as the film continues. At first they live contentedly together, in one scene rough-housing with a young boy. Later they are brought before Pontius Pilate and Herod, tormented by a group of young off-duty policemen,[29] and, finally, forced to carry a cross.

In this film Jarman has rewritten the Passion as a Queer story. As he has claimed in a different context, "Jesus was a Drag Queen".[30] While readers may consider this a provocative or shocking comment, it recognises the generally accepted fact that the Bible depicts Jesus rejecting a heterosexual lifestyle. Like the Christ couple in *The Garden*, the Biblical Jesus has no female lovers or children, and lives in an all-male community. Furthermore, Christ's radical life of poverty met with relentless persecution. By transforming Jesus into gay lovers, Jarman links the Saviour's treatment to the persecution of gay men in contemporary society. The eroticization of the life and particularly the suffering of the gay Christ couple provides another link to Christ – the eroticization of His life and suffering.

The same issues that occur around the Christ couple in *The Garden* – rejection of societal authority, persecution, the eroticization of suffering, and a suffering unto death – are also played out in Jarman's first feature, *Sebastiane*, although visually the two films are very different. The Roman soldier, Sebastian (Leonardo Treviglio), banished to a remote outpost, attracts the attention of the Commanding Officer, Severus (Barney James). For Severus, sexuality depends on maintaining rigidly-prescribed positions. In refusing his overtures, Sebastian does not struggle against an acknowledged authority; he refuses to recognise it as authority. Severus's obsession interrupts the growing affection and slow-motion frolicking of Sebastian and his friend, Justin, who share a relationship of some equivalence. (Nevertheless, Sebastian, as the protagonist, is more dominant within the context of the film.) Sebastian is ultimately crucified, but famously and beautifully by a hail of arrows. He dies rather than submit his erotic life to an authority established by the state.

Edward II also figures the equality of male lovers, linking their union explicitly with the elision of the father. Jarman's very adaptation and production of the film actually writes in the father only to write him out again. Jarman includes in *Queer Edward II*, an annotated script of *Edward II*, an opening scene not found in Marlowe's play and later cut from the film. It depicts an infirm Edward I accompanied by his grandson, the future Edward III. The dying King says, "Edward, Edward",[31] but it is not clear whether he refers to himself, his son or his grandson.

The film actually begins: "My father is deceased; come Gaveston". Lightborn, Edward II's executioner, first says the line in the dungeon cesspit where the King is held; Edward repeats the line. The play then returns to the beginning of events (where Marlowe's play begins), as Gaveston reads: "My father is deceased; come, Gaveston, And share the Kingdom with thy dearest friend". The line repeatedly announces a shift away from the patriarchal relation of father and son, here represented by the significant inheritance of the Kingdom of England – second only, in patriarchal terms, to the Kingdom of Heaven. The gay male couple in this film serves as a total rejection of the father, Edward I's, inheritance which, Jarman has elsewhere suggested, was less impressive than has been popularly thought: "Longshanks [Edward I] had left his son a bankrupt land...For all this he is credited with being one of our greatest kings".[32]

Refusing this distorted inheritance, Edward refuses to position himself above Gaveston. Jarman – severely editing, but definitely faithful – emphasises those aspects of Marlowe's text where Edward expresses parity: "Share the kingdom with thy dearest friend"; "Kiss not my hand,/Embrace me, as I do thee,/Why shouldst thou kneel?/ Knowest thou not who I am?/Thy friend, thy self, another Gaveston";[33] "Were he a peasant, being my minion,/I'd make the proudest of you stoop to him".[34] Gaveston is awarded high titles and even leaps onto the throne. The casting of Edward and Gaveston, like the casting of the Christ figures in *The Garden*, reinforces the equality, even self-identity, implied by the play's speeches. The two look very much alike and frequently dress in the same clothes.

Edward II is most explicitly political in its depiction of the opposition ranged against the lovers – opposition which focuses on their personal connection and the public blurring of their roles. The chorus of nobility "resemble[s] the benches of the House of Commons",[35] and is relentlessly antipathetic to the King's relationship with Gaveston. The structure of heterosexual society, which requires the King to be set above all others, violently separates the lovers.

Jarman continually emphasises the destructive intolerance potential in all societies, particularly when they are forced to confront equality. In *Sebastiane*, Sebastian and Severus act out their conflict within a small, isolated community – less than a dozen men on an otherwise unoccupied Sardinian beach. Even the existence of this tiny society problematises relationships – the group functions only as part of an immense Roman system within which gay lovers cannot be together as equals. Only in *The Angelic Conversation* does Jarman provide a loving couple not thoroughly destroyed or torn apart by the social structure. The film depicts two men who look alike and are dressed and photographed similarly. Early in the film, the two remain separate; they then spend some time offering attendance to an arrogant King; eventually they come together in a loving sexual union. Although they do not appear to be together at the film's conclusion, their separation is not due to violence. The voice-over narration of Shakespearian love sonnets, because it is spoken by a woman (the actress Judi Dench), can be attributed to neither of the lovers, suggesting their equivalence. Neither controls the point of view of the film, nor can be set above the other.

For Jarman, undifferentiation is almost always shown to be an unequivocal good, as well as a political position; he consistently asserts the radical nature of the same ("Homo means same means equal").[36] René Girard has discussed the danger that societies perceive in the equivalence Jarman celebrates. For Girard, the threat posed by close identity between individuals can affect an entire social system and can often erupt into violence. An organisation based on hierarchy – as most are – systematically resists the same, creating a widespread "phobia of resemblance".[37] Jarman puts the doubleness of gay lovers in place of the singleness of the father and condemns the violence which ensues, locating it not in their equivalence, but in the differentiation triggered by the father's presence.

Girard speaks frequently of twins, but he extends his discussion to other situations where "[t]wo individuals suddenly appear, where only one had been expected".[38] Brothers, even when they are not twins, are frequently too close for comfort. The theme of enemy brothers is prevalent in many myths, and the conflict between brothers often leads to bloodshed. Rather than show conflict between brothers, Jarman puts them in bed together, as in the incestuous brothers of Gawain's tale. *Jubilee* also features a pair of brothers who share a sexual relationship. Angel and Sphinx are always together and affectionate – the most appealing characters in the film. Through them, Jarman depicts Heterosoc's hostile reaction to gay men – even those engaged in socially-sanctioned activities. The brothers are gunned down while playing bingo.

The characters in *Jubilee* raise a related and crucial pcint: Jarman's representations of female characters. In general, Jarman's written and film work demonstrates tolerance for most of the imbalances which can exist between people. Only gender, among such distinctions as class, age, race, etc., is reinforced, rather than erased, by sexual relations. Women's sexuality becomes emblematic of Heterosoc – violent, destructive and unsympathetic. In *Jubilee*, an increasingly dismayed Elizabeth I and John Dee investigate a dysfunctional household during 1977, Elizabeth II's Jubilee year. The men of the house share names which evoke the transcendental, timeless and ungendered: Angel and Sphinx. Their lovemaking consists of soulful kisses and long looks, in a tastefully underdecorated bedroom and outdoors. The women's names – Bod, Crabs, Mad and Amyl Nitrite – suggest their more graphic, nitty-gritty approach to sex. They victimise their sexual partners, at times to the point of death, in cluttered rooms. They speak to each other in harsh insults. The women's ambition to enter media society fuels their destructive rampages, a characterisation which reinforces the familiar linkage of femininity with consumption, consumer society, predatory sexuality and uncontrollability. The only exception to this portrayal, Viv – whose name at least suggests life – acts as a third wheel to Angel and Sphinx. After telling the brothers that she loves them, they tell themselves that they love each other. She is irrelevant to their romance and to their death.

Many critics have noted – only quickly to ignore or rationalise – Jarman's depiction of women, particularly in *Edward II*, where the most objectionable moment appears to be when Isabella kills Kent by biting into his neck.[39] While it is not helpful to label Jarman a misogynist, his depiction of women is neither peripheral to his work nor something to be simply explained away in order to maintain Jarman's films as good objects. Rather, the representation of women demonstrates a basic attitude not unconnected to the manner in which fathers are depicted.

The refusal both of the father and of femininity can refer to a yearning for a state characterised by the absence of the father and the absence of the differentiation of gender; a state before the metonymies of the middle give birth to a metaphoric totalization; a pre-Oedipal state where the motor of linear narration – the conflict between desire and the law – does not apply.[40] Jarman implies that relationships can thrive only in this state. He quotes Shakespeare at the beginning of *The Angelic Conversation*:

> Love is too young to know what conscience is;
> Yet who knows not conscience is born of love? (Sonnet 151)

The arrival of the father announces the differentiation of gender and induces conscience; it poses the barrier to love, as well as establishing the basis of hierarchy.

Just as Jarman interrogates hierarchy thematically in his books and films, he also does so formally, contributing both the sense of experimentation associated with his work, and a principle of non-narration. Jarman typically ignores the imperatives of filmic conventions, rather than challenging them in a confrontational manner – as, for example, Godard systematically did. His work recognises and uses the formal hierarchies of film. They include the placement of objects within the frame; temporal order; duration; association with other elements; and movement vs. stillness. Jarman's images nevertheless work against the perception of narrative flow. Non-narration on a formal level can be analyzed in three areas: intertextuality; specularity; and the manipulation of narrative form.

As well as playing on avant-garde film and British literary traditions, Jarman's films play on an intertextuality with his own œuvre to an extraordinary degree. Many of his cinematic techniques recur across several films: mirrors reflecting into the camera (often affecting the Super 8 camera exposure and revealing the low-tech nature of the equipment); manipulations of the image (the complicated and image-degrading stop-frame system used extensively in *The Angelic Conversation*);[41] and temporal distortions (sped-up or slow-motion). Visual motifs also recur: the filmmaker at his labours, angels, rough-trade young men, and so on.

The written texts, published independently, serve as companions to the films, commenting on their themes and discussing Jarman's production methods and conditions. Although the films stand on their own, layers of significance are added by reading the books, which concentrate on Jarman's creative life and influences. Conversely, the films illuminate the written texts. This intertextuality between Jarman's books and films interrupts the belief – in effect, just a convenient fiction – that the film text is discrete with a locatable beginning, middle and end.[42]

If intertextuality calls into question the borders of the text, Jarman's particular use of spectacle display interrupts the narrative flow and logic within texts. Jarman often incorporates musical interludes that stop the narrative action and isolate the visual elements. This technique is common, although more severely contained, in mainstream cinema. While spectacle is normally in the service of a seamless transparency – the generation of totalizing moments – for Jarman, specularization is so total and not confined to special moments that it places ideological origins outside the world of the film rather than within it.

Some of Jarman's spectacles emphasise a camp sensibility. The "Stormy Weather" sequence in *The Tempest*, in which a chorus of sailors prances through an anachronistic dance routine, defiantly up-ends a Shakespearian attitude already challenged in the film with less extravagance. In *The Garden*, a woman in a pink evening gown, not clearly linked to the life and Resurrection of Christ, lip-synchs to the "Think Pink" number from Hepburn and Astaire's *Funny Face*. The inane optimism of this song and the scene's Kenneth Anger-inspired visuals contrast with the depictions of sincere affection in the Christ couple, their persecution, and many of the film's other images.

Other disruptions of narration through specularization are less dependent on a camp sensibility. In an extended take in *Caravaggio*, an acrobat posing for Caravaggio steps away from her prop pair of wings and does a graceful routine. In *Edward II*, the action halts to display a mostly-naked man with a snake; and subsequently halts again for a music video-like sequence in which Annie Lennox sings "Every Time We Say Goodbye".[43]

While these examples are all based on a character or characters performing before the camera, Jarman's films work towards pushing all visual elements into the realm of the spectacle. Techniques such as shifting exposures, shooting on grainy film stock, and the juxtaposition of varied stocks distort the image, emphasising its surface and the external mediation of the filmmaking process. A sense of spectacle is also created by the frontal orientation of Jarman's compositions which often slide into tableaux, most notably in *Caravaggio* and *War Requiem*. The refusal of master-shots, eyeline-matches and the creation of 3-dimensional, realistic space implicit in this frontality mark even Jarman's more narratively conventional films as avant-garde. *Sebastiane* even includes what has become the ultimate spectacle – an erect penis which briefly enters the frame.

Finally, Jarman disrupts narrative progression through his manipulation of narrative elements such as the story-world. The eruption of spectacle can signal a shift in a film's level of abstraction;

specularization is therefore crucially connected to Jarman's film "worlds" which continually move between varied levels of abstraction. *Wittgenstein*, for example, moves between biography, history, philosophy, memory, dramatisation, symbolism and a fantasy space where a small, green Martian can appear to give advice. The creation of multiple levels also occurs in the written texts. *Queer Edward II* contains several tracks of information which exist simultaneously: the script to the film; slogans; photos; and production notes by Jarman, "Ghost Director" (Ken Butler) and "Isabella Regina" (Tilda Swinton). Shifts between film stocks – as in *The Last of England* – and image quality – as in *The Angelic Conversation* – not only specularize, but also create a slippage between levels of abstraction within a single text.

With few exceptions, Jarman's development of conflict and resolution also confounds narrative. Conflicts are not embodied by characters in a simple and obvious manner – other than in, perhaps, *Sebastiane*. Characters such as Tilda Swinton's besieged Virgin Mary in *The Garden*, or her troubled bride in *The Last of England*, reappear but do not continue throughout the texts along a line of character development. The personalities and concerns of these characters, to the extent that they are even depicted, do not resolve. The conflict may evaporate, as in *The Angelic Conversation*, or persist unsolved as in *Jubilee*. Or the film may simply stop, without having suggested that a clear solution – through the agency of any character – could satisfy, as is the case in *The Last of England*.

The lack of character development and agency heightens the sense that Jarman's characters are images rather than particular points of view. In fact, point of view and its relation to hierarchy is at the crux of all the issues of intertextuality, specularization and manipulations of narrative form. Through his experimentation with these formal elements, Jarman refuses to erect those hierarchies of knowledge which typically help to motor narrative. Edward Branigan discusses hierarchy, or disparity, as a crucial aspect of narrative:

> Narration comes into being when knowledge is unevenly distributed – when there is a disturbance or disruption in the field of knowledge. Informally, one can grasp the importance of disparity by imagining a universe in which all observers are perfect and all-knowing.[44]

For narrative to function, knowledge must be "intermittent".[45] Information can then be proffered or withheld in several ways, among them the position of the camera – position already implying hierarchy.

Jarman's films rigorously reject this development of disparity. They are never structured on suspense. The spectator may not understand every image, but the films do not play on the desire to know more, or imply that solutions will be forthcoming when the film/camera/character shifts to a new perspective. Controlling looks, privileged glances, and those other structures of seeing associated with the concept of "suture" are almost entirely absent.[46]

Frontal and self-contained compositions help avoid the development of narrative suspense. To use Eisenstein's terminology, Jarman's images are organised centripetally rather than centrifugally, so that the frame does not appear to withhold objects from the spectator. The fast-motion home-movie of Jarman's Sloane Street apartment (included in *Glitterbug*) is a clear, early example. Within a short length of film, a stationary single shot depicts a period of several days. In the sole composition, a wall-sized mirror reflects the comings and goings of Jarman and several friends with relentless claustrophobia; here, out of the frame means out of the film. The centripetal effect becomes especially profound in Jarman's later films. The objects and characters of *Wittgenstein* are surrounded by blackout space, making them totally self-contained and unconnected to any suggestion of a reality which is not being seen.

These visual and narrative strategies are far more abstract than Jarman's explicitly stated disagreement with hierarchical institutions in his written autobiographical texts, yet they are fundamentally linked to those attitudes. They consistently erode narrative progression and experiment with point of view. Intertextuality, specularity and Jarman's manipulation of narrative all work against the development of a stable point of view – a privileged position – located within the film.

Jarman's final film, *Blue*, for the first time in his career combines film and autobiography. This combination presents as a cinematic problem how a depiction of the life-span becomes narrativized – with disparities, asymmetries and significances imposed. In *Blue*, Jarman begins by upsetting the most basic dominance in cinema: that of image over sound. The audio-track is rich, complex and layered, and contains almost all sensory information using narration, music and sound effects; the image-track has been impoverished, reduced to a continuous blue screen.[47]

The screen's meaning is carried by colour, duration and juxtaposition to audio, but it foregoes many possibilities of the filmic – movement, change over time, representation, repetition and editing. As a result, *Blue* has none of the structures of seeing typically used in film, although it is crucially concerned with vision. In the film, Jarman asks: "My vision will never come back...If I lose half my sight will my vision be halved?";[48] and "How are we perceived, if we are to be perceived at all? For the most part we are invisible".[49] He describes the

25

physical appearance of his eyes and details the range and condition of his deteriorating sight. The "vision" which Jarman discusses is fragile, ever-changing and non-locatable; unlike most films, vision never becomes inextricable from point of view.

In fact, like other Jarman films, *Blue* diffuses point of view. Film viewers become film auditors, a role with which they are less accustomed and adept. While they only listen, film-goers are less able to determine origin; the position from which a sound emanates is never as clear as the place of the image. Jarman further confuses the issue by using four different voices – John Quentin, Nigel Terry, himself and Tilda Swinton – to express what is entirely his own poetically rendered world. (Significantly, the published text does not distinguish between voices.) In keeping with this diffusion, Jarman never fixes the symbolism of the "blue". It is variously a colour, a person or agent, a mood, a concept and a thing.

Jarman manipulates hierarchy in this film by experimentation with film's visual/audio dynamic and, by his very selection, of the autobiographical form. Peter Brooks states that "[t]he telling [of a life] is always *in terms of* the impending end",[50] but in autobiography, unlike biography, the end can never be represented, and will never provide the terms of what had gone before – the beginning and middle. *Blue* certainly alludes to the impending end, or rather what occurs after the end – mourning. The film is full of losses, both public – a plane gone down – and private – shoes Jarman will not need to buy. He speaks of lost sight and lost friends: "I have no friends now who are not dead or dying".[51] The final line in the film speaks to a moment of mourning beyond the end: "I place a delphinium, Blue, upon your grave".[52] We are brought to the edge, the moment when life will "pass like the traces of a cloud...like Sparks through the stubble",[53] but the moment can never be shown.

Finally, the cryptic quality of *Blue*'s autobiography – short, non-chronological, a mixture of poetry and prose – reveals an inherent quality of the genre, one which is fundamentally at odds with narration. In film or writing, it simply is not possible to include every aspect of even a very short life. Many events, experiences and feelings will be forgotten, distorted or ignored as irrelevant. Autobiographies confer importance on events less by their position in the causal chain than by the very fact that they are presented. Inclusion becomes at least as important as ordering. In *Blue*, Jarman employs strategies both thematic and formal to continue an emphasis which carries through all his work: the rejection of place and position to stress the importance of presence.

Notes

1 Derek Jarman, *Blue: Text of a film by Derek Jarman* (London: Channel 4 Television and BBC Radio 3, 1993): 15-16.

2 Peter Brooks, *Reading for the Plot: Design and Intention in Narrative* (New York: Vintage, 1985): 29.

3 Brooks: 52. Emphasis in original.

4 Simon Field, "The Troublesome Cases", *Afterimage* (London) 12 (autumn 1985): 3.

5 Derek Jarman, *At Your Own Risk: A Saint's Testament* (London: Hutchinson, 1992): 57.

6 Ibid: 90-91.

7 Ibid: 28.

8 Ibid: 66.

9 Ibid: 18.

10 Derek Jarman, *Dancing Ledge*, edited by Shaun Allen (London: Quartet Books, 1984): 51.

11 Jarman (1992): 28.

12 Ibid: 46.

13 Ibid: 30.

14 Ibid: 38.

15 Derek Jarman, *Modern Nature: The Journals of Derek Jarman* (London: Century, 1991): 249.

16 Jarman (1984): 53.

17 Jarman (1991): 265.

18 Jarman (1992): 17.

19 Jarman (1991): 265.

20 Jarman (1984): 38.

21 Jarman (1991): 266.

22 Jarman (1992): 4.

23 Ibid.

24 Jarman (1984): 95.

[25] Jarman (1992): 38.

[26] Ibid: 7.

[27] Psychoanalytic theory requires the removal of the father for the possibility of the adult male self. Lacan's "symbolic Father is, in so far as he signifies [the] Law, the dead Father" (Jacques Lacan, *Écrits: A Selection*, translated by Alan Sheridan [London: Tavistock Publications, 1977]: 199). Laurence A Rickels places this imperative in the realm of mourning: "As locus of testamentary substitutions, the father's death is that mournable death which, according to Freud, allows civilization itself to survive" (Laurence A Rickels, *Aberrations of Mourning: Writing on German Crypts* [Detroit: Wayne State University Press, 1988]: 20).

[28] Aspects of this home-movie sensibility include working with and casting friends, cheap, small and low-tech production, and working without a script.

[29] Jarman describes *The Garden*'s spontaneous, eight-day shoot in *Modern Nature*. He says of this scene, shot in December 1989: "Then we all went into B stage and filmed the Mocking – Guildford Four style. Off-duty policemen – the boys tied to the canteen chairs and gagged. The day before, Sarah Swords, who had the thankless task of holding this shoot together, found an actor with a penchant for opera who played a policeman. At the last moment Dawn Archibald put on a waitress outfit and produced the black treacle for the tarring and feathering." (Derek Jarman [1991]: 201.)

[30] Derek Jarman, *Queer Edward II* (London: British Film Institute, 1991): 123.

[31] Ibid: 2.

[32] Jarman (1991a): 211.

[33] Jarman (1991b): 18.

[34] Ibid: 30.

[35] Ibid: 32.

[36] Ibid: 26.

[37] René Girard, *Violence and the Sacred*, translated by Patrick Gregory (Baltimore: The Johns Hopkins University Press, 1977): 59.

[38] Ibid: 56.

[39] Colin MacCabe writes that the misogyny suggested by Edward's rejection of the Queen's body in the beginning of the film "is itself horribly overtrumped at the end when Isabella literally tears the life out of Kent with her teeth: the vagina dentata rendered into all too palpable an image" (Colin MacCabe, "Throne of blood", *Sight and Sound* 1: 6 [1991]: 13). Bette Talvacchia argues that the scene evokes vampirism: "The sexual nature of Isabella's vengeance receives a most disturbing allusion in the murder that she resolutely enacts on Kent, the brother of her husband...The vampiric

image is so overdetermined...that its use has warranted accusations of misogyny" (Bette Talvacchia, "Historical Phallicy: Derek Jarman's *Edward II*", *Oxford Art Journal* 16: 1 [1993]: 112-128). Like Talvacchia, Michael O'Pray attempts to blunt the import of the vampiric moment by comparing Isabella's action to that of Edward: "The violence is characteristically brutal and ambiguous. Isabella's murder of Edward's brother Kent by biting out his throat is horrific and intensely erotic, as is Edward's murder of Gaveston's assassin" (Michael O'Pray, "Damning desire", *Sight and Sound* 1: 6 [1991]: 8).

[40]   In a Lacanian system, the Oedipal conflict of law and desire becomes a motor for activity as well as a means of differentiating the individual. Anika Lemaire notes that the "singularity" of the self depends on this conflict: "The first dual relationship between the child and his like – another child, his own image reflected in the mirror, the mother herself or her substitutes – does not provide the child with 'subjectivity' in the sense of 'singularity' given above to that term. According to Lacan, the most this relationship can do is to constitute a registration of the totality of a body previously lived as fragmented." (Anika Lemaire, *Jacques Lacan*, translated by David Macey [London; New York: Routledge & Kegan Paul, 1977]: 78.) My thanks to Jon Wagner, with whom I discussed these issues.

[41]   Aside from its artistic value, this process also had an economic – therefore, political – significance. In an interview with Simon Field and Michael O'Pray, Jarman reports: "It was just a button on the NIZO camera. It simply occurred like things do. I just realised when I got that particular projector (a Bolex) that here was a way of recording an awful lot with very little film. It has an economic basis. You can take a three minute cassette and spin it out to twenty minutes. It's a very cheap way of documenting things. It also has a slightly hypnotic effect." (Simon Field and Michael O'Pray, "*Imaging October*, Dr. Dee and Other Matters: An Interview with Derek Jarman", *Afterimage* [London] 12 [autumn 1985]: 55.)

[42]   Jarman's published autobiographical works demonstrate varying levels of connection to his films. For example, *At Your Own Risk* and *Modern Nature* both discuss aspects of film production, but concentrate more significantly on political awareness and Jarman's life as a gardener, respectively. On the other hand, *Queer Edward II* and *Caravaggio* both include scripts from the films with which they are centrally concerned.

[43]   Talvacchia (117) recounts that Jarman had planned to film Lennox's version of the song for "Red, Hot & Blue", but was too ill at the time. *Edward II* provided a second chance for their collaboration.

[44]   Edward Branigan, *Narrative Comprehension and Film* (New York: Routledge, 1992): 66.

[45]   Ibid: 69.

[46]   Daniel Dayan's concept of the suture argues for specific psychological and ideological effects of the shot-reverse shot formula. Most crucial, in contrast to Jarman's films, is the argument that this editing strategy locates the origin of the film within the film's own fiction. (See Daniel Dayan, "The Tutor-Code of Classical Cinema", *Film Quarterly* 28: 1 [autumn 1974]: 22-31.)

[47] As the text of *Blue* makes clear, Jarman had by the time of its production lost much of his sight. Yet, his illness does not entirely account for his decision to abandon the image in this film; Jarman previously had had directorial assistance on *The Garden* and *Edward II* because of his health. Furthermore, he was not at all uninterested in the visual. Jarman's final published book, released posthumously, is *Chroma: A Book of Colour – June '93* (London: Century, 1994), an intense investigation of colour.

[48] Jarman (1993): 7.

[49] Ibid: 12.

[50] Brooks: 52.

[51] Jarman (1993): 7.

[52] Ibid: 30.

[53] Ibid.

Perverse law: Jarman as gay criminal hero

David Gardner

The time has come to reckon with the criminal. Not merely as a scapegoat relegated to the fringes of social acceptability, but as a powerful emblem of opposition to the constraining forces of a dominant order, in whom the most marginal – or marginalized – communities may read the possibility of resistance to that order. In this light, the outlaw is figured as both an object of admiration and an agent of transgression, as both hero and subversive. This dual figuring is crucial, for he (or she) is thereby the site of both attraction and action, a model for desire and political resistance. It is the connection between the latter that provides an *entrée* for gay and lesbian studies. Resistance and desire are prominent axes around which myriad representations of homosexuality may be and have been organised. In their orbit we discover a series of evocative oppositions: acceptance and rejection, visibility and invisibility, strength and weakness, among others. The criminal thus models as an image of what is desired and as an image of competent activism, whose (anti-) authority is constituted around his or her own desire. In representations where the desirer and the desired are identified, "sameness" (of sex, of marginality) signifies difference rather than conformity to the norm, and is therefore perceived as a liability – or worse, as a stigma.

It is the project of many lesbian and gay authors, whether cinematic, literary or otherwise, to invert the norm, particularly when that norm denies them existence. Hence, what is unacceptable is recast as acceptable, and what is forbidden becomes permissible. There is a strong tradition within such representations, largely neglected thus far, to cast the criminal as hero, as one to be admired, emulated and, ultimately, desired. The myth of the outlaw figures significantly in non-gay and non-lesbian contexts, of course, serving a challenge to the normative forces of any society. As an uneasy, potentially disruptive presence, however, the criminal has been conspicuously central to representations of homosexuality, giving rise to a number of configurations: theft as an act of love, the outlaw as comrade, and the criminal as artist.

Whether rendered as outcast, artist or even king, the criminal fascinated Derek Jarman. This preoccupation aligns Jarman with many of his idols – such prominent homosexual writers, filmmakers and criminals as Genet, Pasolini, Eisenstein, Cocteau and Anger. Their influence is felt continuously in Jarman's œuvre, including *Sebastiane* (1976), *Caravaggio* (1986) and *Imagining October* (1984). The achievements of such a pantheon – radical, subversive, but no less important for its marginality – point to an underlying current which, forced to posit gay identity and representations far beyond the margins of an accepted social order, rewrites that order in terms that both privilege and give voice to an alternate aesthetic.

If Genet and Pasolini revelled in that mythical criminal hero of their imaginings, Jarman paid tribute to their longings by addressing a workable model of gay heroism, one that progressed from the underworld (Genet's prison milieu, Anger's film culture) to the pageant of politics and letters (Eisenstein and Pasolini's realm) in films from *The Last of England* (1987) to *Edward II* (1991) and to *Wittgenstein* (1993). Such a "workable" model envisages yet another array of binary axes evoked by the combination of gay artist with heroic criminal: love/violence, art/crime, acclaim/notoriety. The goal, in a sense, is to invert the positive/negative binarism and thus pervert what is oppressive in the norm. A hero is someone admired individually, but also by some collective definition in respect to a certain community. How does a marginal subculture air its communal interests in the absence of conventional or legal channels? Moreover, is it the task of gay fiction, documentary or even textual criticism to rework or correct the "missing" or hidden histories, and, in the attempt, to mobilise, define or merely represent this subculture? Often, as in gay subculture, what is admired from the margins is simultaneously unacceptable to the norms of the society at large. To the extent that the dominant order responds to marginal culture with intolerance, even repugnance (in the form of legal suppression[1] and condemnation) resistance can be organised around society's proscription. Social taboos are easily adapted to highly charged forms of protest, both cultural and political, by virtue of their mere representation. What is proscribed or even unspeakable, such as criminality or homosexuality, is not only spoken, but also deployed as a weapon of resistance.

Jarman explored the history of this criminal and "heroic" identity within his film texts, but himself progressed, through political engagement, from the potentially passive role of filmmaker (as social commentator) to both public activist and hero. This heroism (or martyrdom, in the fashion of Genet) can be quite readily attributed to his resilience in working outside the system: not surprisingly, the mainstream film industry was reluctant to embrace his films; more to the point, in his later career the broader society never sufficiently recognised his political constituency, much less responded adequately to the dire health crisis afflicting both his community and him personally.

There is a danger inherent in this investigation. The line blurs easily between Jarman's work and his persona, due in part to his self-identification within the films, achieved through voice-over, self-portraiture and the extensive writings he published about his life, work and beliefs. But this is due equally to the impossibility of separating the criminality – the outlaw nature – of the mere representation of "criminal" acts from that of the act contained *in* the representation. Censorship laws, even laws that proscribed homosexual acts in Britain far later than in other modern states, compound the difficulty of distinguishing between the transgressiveness of what is represented and that of the underground culture which seeks to represent itself.

Through a reading that foregrounds both the representations and the extratextual "work" of Jarman's life, I propose to trace the developments of varied strains of criminal aesthetics, outlaw artists and heroic figures that fill out Jarman's film work, together with the effects and exchanges that his artistry in turn exerted over his life – his political life in particular. The aim of my analysis, in view of other possible contexts in which Jarman has been read, is to place him anew within a framework that offers the richest understanding not only of the imagery he furnished, but also of the impetus that led him to represent in the first place. At the same time I hope to suggest a fresh approach to the study of gay texts and authors, by examining a tradition that, however prevalent, has yet to be charted.

In its potential for locating or authorising a discourse from the margins, film is particularly potent. Even as traditional cinematic forms have come under attack for perpetuating dominant myths and excluding experiences which fall outside the norm, cinema harbours the power to erase or undo marginality by excluding or rewriting the dominant order. If this potential has been exploited by the mainstream where marginal culture has long remained invisible, what is to prevent the latter from appropriating the very tools of the dominant culture? What is visualized and then made visible assumes a particular force.

Behind the vision is the author, whose authorship in this case is neither the product of a systematic analysis nor a structural resemblance among a body of a given filmmaker's films, so much as a text unto itself. A politicized image of a radical individual emerges alongside the cinematic texts he or she has produced, offering clues about concerns and interpretations of the less-than-hermetic film texts. Rather than read biography in the text, we read the text in the biography. In the end, we have not only identified authors whom we would claim within a certain heritage, but also formulated a new kind of authorship.[2]

My argument depends on a reading of Jarman's life and work that, as already suggested, proceeds on slippery terrain. The task is to an extent made easier by the substantial amount of light Jarman shed on his films in a number of volumes compiled from journals and production notes. I will freely consider Jarman's life and those of his peers and influences within my discussion. There is naturally a hazard in inferring biography from an author's works. The terrain of autobiography is even more treacherous, yet can hardly be ignored. What are the risks of reading identity or sexuality within a given text, in view of or despite the body of biographical material? In his book on homosexuality in Spanish writing and film, Paul Julian Smith addresses the risks of naming identity and ascribing to it a set of socially constructed attributes or values.[3] The difficulty lies especially in negotiating codes of "recognition" or identification among the members of a community that is not easily defined or generalised. Where does one begin to locate a gay text or spectator in the absence of a clear starting-point? Must one establish a consistent practice of reading homosexuality either in the constructions of the text, its author or its audience?

In discussing what he terms "the ends of autobiography", Smith cites another literary critic who suggests that "homosexual writers so consistently take as their text the construction of the self that one is tempted to claim there is only one genre of homosexual writing: the autobiographical".[4] Likewise, writers on Third Cinema, such as Teshome Gabriel, have proposed a "third phase" of cinema, which addresses the inevitability of autobiography in marginal discourse.[5] Jarman himself suggests that gay biography was not possible, given social attitudes, until very recently: "Most of our biography is located in fiction. Genet's prisoners, Cocteau's sailors; it was not possible to write in the first person, so we have a lack of information".[6] In fact, what is intriguing about such representations is how difficult it is to separate the autobiographical elements from the work. Genet reworked his experiences through a number of ostensibly fictional works, and relished his skill at confounding efforts to distinguish the life from the legend. Ultimately, he generated a myth of the self that transformed his lived experiences into a credo, a model of identity. Jarman similarly found himself unable to represent without suffusing the work with his own history. More importantly, Jarman's autobiographical strategy not only emulates or alludes to those of Genet, Pasolini and Caravaggio, but also is projected over them, re-instigating the production of those other autobiographies to arrive at an entirely new meaning. Jarman reinvents his life not only in the fashion of Genet, but also by borrowing from him and from a host of others. Autobiography, as such, is a mode that is conveyed across a variety of genres, and identity is a device that amplifies the reader's ability to consider, assume or even reject a number of provocative social roles.

Risking an autobiographical reading may produce richer, more complex meanings in otherwise banal or insignificant texts. There is a far greater risk, however, in a simplistic or singular approach to texts that are complex or polysemic in their engagement with autobiography, politics and cultural history. The danger there lies in inadvertently reducing complex meanings to the banal: Jarman's works cannot be read merely in terms of identity, the law, or society alone. For the 1991 reprinted edition of *Dancing Ledge*, Jarman wrote a new preface that provides a definitive key to reading both his work and his life, sadly halted three years later:

> When I started to write *Dancing Ledge* in a Roman hotel room (Croce di Malta) late in 1982, my worklife was becalmed, deserted by the funding bodies and the British cinema renaissance running hard for Mrs Thatcher's new Jerusalem – absolute beginners all. My own renaissance (*Caravaggio* made on the Isle of Dogs for £475,000 from the BFI) was three years away. Angry, Nico said why don't you write it out. One thing led to another and what started as a book on the frustration of funding led to the writing of an autobiography at forty...Now a decade later my Queerlife is reprinted...The years since have seen the renewal and reinvention of my cinema (*Angelic Conversation, The Last of England* and *The Garden*), the reclaiming of the Queer Past in *War Requiem* and *Edward II*, my move to Prospect Cottage, the building of the garden, catching the virus and falling in Love.
>
> My body was thrown into the struggle, bringing me into a spotlight in a way I never expected or wanted. On 22 December 1986, finding I was body positive, I set myself a target: I would disclose my secret and survive Margaret Thatcher. I did. Now I have my sights on the millennium and a world where we are all equal before the law.[7]

The author here seems little troubled by a reading of his autobiography that risks essentializing his identity or, worse, conflating him with the text. His body itself is in the struggle, a struggle that is social as much as medical. As confirmation of this, Jarman films himself in *The Garden* (1990), washed up on his sickbed in the surf near Prospect Cottage.

I will leave aside the larger question of assigning authorship to a filmwork produced by a collaborative effort. Jarman, in extensive writings, reveals a great deal of the process of realising his various projects, and is quite clear in his acknowledgement of others' contributions to the works, even as he claims authorship and shows himself to be the orchestrator of a particular cinematic vision. With such an unconventional filmmaker, however, who worked apart from, and even in spite of, orthodox means, identity, autobiography and society are deployed in an entirely subversive fashion that demands an alternate approach, and in fact denies the possibility of ignoring this deployment. What is truly transgressive about Jarman is that his films solicit both an aberrant ideal reader and an aberrant reading practice.

*　*　*

Within a British context, Jarman may be aligned with such filmmakers as Stephen Frears, Hanif Kureishi, Isaac Julien, Julien Temple, Terence Davies, Neil Jordan, Mike Leigh and Sally Potter, who explored fractured racial, class and sexual identities during the Thatcher years. Here was the vanguard of the true renaissance, as opposed to Thatcher's "Renaissance", the enemy of innovation and free expression, which Jarman ascribed to the revival of Empire epics such as *Brideshead Revisited* (1981) and *Chariots of Fire* (1981) during David Puttnam's ascendance. Working with considerably less funding than most of his peers, however, Jarman saw his role and position differently. The struggle entailed in bringing his projects to the screen forced him to consider his identity as both an artist and a homosexual in relation to the film industry, as well as to society at large. He thus was as apt to identify with Pasolini or Eisenstein as with other British filmmakers. Gradually, he saw his stigmatized position as outcast evolve into a more dynamic role, that of agitator and outlaw. In so doing, Jarman pledged affiliation with a wholly *other* tradition. It is a tradition of criminal-artists, and its spokesman is Jean Genet.

Michel Foucault's *Surveiller et punir: Naissance de la prison* (*Discipline and Punish: The Birth of the Prison*, 1975) documents the prison world as an elaborate structure that pervades the whole of society. His description of the carceral alludes often to Mettray, a boys' colony where Genet was housed and to which the latter referred often in his own writing. In fixing a time for the birth of the French penal system, Foucault speculates: "perhaps, that glorious day, unremarked and unrecorded, when a child in Mettray remarked as he lay dying: 'What a pity I left the colony so soon'...This marked the death of the first penitentiary saint."[8] He evokes a literary tradition with his imaginative analyses, but prefers not to follow through:

[T]he lyricism of marginality may find inspiration in the image of the 'outlaw', the great social nomad, who prowls on the confines of a docile, frightened order. But it is not on the fringes of society and through successive exiles that criminality is born, but by means of ever more closely placed insertions, under ever more insistent surveillance, by an accumulation of disciplinary coercion.[9]

Foucault's account of institutional discipline instructs us to resist docility or be preyed upon. Detention inspires recidivism, and, as Foucault indicates, "those leaving prison have more chance than before of going back to it".[10] If Foucault is trying to draw out possible resistance to this system, why not turn to Genet, who rendered explicit the erotic wish behind the inevitable return to prison? Like Jarman, Genet attended closely to the "insertions" within the centre of the society that would cast him out. This is to say that his recidivism was not merely a gesture towards the exile Foucault spoke of – the return to prison – but a staging of the criminal act in full view of the public. Once incarcerated, the criminal had less to fear from future sentencing, to the extent that the stigma of prison – of the *first* incarceration – had already been sustained. The criminal who had also experienced the theatrical pleasure of the criminal act would find it difficult to resist the next opportunity to perform. As if setting the stage for one of Genet's plays, *Discipline and Punish* reveals prison as a model for the interworkings of power, social confinement, illegality, authority and surveillance. The marginal – and yet, as both Foucault and Genet cast it, lyrical – world of delinquency is the most appropriate place for introducing resistance, as illustrated in the prison erotics of Genet's film, *Un Chant d'amour* (1950).

Richard Dyer, despite a myopic tendency to catalogue "good" and "bad" representations, provides an insightful account of Genet, in whom he sees the fetishization of crime, masculinity and rough trade as subversive attractions.[11] The richest portions of Dyer's analysis emphasise Genet's aesthetic of beauty, which ran counter to the clean, delicate refinement of classical French cinema. The "rhetoric" of beauty which Genet explored is applied in a subversive way to a sordid and dangerous criminal world.[12] Dyer cites Sartre (from his tract, *Saint Genet*) as further evidence: "Genet turns everything designated criminal – murder, theft, homosexuality – into things to be sought, desired, pursued and venerated, not to be avoided or disavowed".[13] Even the relationship between prisoners and guards, determined and constrained though it may be by prison bars, permits an unequivocal representation of subcultural desire – one which can be mapped onto analogous relations that Genet eroticized, between murderer and victim (*Querelle de Brest*), hero and traitor (*Pompes funèbres* [*Funeral Rites*]), or master and slave (*Les Bonnes* [*The Maids*]).

Avant-garde films that, according to Dyer, derive from Genet's work reiterate the prison setting. Dyer indicates the interplay of pastoral, Romantic scenes with cold, brutal prison cells as an elaboration of Genet's rhetoric of beauty. This alternation is important in explaining the connection between the political space of prison and what is being represented – i.e. desire and freedom, or the freedom to desire – but Dyer misses the irony of such a comparison. Genet is not idealising pastoral romance, but rather the transformation of prison into a lyrical world, rendered through the force of words and representation as a poetic subject. In Fassbinder's *Querelle* (1982), based on Genet's novel, representations of the external world of a French seaport – the dungeon in an abandoned battlement that serves as both hideout and trysting point, for example – invoke the architecture of prison, while at the same time foregrounding the dysfunction of homosexuality outside prison, i.e. its marginality in respect to the norm. Despite the regulated confinement of prison, Genet and those who followed argue for its liberating potential: imprisoned, one is somehow freer to love.

Dyer's critique of *Querelle* concentrates on the power relations of passive and active sexuality centred on the penis and anus, neglecting the richer configurations of symbolic roles that Genet explored, such as murderer/victim, betrayer/betrayed, guard/prisoner.[14] For Genet, in fact, these positions shift, and the investigation of power between active and passive role-playing can subvert the expected outcome. At the peak of modernism, Genet demonstrated admirably that there is ample power in a "bad" representation, provided that the result is the upheaval of societal norms.

The language in some of these systems of representation, like the language of Foucault, evokes some of the most negative associations for homosexuality within dominant culture: sickness, criminality, perversion, delinquency, murder, thievery, plague. The coincidence of these as metaphors in both Foucault's theory and in film practice (witness recent gay independent projects such as Haynes's *Poison* [1990], Araki's *The Living End* [1992] or Kalin's *Swoon* [1992]) is intriguing, suggesting that we are on the right track – if we can be assured of appropriating such descriptives for the subversive shuffling of dominant cultural norms. Martyr and scapegoat become the terms of desire; they voice a powerful subjectivity wrought from disadvantage or ostracism.

Genet, whose sexual and social existence outside prison was uncertain, was forced to turn that prison inside out and expose society to the terms of his prison aesthetic. This resistance served not only to promote Genet's work, and with it the influence of his aesthetic commentary, but also to liberate him. His writing caught the attention of established intellectuals such as Sartre and Cocteau, who intervened on his behalf and persuaded the state to pardon his life sentence. In other words, Genet defended his sexuality, criminality and philosophy through the action of his representation. By taking prison as the preferred space for his self-representation, he paradoxically demonstrated that he did not belong in that space.

Jarman's work is illuminated by the world Genet revealed. The potential of the prison cell as a space of representation, together with the charged relationship between gaoler and gaoled, murderer/thief and victim, figure prominently in Jarman's films. Prison is a privileged space of desire in *Edward II*. The relationship between the prisoner and his gaoler is exalted, only to end in betrayal transformed by love. In Jarman's extreme rendering, homosexuality is so resolutely an anathema to the state that when its emblem, the King, is discovered to be hómosexual, the state itself is outlawed. Edward II, as supreme authority, is powerless to institute his love for Gaveston as equal to or compatible with his love for kingdom. His desire is therefore read as treason, and he is imprisoned. Deep in his dungeon, love takes root where it would not in the aboveground. Lightborn, his gaoler, becomes his solace and only companion. Covered in soot, he stokes the fire in his boiler suit – evoking a tradition of gay iconography, found in Eisenstein's *Bronenosets Potemkin* (*Battleship Potemkin*, 1925) and Fassbinder's *Querelle*, of shirtless men tending coal engines. His own desire remains enigmatic and replete with possibilities.

In a film that presents explicit gay sexuality as a set piece and as provocation, the understated romance between Edward and Lightborn serves as the film's most eloquent argument for desire that is not permitted in the open. Jarman writes:

> the general public has returned home to pore over the salacious Sundays, ferreting out another middle-aged victim driven into the not so secret arms of a boy starved of attention and affection who has spilt the beans for the illusory security of cash. 'He pulled down the boy's pants and blew him for £20 in the corridor of a cinema/a public lavatory/a deserted station, they met in a seedy club/Half Moon Street/the Dorchester.' Two young men holding hands on the street court ridicule, kissing they court arrest, so the worthy politicians, their collaborators, the priests, and the general public push them into corners where they can betray them in the dark. Judases in the garden of Gethsemane.[15]

Jarman writes often of these dark corners, and of his own experiences of illicit sex on Hampstead Heath, which, despite its secrecy, is rendered with jubilance in Jarman's writing as a site of marginal festivity. In the end, Edward is betrayed by Lightborn who becomes his executioner. The ecstasy of his death, exactly as Genet would sketch it, is matched by its horror. Edward has a red-hot iron poker shoved up his anus in a highly telling gesture (given his "crime") that is supported by historical fact.

Along different lines of Genet's tradition, Jarman's first feature, *Sebastiane*, depicts the all-male community of a Roman legion camped in the desert. The undercurrent of sexual and violent tension simultaneously subverts and reinforces the institutional authority of the soldier's world, a world that is both desired and resisted. Sebastian, the Christian, will neither renounce his conversion nor accede to his desire for his commander, who would free him:

> Sebastian. Renaissance. Pretty boy smiles through the arrows on a thousand altar pieces – plague. Saint. Captain of Diocletian's guard. Converted, stoned, and thrown into the sewers...Androgyne icon banned by the bishop of Paris... Impersonated by Mishima. In love with his martyrdom.[16]

In Jarman's film, Sebastian's stubborn piety is rendered as perverse, more so even than the denial of his desire. Yet his suffering is at the same time attractive, and the only consummation of his desire will be his martyrdom. It is all he believes in; he mistakes it for faith, even love. Like Genet, Jarman up-ends and profanes the terms of religious iconography in view of his own desires and ends. Not only does he recast a society in which piety is perverse and homosexual desire the norm, but also he indicates how the norm is oppressive in any light. On the one hand, Jarman presents a homosexual "order" which will not tolerate the self-denial of Sebastian. On the other hand, Sebastian's apparent sexual repression ("dis-ease", for Jarman) is also represented as a principled resistance, one which is celebrated in Christian hagiography (even as the eroticization of Sebastiane's martyrdom in Renaissance painting is eschewed). By highlighting a moment when Christianity itself was marginal, a moment which also privileges gay desire, Jarman vindicates his own marginal position in the context of Christian martyrdom – martyrdom as apotheosis, martyrdom as pointless waste, Passion as passion.

There can be no question that Jarman modelled his ideal of sexual outlaw according to the subversive, resistant aesthetics of Genet's brand of criminality. Jarman is called "Saint Derek of Dungeness"[17] by his admirers, and one of his published writings is called *At Your Own*

Risk: A Saint's Testament (1992). Like Genet, Jarman reconstituted his martyrdom as an aggressive pulpit for civil rights – Genet espoused the causes of Palestinians and Black Panthers in an era before AIDS and gay consciousness prompted a new brand of activism; it is not clear whether Genet, who, like Pasolini, harboured ambivalence about communal gay identity, would have embraced gay liberation as such – and the normalisation of his marginal existence by its imposition upon the centre. Jarman's life and imminent death with AIDS provoked him to expand the metaphor of sexual criminality to account for both popular perceptions and state oppressions of homosexuals in the age of the plague.

* * *

Even before illness, Jarman was drawn to the identification of criminal and artist, which came together in his film, *Caravaggio*. Jarman speculated that if the 16th century painter Caravaggio lived in the 20th century, he might be a filmmaker such as Pasolini. Jarman's own identification with the latter is evident from *Sebastiane*, an adaptation of the martyrdom of Saint Sebastian filmed in the desolate landscapes of Sardinia in homage to the poet/filmmaker. After its release, he was told that it was a film "Pier Paolo would have loved".[18] Later, filming *The Garden*, Jarman digs out a cape worn by one of the Roman soldiers in *Sebastiane*:

> I threw the cape over [the actor's] shoulders, handed him the crook and knife...He hid himself from the camera behind the cape. I filmed this, and later him sleeping in the sun. Felt Pier Paolo smiling over my shoulder. Secret camera work...There is a romance in the camera that I touched in *The Angelic Conversation*. I see it all over the Pasolini films – something vulnerable, an archaic smile. I see it in our films, nowhere else. This is all I really want to film.[19]

Nor is Jarman's identification with Caravaggio disguised in the slightest. While working on the *Caravaggio* script, he complained: "[t]he problem is that I've written a self-portrait filtered through the Caravaggio story, which is of course not in any way Caravaggio's life".[20] Earlier, Jarman had seen this strategy as a profitable one, providing an innovative use of period (through the insertion of contemporary values, and anachronistic objects such as typewriters, calculators and motor cycles) and the means to infuse his film with his own life: "My Italian childhood in Villa Quessa would make a perfect start, a few miles down the road from Caravaggio".[21]

In fact, *Caravaggio* allowed Jarman to insert his own life into Caravaggio's story in further homage to Pasolini. He shared Pasolini's divided allegiance to two Italys: the childhood idylls in northern Italy and the adult fascination with the rough street culture of Rome and Sicily further south. Jarman's earliest memories are of his father's postings in Pakistan and Italy. In his writing, he periodically calls upon these vague traces of the past:

> May 1946. Lago Maggiore – 'Dolce Fa Niente'. Four years old: the sound of swallows, *itys itys itys*. I lie awake in a grand old mahogany bed, staring at the high ceiling of my bedroom, which glows pearl-white in the early morning sunlight. *Itys itys itys*. In the yard Davide, the handsome one, who rows across the lake and throws me high in the air and takes me hunting on the handlebars of his bike is whistling 'Dolce Fa Niente.' A swallow sweeps in through the window along a random sunbeam...Then Cecilia, *'Zia di questo bel uomo'* bustles in with a long bamboo feather duster swearing incoherently at the swallows, the mess they've made building their nests.[22]

Jarman elaborates on this memory ten years later, in *Modern Nature*:

> After breakfast Davide, [Cecilia's] handsome eighteen year old nephew, would place me on the handlebars of his bike and we'd be off down country lanes – or out on to the lake in an old rowing boat, where I would watch him strip in the heat as he rowed round the headland to a secret cove, laughing all the way. He was my first love.[23]

There is an enigmatic coda in *Caravaggio* after the artist's death, which is ambiguously cued as a flashback to Caravaggio's childhood. A small boy dressed in an angel's costume watches a night-time procession that re-enacts Christ's final march along a narrow village street. He holds the hand of a handsome young man (in the tradition of Pasolini's *ragazzi*). The boy slips into a doorway and calls out to the youth, Pascualoni, who responds by asking Michele (Caravaggio's name) what it is he sees. Then young Caravaggio leads his guardian into a church, where a living tableau of Caravaggio's "The Entombment of Christ" is staged at the altar. The voice-over narration by the adult Caravaggio that leads into this sequence begins in the previous scene, in which he slits the throat of his lover, Ranuccio. The murder itself is a flashback from the end of the painter's life. As the dying Ranuccio is held in a final embrace by Caravaggio, we hear the voice-over repeat Jarman's childhood recollection of the swallows in his bedroom at Lago Maggiore, with a few variations. The mahogany bed has become a death barge, and the sleepy young boy presses his face into the pillow and dreams of Pascualoni, his "true love" (the name itself seems to combine the idea of Pascua – Easter, the Passion – and Pasolini). Cecilia, the housekeeper and aunt of that "handsome" man, remains intact. But the fictional Pascualoni substituted for Davide refers us to an earlier moment in the film, when the former figured as the teenaged Michele's street companion. The sequence, drawn from Jarman's childhood memory, creates a cinematic link between Ranuccio's murder and Caravaggio's own death barge. The Passion tableau in the little village church depicts Caravaggio's passion; it is as Christ that Caravaggio encounters the boy Michele in his final death-scene fantasy.

Because Jarman does not account for the Easter pageantry in his writings, this sequence remains somewhat mysterious, as though it has been culled from the deep recesses of memory in an obscure declaration of Jarman's own position within the film. Although Pascualoni connects it to the rest of the film, there is a rare, ephemeral quality which also distinguishes the sequence. The boy seems to intrude from another world or era, even class, so that the images represent something more remote than Caravaggio's life: Jarman's childhood. As impossible to conceive as Michele, the boy, face to face with the image in death of the adult Caravaggio, is the boy Derek before the grown man's camera.

Jarman, who trained as a painter, referred directly to Caravaggio's work for clues to the painter's life and the narrative line of his film, undertaking a kind of sexual archaeology:

> To Caravaggio's sexuality there are two references. One to the girl Lena, his girl, in the police records, and the second to his involvement with some schoolboys in Sicily which led to his leaving town rather quickly. Neither is in any way conclusive; so the evidence is to be sought in the paintings. This, as all the work was painted from life, is much easier than might be imagined. With so little documentation on such a taboo subject it's difficult to know how the seventeenth century understood physical homosexuality. How it was viewed obviously depended, as now, on who you were...The term 'homosexual' which identifies and ostracizes a group because of their desires and inclinations, is a nineteenth-century clinical invention, c. 1860.[24]

Jarman subscribes here to Foucault's view of the modern construction of homosexuality; he goes on to describe the urban underground in which homosexuals must have identified their desire, and the peasant society's indifference to "urban moralists".[25] Moreover, the Church propagated a contradictory view of homosexuality as heresy (Jarman attributes the expression "faggot" to witch trials and the burnings that invariably ensued), while at the same time celebrating the male nude and images of homosexual "passion" in Renaissance painting.[26] Cognizant of this tradition, Jarman relies on his own experience to give logic to the grey areas of the canvas and to provide an impetus for the political edge of his portrait of Caravaggio. His film therefore manifests, between the layers of his and Caravaggio's lives, an effect of *pentimento*, a phenomenon of oil painting where ghostly traces of an earlier painting are discernible over time beneath the surface of a canvas that has been painted over.[27]

Pasolini depicted similar glimpses of early childhood that eroticize his memories in the light of his adult desires. In *Edipo Re* (*Oedipus Rex*, 1967), Jocasta and Laius are represented as an elegant 1930s couple with an air of rural (northern) gentility. Oedipus's father is a handsome young military officer with Fascist sympathies. While the rest of the film is clothed in classical garb, Pasolini, like Jarman, avails himself of anachronism to work in his own background, and to propose for the infant Oedipus an inverted Oedipal scenario, where attraction for the father is also indicated along the lines of Pasolini's desire.[28] Although the modern setting does not correspond historically with Pasolini's life (he was an adolescent rather than an infant in the 1930s), it enables him to establish the political context for the antagonism between Laius and the infant who has already supplanted him in Jocasta's affections.

Il Vangelo secondo Matteo (*The Gospel According to St Matthew*, 1964) proposes the desert hillsides of southern Italy for its Holy Land. Pasolini idealised the peasant villages in much the same way that he fixated on the urban sub-proletariat of Rome – both offer resistance to the *miracolo economico* of the 1950s that threatened to erase the last traces of Italy's pre-capitalist past. As in Jarman's *Caravaggio*, it is a past where sexuality and art have a more ambiguous, important relationship to the law and the Church, one better suited to Pasolini's ambivalent sexual identity. The Italy of his fantasies was vanishing, but this does not prevent Pasolini from representing his fantasy past. Matthew's Gospel in Pasolini's hands also reveals an Oedipal melodrama, wherein Joseph is relegated to the sidelines by the saintly missions of his wife and the son he did not father.[29]

Jarman's identification with the Roman underclass culture of Pasolini's *ragazzi* is explicit. In his production diary, he notes that "[t]he streets of Rome will be ridden with violence as they were in the beginning of the seventeenth century. Not the Red Brigades, but religious factions."[30] *Caravaggio* underscores the connection between violence and desire that is as much a part of Pasolini's criminal aesthetic (in films such as his first feature, *Accattone* [1961]) as Jarman's. In his journal, Jarman recounts an episode in which he is attacked by a gang of youths, out for thrills and a few lira. It is chilling in its resemblance to the circumstances of Pasolini's death. A few days later, he learns that a businessman from Turin was killed at the same spot.[31] Jarman's diary invokes *Una vita violenta*, the title of a novel by Pasolini, who in *Accattone* prefigured his death with a similar scene of a prostitute attacked by a gang of toughs on the outskirts of Rome. Of course, not all of Jarman's identification with Pasolini's aesthetic is violent or self-destructive:

> Had Caravaggio been reincarnated in this century it would have been as a film-maker, Pasolini...painting has degenerated into an obscure, hermetic practice, performed by initiates behind closed doors. There is a remarkable lack of emotional force in modern painting. Who could shed a tear for it now? But you *can* weep at Pasolini's *Gospel According to Matthew*, and *Ricotta* can make you laugh. In 1600, who knows, painting might have evoked the same immediate response. Of course Pasolini painted very badly.[32]

By examining his portrait of Caravaggio, we can also understand how Jarman heralded Pasolini as a hero, rather than as a tragic victim. As Jarman suggested, society's view of the homosexual depends on "who you were". Pasolini was firstly a celebrated poet admired as a national figure in Italy, and secondly a filmmaker whose marginal representations received far more attention abroad.[33] For Jarman, it was Pasolini's marginal vision that earned admiration.

This admiration is reworked in Jarman's identification with Caravaggio, who embodies the ideal of criminal-artist in Jarman's work:

> Not a victim like Orton or Pasolini but a murderer who happened to be an artist. Caravaggio painted some of the most powerfully religious images of the seventeenth century; and changed the way an entire generation *looked*. Notorious amongst his contemporaries as a dangerous and dangerous-looking young man, the violent trajectory of his life calls assumptions about an artist's relation to society into question... casual pickups painted as Saint John, dead prostitutes hauled from the Tiber hung as Virgins over the counter-reformation altars of Rome...Artists steal the world in order to re-present it as art.[34]

45

Caravaggio painted from life – one reason why Jarman looks to the paintings for his film's narrative. *Caravaggio* is peopled with the subjects of those paintings – they are also the characters from Pasolini's film. As he sifts through Caravaggio's life, Jarman is at times explicit in his identification with the painter, at times oblique. He confirms from what little recorded history there is that Caravaggio suffered from a malarial illness, then painted himself as Bacchus with a hangover: "The Jaundiced Bacchino Malato".[35] In his journal, Jarman also recalls a summer in childhood when he himself was afflicted with jaundice.[36] He continues to seek out his own history in Caravaggio's life:

> Caravaggio breathed his life, himself, into old ideals. Bacchus was the androgyne god and this was a reflection of the painter's sexuality. At first Caravaggio was probably bisexual, at eighteen or nineteen growing up with the conventions that surrounded him. Later you hack them away, but the strictures of Church and society leave a cancer, a lingering doubt, which leads to dis-ease in this painter, and to the extraordinary force of his work as he attempted to overcome it. He brought the lofty ideals down to earth, and became the most homosexual of painters, in the way that Pasolini is the most homosexual of film-makers. In a hostile environment this extreme of self-analysis became self-destruction. It's worth noting how many 'gay' artists die young: Murnau, Pasolini, Eisenstein, Fassbinder, Marlowe, Orton, and Caravaggio...From the moment he grew up and identified himself with the murderer in 'Saint Matthew' – the murderer imaged as god – he unconsciously took on the Church as his true and deadly enemy – after all, its authority, its over-selective reading of its holy texts, had led to the outlawing of the centre of his life.[37]

When Jarman compares Caravaggio to Pasolini as the self-destructive victim of a hostile society, he is not entirely contradicting his earlier claim that Caravaggio was different from Orton and Pasolini. What matters is the "extraordinary force of his work" in the face of social opposition. In a discussion of Stephen Frears's film about Orton, *Prick Up Your Ears* (1987), Jarman muses on the irony that some of the important "gay" films of the 1980s were made by straight directors. Jarman does not believe he could have done a better job than Frears, but he is nonetheless frustrated that the same film – given the hostile commercial environment of the time – more than likely could not have been made by a gay filmmaker. In fact, Jarman is certain that his version would have been markedly different: "It would have been difficult, even unacceptable to suggest that the hero of the Orton film was Halliwell [Orton's lover and murderer] – a much more attractive character than Joe".[38] Jarman points to Halliwell as co-author of the plays, one who did not suit society's image of the artist as well as Orton did.

In Caravaggio, Jarman saw both murderer and victim, and a way to admire Pasolini and even Orton for their depictions of the criminal milieu. Given society's enmity, Orton's self-destructive inclinations provide a brief but powerful model of resistance before they are extinguished. Rather than view their lives merely as cautionary tales, Jarman would celebrate and build upon what Pasolini, Orton and Caravaggio achieved. Perversely, Jarman sympathises with Kenneth Halliwell, and posits a murder as the central heroic act of *Caravaggio*.

The "murderer imaged as god" is the key to Jarman's reading of Caravaggio's paintings. Their subjects are crucial for unravelling the narrative that the filmmaker traces: heroes, gods, assassins and saints play their different roles both on and off the canvas. The models are the painter's lovers, according to Jarman, but Caravaggio also cast himself in all the parts:

> Through his patron the Medici Cardinal Del Monte he received his first major commission, the 'Martyrdom of Saint Matthew' in the Contarelli Chapel, in which a handsome assassin – he occupies the centre of the canvas – is cruised by the artist gazing guiltily over his shoulder; it is a self-portrait of one in his late twenties whose good looks have been prematurely destroyed. Meanwhile, the martyr lies abject, a cypher of holiness, at the feet of a murderer reminiscent of the triumphant Christ in Michelangelo's 'Last Judgement.'
>
> Caravaggio, the theatrical hard boy, fades into the chiaroscuro, the light and dark of his schizoid vision – gambling in taverns, stones through windows, artichokes thrown at waiters, the endless petty sword fights. Finally he murders Ranuccio Thomasoni (his lover?) after a game of tennis then goes on the run. Safely in Malta, he signs a confession in the blood of John the Baptist, 'I, Caravaggio did this.' In one of the final paintings the hollow eyed severed head of Goliath which the young David holds in his hand is recognizably the artist's own. David is not pretty; he is a rough little number, one of those Roman street boys in whom, like Pasolini, C. continually sought 'perfection.'[39]

Jarman seems to have caught "C." cruising the paintings, with looks exchanged between the murderer and his victim, the artist and his model, or Caravaggio and the painting's intended viewer (a patron such as the Cardinal). Jarman traces the history of these looks in the tableaux of live models which Caravaggio staged in his studio. The film reveals that painting for Caravaggio was a process of intense *looking*. Caravaggio's concentration is divided between the labour of painting and the seduction it represents. Jarman's film unpacks these looks in its narrative with the spatial and temporal dimensions that film montage allows.

Its story unfolds in the relationships implicated by the various gazes: we first see the youth Caravaggio as a hustler who passes the late summer evenings on the street painting (a self-portrait) until his next trick arrives. An older "art patron" uses the pretext of the painting to approach Michele. Thus the painting is incorporated as the site of looking, an invitation from the unaware youth (since the look of the painting is knowing where Caravaggio's look is unknowing, or its significance hidden). The would-be patron asks the price of the painting, but his gaze makes it clear that it is Michele he desires. Seated nearby is Pascualoni – older than Michele, perhaps his pimp. He too sees the look of the older man, and when he glances covertly at Michele, his look signals the go-ahead.

Caravaggio is the "pretty vain boy of the early genre paintings"[40] who studied and painted himself in the mirror: "When Caravaggio paints the reflection of Narcissus it is no true reflection but a comment on all vanity and our film should treat his life in a similar way, penetrate the surface".[41] In Jarman's film, the youth Caravaggio secures the Cardinal's patronage with a seductive inscription on another self-portrait – the lyrics of a popular song – "You know that I love you". Years pass, and the painter is implicated in a more complex system of identification with his paintings:

> Michele gazes wistfully at the hero slaying the saint. It is a look no one can understand unless he has stood till 5 a.m. in a gay bar hoping to be fucked by that hero. The gaze of the passive homosexual at the object of his desire, he waits to be chosen, he cannot make the choice. Later his head will be cut off by a less godlike version of the young assassin; his name is now David and all the weight of society is behind him and he can cut off the head without a trace of pity.[42]

The tension I described earlier between identification and desire becomes evident here. In the painting of Saint Matthew, Caravaggio is cruising the murderer. The murderer is the "hero" in Jarman's analysis. When he paints his lover, Ranuccio, in the "Execution of Saint John", we discover that Caravaggio is also attracted to the victim

– an attraction that leads ultimately to Ranuccio's murder. Jarman reads Caravaggio's succession of identifications as a process of decay. As the artist's beauty fades and his identifications evolve with maturity, he casts himself in the end as the destroyed victim.

Not only does this narrative progression indicate how sex and violence are fused in the alternation between identification and desire in Caravaggio's painting, but also it allows us to consider where Pasolini and Jarman fit among the possible positions mapped out in the film, how Jarman recuperates Pasolini as a hero, and how he formulates for himself a method of cinematic resistance. Jarman returns again and again to the same motifs in Caravaggio's work, to a pattern of violence and its representation, and to the foundation of his own criminal aesthetic. Obsessed, Jarman rehearses the progression of Caravaggio's career:

His first major commission was the violent Martyrdom of Saint Matthew; before that it was wine and roses. Then the violence escalated until the murder was committed. After 1606, when he was on the run, the paintings became more introspective. The violence of 'The Beheading of Saint John' is confessional; in 'David and Goliath' he notes his own destruction. In his last, and only recently discovered painting, 'The Martyrdom of Saint Ursula', there is resignation in death. The saint looks at the arrow which has pierced her without a trace of horror (we must bear in mind the taste, at this time, for dramatic explosions on canvas – a violent deed evoking a violent response). Less in anguish and more in reverie, Ursula is oblivious to her executioners. The arrow is an object of contemplation.[43]

Gradually, Jarman's exhaustive study gives way to the rudiments of his scenario. The images, the ways in which he will update the story, begin to take shape:

At first the painter is unaware. All the boys together chant the latest song, 'You Know that I Love You', and share his bacchic orgies. The boys are beautiful, healthy and young; the worst they can do is play at being Medusa and frighten nobody. Then comes the pent-up violence, and the destruction of his looks with the wine, over-indulgence and success. He hasn't identified the enemy: it's his landlady, some boys in a restaurant. He bolsters up his insecurity with hostility and he numbs the hurt with *wine*. He paints his lovers as Saint John, the wild one in the wilderness, who will be destroyed by a capricious woman. When he's not gazing at these heroes he paints himself as Saint Francis, contemplating death. He paints with a knife: painting is a revenge; on the knife is written, 'No hope, no fear'. He hacks his way through altar pieces, Isaac and Holofernes, crucifixion, wounds, flagellations. It culminates one morning in the real murder of Ranuccio.

'For each man kills the thing he loves'; following that, shadows envelop his work; but after the confession of 'Saint John' at the end there is complete awareness of self. Even if his head has been cut off, he can contemplate the wound and venerate the arrow in the Saint Ursula. The battle is inevitably lost, but the understanding is gained. He is the most self-conscious of artists, a man who understands the Passion, the most powerful religious painter of the Renaissance.[44]

The arrow wound evokes another martyrdom, that of Saint Sebastian, indicating how the fantasies of Jarman and Caravaggio may coincide. Jarman finds a place for the wound in the film, where it becomes the symbol of violence figured as desire. Ursula's resignation, like her reverie, is explained in the relationship between Caravaggio and Ranuccio.

A violent sequence signals the consummation of their desire for each other. While the prostitute Lena and others look on in fear, artist and model banter with knives. They seem equally matched. Ranuccio moves in gently as if to kiss Michele, who lets down his guard. Ranuccio stabs him unexpectedly. The wound is serious, but not mortal. Caravaggio studies the gash, then smears his bloodied hand across the treacherous Ranuccio's face with an intonation, "Blood brothers". This is an appalling and yet compelling image of sexual violence, the explosion of violence evident in the paintings, which cannot escape the deeper signification today of the term "blood brothers" in the context of gay sexuality and the communication of the HIV virus. The implication is that this exchange is even more dangerous than it already appears – that every gay sexual encounter has the same violent potential; we are all blood brothers.

One is tempted to consider this exchange in light of Jarman's own HIV status, despite ignorance of his infection during the filming of *Caravaggio*. Perhaps the "distant shadow" of AIDS had somehow darkened his view of art and desire, but it is difficult to say to what extent. A violent, erotic vision was already evident in *Sebastiane* before AIDS. Art and criminality are inseparable in both Jarman's and Caravaggio's worlds. At the unveiling party for one of his paintings, Caravaggio seduces a hostile art critic and then steals a gold ring from his finger, warning him of the fact that "Mercury invented the arts with

50

an act of theft", a sentiment which Jarman shares.

But Caravaggio must hover between the positions of victim and murderer. Towards the end of the film, he arranges for Ranuccio's release from prison, clearing him of the charges of Lena's murder. Ranuccio confesses that he did in fact murder Lena, as an act of love for Caravaggio. Perhaps to avenge Lena (who in the film models for Caravaggio only in death, after she is dragged from the river), or perhaps only because of his criminal destiny, Caravaggio in turn kills Ranuccio, the object of his desire. Without uttering a word, Ranuccio smears his own blood across Michele's face before dying, the lovers' final exchange.

In adapting Caravaggio's life filtered through his own onto the screen, Jarman offers a specific model of authorship and autobiography. With only inconclusive historical references to the painter's sexuality, Jarman points to the paintings themselves as evidence of his life. In their violent renditions of street culture as religious tableaux, Jarman reads an inversion of the social norm and draws his own conclusions. By gleaning a life of Caravaggio from the painter's work, Jarman is able to construct a text that points to his own life outside the film, even society, identifying himself as a criminal, someone who steals from life to represent, and whose representations in turn transgress the social boundaries that distinguish hero from outcast. Caravaggio murders his lover Ranuccio in the film; in answer to this, Jarman quotes Oscar Wilde: "each man kills the thing he loves".[45] It is a refrain heard in Fassbinder's *Querelle*, and also a summary of Genet's aesthetic. For Jarman, it has the dark implication that homosexuality equals crime, love equals murder, an implication brought to the forefront by the sexual transmission of the AIDS virus.

Yet these equations open the way for struggle if they do not accede to the dominant notions of criminal and homosexual. In a resistant reading, they signal strength and activism: the shock value of a declaration of one's marginal desire, the insistence on one's existence, the dramatisation of the struggle itself. In Jarman's film, Caravaggio murders not only to avenge Lena's death, but also to rescue Pasolini from his status as tragic victim. If Jarman is aware of Genet's influence as a model of marginal resistance, he most identifies with Pasolini's approach to "the reclaiming of the Queer Past". Like Pasolini, he has engaged wholeheartedly with the homoerotic, mythic potential of the Passion (*The Garden*), history (*War Requiem* [1988], *Edward II*) and modern thought (*Wittgenstein*) through his works of adaptation. Jarman understands the context of Pasolini's reluctant homosexuality – the source of the artist's "dis-ease" – and is better equipped to move beyond:

Pier Paolo, living with his mother and hitting the streets nightly to give blow-jobs to his street boys, illustrates the situation well. Though open, his sexuality was a tortured confusion, made worse by the Communist Party's adoption of bourgeois restraint. In *Salo*, his last film, all homosexual relationships are shown as decadent, unpleasant and power-based. At the centre of the film is a significant line of betrayal. Photos of loved ones lead the inquisitors on a hunt to destroy the last vestiges of private and pure relations.[46]

On the one hand, *Salò: o le centiventi giornate di Sodoma* (*Salò, or the 120 Days of Sodom*, 1975) fits the pattern of Genet's explorations of power-based relationships, role-reversals and betrayal, which Jarman evokes in Caravaggio's act of murder. On the other hand, Jarman seems sceptical about the sincerity of Pasolini's attempt at such a formulation. Its dark political premise is taken to sombre, excessive extremes of both aesthetics (the flawless *modernismo* décor) and representation (to the extent that an adaptation of Sade clothed in Fascist decadence is obscene, nearly *un*representable). Like Caravaggio's later works, it is a "self-portrait of deepening disillusion".[47] Jarman speculates that Pasolini's heart could not be in a project that represents predatory homosexuality as a metaphor for Fascist decay and inhumanity.[48]

Unquestionably, *Salò* is a monumental film, all the more striking because it was the last Pasolini made. Jarman recognised it as a cry of despair from a filmmaker whose self-destructive sexual ambivalence would soon lead him to his death. Jarman locates the heroic Pasolini in the rest of his work, where his sexuality and the representations of resistant desire may be sought out. At the heart of Jarman's identification with Pasolini was sympathy for the marginal position from which he operated, and admiration for the quality of his work, its "extraordinary force". This identification acknowledges both the inspiration and lesson Pasolini afforded, and Jarman seemed grateful to follow in his footsteps, if wary of ending up a victim.

* * *

Sexuality colours my politics – I distrust all figures of authority, including the artist. Homosexuals have such a struggle to define themselves against the order of things, an equivocal process involving the desire to be both 'inside' and 'outside' – a source of that dis-ease in the work of Caravaggio and Pasolini. I distrust those with blueprints for our salvation. As a group we have suffered more than most at the hands of the ideologically 'sound'.[49]

Long before his battle with AIDS, Jarman struggled against social "dis-ease". He extended the notion of the criminal-artist in his work as a template for his own political life, drawing force not only from the marginality of his social position, but also from the transgressiveness of his public persona. Refusing to be outcast, he marshalled the forces of his mild notoriety into fringe militancy. Even with AIDS, Jarman defied illness and commercial film institutions to complete *Edward II*, *Wittgenstein* and *Blue* (1993). His public condemnations of those he saw as complicit with hateful traditions, such as Ian McKellen, an openly gay actor who accepted a knighthood, divided gay popular opinion in Britain, sending Jarman into yet more radical exile. Whether by choice or necessity, he found strength in conflict, which on its own would hardly constitute a "criminal" resistance. What was most transgressive about the filmmaker, in view of the cultural context in which he worked, was his assault on the mythologies of the British past. If that tradition was oppressive, Jarman's irreverence was all the more intransigent.

He declared open war in *The Last of England*, eschewing both the deadly literary tradition and the conventions of narrative cinema. Thatcher's Britain is rendered as a terrorist state – not the anarchic, sexual terrorism of *Jubilee* (1978), where punk sensibilities battled centre-stage with pop consumerism, but the authoritarian, faceless surveillance which Foucault described in *Discipline and Punish*. Punk iconoclasm is pushed back to the margins, and the icons are already emptied of meaning as Jarman films "home-movies" of a travestied royal wedding. Even here, Jarman eroticizes the conflict along the lines of Genet, as private desire overcomes the chasm between soldier/terrorist and another man who make love on the outspread Union Jack in an abandoned warehouse. It is the most forbidden of images, one that envisions an end to the discord between the IRA and the Special Forces in Ulster, or mediates an unimagined resolution to the Falklands conflict. And yet it is no more surreal than the images of the tabloids, in which the luxury liner QE2 is transformed into Thatcher's "Battleship England". Later, Jarman realises his own transformation – QE2 becomes "Queer Edward II". In the end, Jarman's frustration with the weakness of both his social and artistic positions only strengthened his sense of mission, and further radicalised his work and his rhetoric.

Like Pasolini, Jarman frequently engaged himself with established myths, rescuing them from the deadly reverence with which they are preserved, and reading in them his own desire. More importantly, Jarman read the possible traces that suggested gay desire had figured in these myths, only to be suppressed from the historical record. He tackled Shakespeare in *The Tempest* (1979) and *The Angelic*

Conversation (1985), Britten's *War Requiem* (adapted from Owen's epic poem), Marlowe's *Edward II*, Wittgenstein's Bloomsbury circle, the legend of Saint Sebastian (in Latin), and Caravaggio's Renaissance. At every turn, Jarman advanced the possibilities of cinema's power to disturb, re-order and invent.

In this invention and in his fascination for mythology, Jarman may be compared to Jean Cocteau. Cocteau's *Orphée* (*Orpheus*, 1950) and *Le Sang d'un poète* (*The Blood of a Poet*, 1930) mix fantasy, period and homoeroticism with both imagination and seriousness of purpose. Like Jarman, Cocteau was remarkably versatile and prolific, producing novels, plays, paintings, sculpture and films, and leaving an extensive record of his work and thoughts in journals and correspondence. In the postscript to his screenplay for *The Blood of a Poet*, Cocteau wrote that he had been reproached for "using film as a sacred and lasting medium, like a painting or a book".[50] Jarman similarly treated images as sacred, even as he sought to provoke with them. Jarman's *In the Shadow of the Sun* (1980) invokes the image of Narcissus, a Cocteau favourite, "a mirror which flashes the sun into the camera so that the image explodes and reinvents itself in a most mysterious way".[51] Although Cocteau enjoyed a more privileged position as an artist and intellectual than Jarman did, due in part to the greater acceptance and support in France of his marginal vision, his films nonetheless provoked scandal.

Cocteau also belongs to the tradition of criminal-artist. Genet's film, *Un Chant d'amour*, bears significant traces of Cocteau's handiwork; Cocteau advised Genet and supervised much of the filming. In places, *Un Chant d'amour* distinctly draws upon *The Blood of a Poet*. Cocteau was equally fascinated by the figure of the murderer and by the act of betrayal. Both *Les Enfants terribles* (1949) and *The Blood of a Poet* feature the character of Dargelos, the desired object and leader of the gang, who with a snowball slays the friend that loves him. In *Les Enfants terribles*, the victim in fact lives, but the betrayal constitutes a symbolic murder, where murder is simultaneously envisioned as an act of love. Fassbinder, in his film of *Querelle*, acknowledges Cocteau's influence by borrowing from his magical cinema. When Madame Lysiane informs Robert that he never had a brother, that Querelle does not exist, the opening sequence of the film is run backwards, undoing Querelle's arrival in the port with a fantastic, ambiguous gesture that immediately evokes *Orpheus*.

For Cocteau, the poet inhabits a marginal and underground milieu. The café that Orpheus frequents is an avant-garde meeting place where a band of subversives on motor cycles creates a stir, and where Dadaist-styled poets orchestrate a provocation. Orpheus's descent into the Underworld merely proceeds further in the same direction.

Beneath this surface hides the more seriously marginal artistic realm in which Cocteau resided. Cocteau himself chronicled his long-standing drug addiction in *Opium*, a collection of his journal entries. Jarman, who wrote often of the flowers in his garden at Prospect Cottage, offers the following observation on an important theme that runs through Cocteau's work:

> Narcissus [the flower] is derived not from the name of the young man who met his death vainly trying to embrace his reflection in crystal water, but from the Greek *narkao* (to benumb); though of course Narcissus, benumbed by his own beauty, fell to his death embracing his shadow. Pliny says *'Narce Narcissum dictum non a fabuloso puero,'* named Narcissus from *narkê*, not from the fabled boy. Socrates called the plant 'crown of the infernal gods' because the bulbs, if eaten, numbed the nervous system. Perhaps Roman soldiers carried it for this reason (rather than for its healing properties) as the American soldiers smoked marijuana in Vietnam...Last year [Matthew Lewis] took a beautiful portrait of a handsome Italian, stripped to the waist, holding a lemon, the juice of which he used to dissolve heroin to fill his syringe. Narcissus, narcotics, self-absorption: benumbed retreat into self.[52]

Jarman links a criminal aesthetic with imagery sacred to Cocteau. But there is much more than this common theme to connect the two filmmakers:

> A story from my childhood still haunts me. It can be found in some of my works. A young boy wounded by a snowball. In *Les Enfants Terribles* the child does not die. In my film, the child dies. I am not reworking a theme. It is a whole mythology that the poet stirs up and examines from different angles.[53]

So, too, we find that Cocteau reworks childhood recollections as part of his mythology, and, in the case of the Dargelos story, to find the means to represent early desires in a new, evocative context.

Jarman's identification with Cocteau is made explicit in his journal – "Dear Jean, am I the only one who, besides you, has funded a film on his name?" – suggesting that perhaps it was his very notoriety, like that of Cocteau, that drove his film projects when all other avenues of subsidy had been exhausted.[54] Whatever independent wealth Jarman had inherited from his family served the films if funds were scarce. Jarman also adopted Cocteau's unsparing and self-critical eye for the contemporary art scene. We see it in monstrous parodies of the commodification of the avant-garde, as in *Jubilee*, or in films such as *Caravaggio* and *Sebastiane*, where period adaptations are invaded by updated visions of a dilettante bohemia out for an art opening or a Roman banquet.

Period and fantasy become weapons in Jarman's hands; violating the stultifying codes of English literary adaptations was paramount in his vision. *Edward II* balances its historical setting with costumes from a variety of periods, while *Jubilee* employs a framing device with Elizabeth I and John Dee walking along the cliffs of Dancing Ledge, Dorset, as a counterpoint to its "celebration" of the Queen's Silver Jubilee in 1977.

> As always, some broke the rules – Dreyer put some large modern glasses on one of his priests in *St Joan*. Eisenstein rebuilt Russia for *Ivan the Terrible*. Cocteau transferred the Orpheus myth to the 1950s. In my film, *The Tempest*, the three-hundred-odd years of the play's age became its period.[55]

In the finale of *The Tempest*, Jarman stages a marriage party, complete with sailors dancing arm-in-arm in modern dress and Elisabeth Welch singing "Stormy Weather". The sequence calls to mind Ken Russell's extravagant reworking of Hollywood spectacle, and Jarman returns to it with the "Think Pink" number (from Donen's *Funny Face*) in *The Garden*.

Russell once asked Jarman what would most upset an English audience: "Louis XIII dining al fresco, carelessly shooting peacocks on the lawn between courses" was the response.[56] A watered-down (or excessively campy, in Jarman's view) version of this image found its way into the opening of Russell's film, *The Devils* (1970), which Jarman designed. While he made it his task to provoke the audience, Jarman shared with Cocteau a reverence for magical cinema. Both filmmakers experimented with the camera, transforming inventive techniques into masterful explorations of dream imagery and fantastic mythologies. Jarman's use of the rich, saturated colours that the Super 8 format lends to *The Last of England* and *The Garden* revealed the filmmaker as a remarkably gifted and innovative film technician, as well as artist. When Jarman first began to work with Super 8 he seemed pleased that few took it seriously. Its simplicity and "built-in meters and effects" allowed him to ignore the technical constraints that hindered the "subsidized 'avant-garde' cinema", and instead move forward to "something completely new".[57] *The Tempest* and *The Angelic Conversation* proved him capable of inventing his own cinema with as much fantasy and painterly beauty as Cocteau's

Orpheus. Jarman's last major film,[58] *Blue* is nothing less than a revolutionary cinematic achievement. It stands alone even among Jarman's works as a contribution to the modern evolution of film art. The intense blue screen and evocative soundtrack have redefined the notion of what is possible in the cinema.[59] Although he has yet to be widely recognised, Jarman's enduring contributions place him in the ranks of film pioneers such as Cocteau and Eisenstein.

In the early 1980s, well before *glasnost'*, Jarman visited Moscow as part of a cultural exchange for British independent filmmakers which also included Peter Wollen and Sally Potter. The result of this trip was the film, *Imagining October*, the title of which suggests yet another journey into a gay artist's past where Jarman might hope to recognise his own. As a prelude to *Caravaggio*, which was long in the making, Jarman turns to painting to render his tribute to Eisenstein. In an attempt to revisit Eisenstein's work through the canvas, Jarman explores the homoerotic relationship between the artist, the iconography of sailors, and Jarman's own identification with Eisenstein. In fact, Jarman's film invokes by analogy the making of an *Oktyabr'* (*October*, 1928) or a *Battleship Potemkin*, attending to the process more than to the finished products or their period. Rather than project his own life onto that of Eisenstein, Jarman projects the relationship between the spectator and film onto that between creator, whether painter or filmmaker, and work. Filmed in Eisenstein's apartments, where his papers are housed, and in England, *Imagining October* also interrogates the relationship between the artist's desire and political engagement.[60]

AIDS, like his disenfranchisement before, became the centre of Jarman's politics from the moment he discovered that he was HIV+. His activism earned him notoriety and the antagonism of the press. There were battles over Ian Charleson (who had starred, improbably, in *Jubilee* and *Chariots of Fire*, and then became one of the first popular actors in Britain to succumb to the AIDS virus) and Ian McKellen, and poisonous campaigns when his films were aired on Channel 4: "*The Last Of England* went out at 11:00 last night; all the other films in the season were out at nine. Special rules for me again."[61] With his characteristic fusion of the contemporary in historical adaptation, Jarman incorporated OutRage protests against Clause 28, AIDS indifference and homophobia in *Edward II*.

In his final years, Prospect Cottage became the setting of Jarman's "corner" of *The Garden*. Jarman combined an history of religious persecution with his own fantasy inventions (a nearby lighthouse becomes his Star of Bethlehem) around "Man's Fall" and the Passion. His writing is most inflammatory when he invokes religious iconography in his challenge to the norm. After participating in

London's gay pride celebration, he entered the following in his journal:

> There are a million psyches to win, and nothing but loss in store for the seedy guardians of the moral majority. Dear Jesus, innocent begetter of an evil and corrupt tradition, we know you would join this march, our entry into Jerusalem, would kiss John and consign the born again to the bottomless pit, or rather enlighten them and put them to bed with their brothers and sisters...We demand one right 'equality of loving before the law' and the end of our banishment from the daylight.[62]

A brief résumé of Jarman's film career illustrates how he sought to end his exile and re-centre his desire onscreen. After designs for Ken Russell's *The Devils* and *Savage Messiah* (1972), there are the "home-movies" shot on the periphery of the Factory, when film in Britain seemed all but dead. Then comes *Sebastiane*, spoken in Latin, a punk *Jubilee* offering to the Queen, and Shakespeare's *The Tempest* in a decidedly non-literary tradition. There follows a long spell where Jarman, prevented from making the films he wants to make, collaborates on music videos with Marianne Faithfull and The Smiths in order to keep active. Finally, with a state-supported visit to the Soviet Union, Jarman begins to lay claim to his "Queer Past" in *Imagining October*. *The Angelic Conversation* sets gay love to Shakespeare's Sonnets, and reveals a new maturity in Jarman's cinematic idiom where poetry and provocation are fused. *Caravaggio* confirms this, although the film is the fruit of over five years' struggle to bring it to the screen. As if in further defiance of the "art establishment", Jarman eschews narrative for a visual assault on "National Mother" – Thatcher's UK and *The Last of England*, a bleak vision darkened by the knowledge of his HIV status, yet still offering the transgressive glimmer of erotic possibility. He continues the assault in *War Requiem*, but experiments with a formal structure new to his work in order to open out Britten's music and national myth in light of its suppressed history. With *The Garden*, Jarman reaches the pinnacle of his abstract iconoclasm, exploding the limits of his violent, homoerotic images, while, beset by illness, he directs from his bed which he includes in the film. His health worsens, and he is temporarily blinded. No one expects that he will recover, and yet he miraculously turns out three more films and sketches the rudiments of two others; *Glitterbug* is released after his death. Before that, *Edward II* brings Jarman his greatest commercial success even as it most directly addresses his social struggle. *Wittgenstein* offers an unexpected and light-handed treatment of another Queer life, while

Blue, a meditation conceived in blindness, reveals a stunning and potent cinematic genius. Shortly before his death, Jarman speculated that all his films combined had been made for less than £1 million.

It is clear that Jarman, given the antagonism he suffered at the hands of the media, acquiesced to become the spokesperson of a certain kind of anger, frustration and also empowerment in the face of prejudice, indifference and ignorance. His films speak for themselves, yet Jarman felt the need to go further in his engagement with the public sphere. The tabloids rattled their scurrilous obituaries at every possible moment ("*Movie Boss with AIDS – Glad to die in a shack!*"),[63] but Jarman, never willing to be written off, took pleasure in reaffirming his presence and sounding a battle cry until the end. Cruising 'the Heath' at night, he was frequently recognised ('"When are you ever off TV, Mr. Jarman?'").[64] He was dangerous, certainly, for the model of resistance that he furnished challenged any threat to banish his desire from the centre of the screen.

Jarman celebrated delinquency and subversion, yet his weapons were words and images, which may at first seem mild or unthreatening. Yet, if their violence was figurative, it was nonetheless potent. His writing and the testimony of those who knew and worked with him reveal an exceptionally kind and generous spirit; he was well-loved, and it was difficult for him to believe that the general public could have despised him. He harmed no one. When Peter Greenaway turned down a project for Italian television, Jarman's friend, Nico, proposed him instead:

> I rang the producer and suggested you knew far more about history than Greenaway and could do his series, they told me they wanted someone who had the reputation of being controversial but was safe. You I'm afraid they saw as just controversial. The problem, Derek, is I know that you're nothing of the sort![65]

From outcast to outlaw to OutRage, Jarman alternated between gentle bohemianism and bitter iconoclasm, offering what can be heralded among the most important images of gay life bursting from the margins of the past twenty years. More significant than this, even, is Jarman's example in claiming the past. Jarman explored the lives and work of those he admired, not only to illuminate or interpret those lives, but also to find the means to represent his own life, to advance his own candidacy within the tradition and politics of Genet, Pasolini, Cocteau and Eisenstein.

Jarman's unusual reworking of his life through the image of Caravaggio (and Pasolini) in particular was an innovation in documenting the hidden, marginalized past he often spoke of. By indicating how the present should serve our investigation of the past, and how that past may, in fact, seduce the present, Jarman assured himself a place among his heroes. More than this, he set his alternative version of that past in firm opposition to an orthodox and exclusive tradition which had erased the traces of marginal, "other" lives which reside there. In doing so, Jarman proclaimed the relevance of the past to our contemporary lives and, much more significantly, the disavowed relevance of those lives, past and present, to the mainstream. Jarman's legacy, which subverted accepted and constraining notions of hero and criminal, will not easily be recuperated or denied by his detractors – all those guardians of what is "normal", moral or simply mediocre.

Notes

[1]   "Suppression" is perhaps a more fitting term than "oppression", given that subcultures, despite their "marginal" positioning, exist within as well as outside society.

[2]   Film scholars such as Alexander Doty have taken up the question of how the author is projected together with the text through the representation of his/her identity, particularly in terms of the cultural negotiation and identification of authorship by a queer audience, whose recognition of either a queer director or a queer system of texts (a Cukor vs. a Hitchcock) adheres to a practice of resistance to Hollywood's dominant ideology. As Doty points out, this becomes complicated when a Cukor has been co-opted within the dominant institution. How can we differentiate between the queer author of a text and the author of a queer text? Or between the author Hitchcock and the *auteur* "Hitchcock", the latter a system of cinematic structures that are the result of close readings of a number of texts? See Alexander Doty, "Whose Text Is It Anyway? Queer Cultures, Queer Auteurs, and Queer Authorship", in *Making Things Perfectly Queer: Interpreting Mass Culture* (Minneapolis; London: University of Minnesota Press, 1993): 17-38.

[3]   Paul Julian Smith, *Laws of Desire: Questions of Homosexuality in Spanish Writing and Film 1960-1900* (Oxford: Clarendon Press, 1992).

[4]   Tom Yingling, quoted in ibid: 53.

[5]   See Teshome H Gabriel, *Third Cinema in the Third World: The Aesthetics of Liberation* (Ann Arbor, MI: UMI Research Press, 1982).

[6]   Derek Jarman, *At Your Own Risk: A Saint's Testament* (London: Hutchinson, 1992): 72.

[7]   Derek Jarman, *Dancing Ledge*, edited by Shaun Allen (London; New York: Quartet Books, 1984; 1991): 7.

8   Michel Foucault, *Discipline and Punish: The Birth of the Prison*, translated by Alan Sheridan (London: Allen Lane, 1977): 293.

9   Ibid: 301.

10 Ibid: 265.

11 What is the critical value of proclaiming, as Dyer seems to, 'Fassbinder good, Pasolini bad'? Certainly, while it is helpful to analyze the context of Pasolini's apparent ambivalence towards his own sexual identity, for example, his works cannot be evaluated solely in terms of their contributions to the struggle for gay emancipation or the positive model they generate, as Dyer would have it.

12 Richard Dyer, *Now you see it: Studies on lesbian and gay film* (London; New York: Routledge, 1990): 55.

13 Ibid: 83.

14 For once, though, Dyer refrains from passing judgment on this movement away from the tender, pastoral depictions of *Un Chant d'amour* that he much prefers, perhaps to open the way for Foucault's "technologies of homosexuality", which have been more commonly applied in gay and lesbian studies than the prison apparatus. It is, however, too restrictive for future studies to focus on the literal realm of practice, i.e. the questions of active/passive sexuality that have figured so predominantly in the identity politics of 1970s' and 1980s' gay culture. Dyer's project succeeds at the level of providing a much-needed history of gay and lesbian representations that uncovers important social contexts, yet fails to move beyond the limits of his contemporary agenda, which at times seems rather out-of-date.

15 Derek Jarman, *Modern Nature: The Journals of Derek Jarman* (London: Century, 1991): 15.

16 Jarman (1984): 142.

17 See Jarman (1992): 117.

18 Jarman (1984): 165.

19 Jarman (1991): 142.

20 Jarman (1984): 28.

21 Ibid: 14.

22 Ibid: 16.

23 Jarman (1991): 11.

24 Jarman (1984): 21.

25 Foucault, in *The History of Sexuality*, translated by Robert Hurley (New York: Vintage Books, 1990), is a major proponent of the notion that

homosexuality, as a clinical and social designation, is a construction of the modern era which has been improperly imposed on earlier cultures, notably that of classical Greece, as part of a misleading "history" of same-sex relations.

[26] Jarman (1984): 21.

[27] As a literary metaphor, this idea was explored by the dramatist Lillian Hellman, whose memoirs (*Pentimento: A Book of Portraits* [Boston: Little, Brown, 1973]) peel back the layers of her past: in particular, her resistance against Nazism, the McCarthy-era blacklist and even homophobia, all of which jeopardised her success as a playwright. Hellman invokes the metaphor of painting to expose the contradictions between her marginal and privileged position as Jew, Socialist and celebrated author.

[28] In Pasolini's *Teorema* (*Theorem*, 1968), this scenario is projected onto a third figure, the character of Terence Stamp, who functions as an intermediary between the multiple Oedipal drives of a bourgeois family, including the homoerotic longings of father and son. The image of the father in these films resonates with the filmmaker's experiences with his own father, a member of the Fascist-leaning middle class. Despite, or perhaps because of, Pasolini's alienation with his father's political orientation, he is able to reframe their relationship according to his fantasies.

[29] Pasolini goes as far as to cast his mother, Susanna, as a wrinkled peasant Mary in old age; Jesus has the dark features of the south (and the Levant, before the Gospels were Hellenized with a blue-eyed, blond Christ).

[30] Jarman (1984): 24.

[31] Ibid: 242-243.

[32] Ibid: 9-10. Emphasis in original.

[33] It is somewhat ironic, therefore, that Jarman's films enjoyed more critical attention and less marginal distribution and televising in Italy than in Britain.

[34] Jarman (1984): 13, 28. Emphasis in original.

[35] Ibid: 21-22.

[36] Jarman (1991): 254.

[37] Jarman (1984): 22.

[38] Jarman (1991): 150.

[39] Jarman (1984): 13-14.

[40] Ibid: 13.

[41] Ibid: 25.

[42] Ibid: 22.

[43]   Ibid: 20-21.

[44]   Ibid: 22, 24. Emphasis in original.

[45]   Oscar Wilde, "The Ballad of Reading Gaol", in *Complete Works of Oscar Wilde*, with an introduction by Vyvyan Holland (London; Glasgow: Collins, 1966): 844.

[46]   Jarman (1984): 242-243.

[47]   See ibid: 13.

[48]   In an earlier study of Pasolini, Richard Dyer objected to precisely this strain of "self-oppression" in the filmmaker's work. Dyer disputes other film critics such as Robin Wood who have framed Pasolini's representations within the context of gay emancipation and the claiming of gay images of the 1960s and 1970s. Wood's approach points to the evolution of a consciousness of gay images available to the liberation movement, even if they were not 'of or for the movement'. Dyer maintains that if Pasolini did not set out to subvert the dominant practices, he was inscribed in them. Yet, Jarman's example illustrates exactly the power of identification and communal recognition which operate despite the impossibility of defining, within the unwieldy and vague body of available texts, one "gay" cinema. Dyer's categorisation of Pasolini would happily sacrifice *all* connections between Pasolini's representations and the gay audience Dyer idealises – an audience apparently incapable of consuming any but positive, prescriptive representations. ("Pasolini and Homosexuality", in Paul Willemen [ed], *Pier Paolo Pasolini* [London: British Film Institute, 1977]: 57-63.)

[49]   Jarman (1984): 241.

[50]   Jean Cocteau, *Two Screenplays*, translated by Carol Martin-Sperry (London: Calder and Boyars, 1970): 61.

[51]   Jarman (1984): 130.

[52]   Jarman (1991): 17-18. Emphasis in original.

[53]   Cocteau: 66.

[54]   Jarman (1991): 281.

[55]   Derek Jarman, *Derek Jarman's Caravaggio: The Complete Film Script and Commentaries by Derek Jarman* (London: Thames and Hudson, 1986): 45.

[56]   Jarman (1984): 104.

[57]   Ibid: 128, 124.

[58]   *Glitterbug* (1994), the final release, was constructed from Super 8 footage filmed in the 1970s.

[59]   Jarman, in his last published work, *Chroma: A Book of Colour – June '93*

(London: Century, 1994), elaborates his colour theory.

[60] *Wittgenstein* also addressed this problem: the philosopher questions his commitment to Socialism, considers abandoning Cambridge for physical labour in the Soviet Union, is reproached by Bertrand Russell for encouraging a working-class student – and lover – to abandon his studies for 'honest work'. Admire the work, or the worker?

[61] Jarman (1991): 172.

[62] Ibid: 102.

[63] Ibid: 75.

[64] Ibid: 84.

[65] Ibid: 189.

"The rose revived": Derek Jarman and the British tradition

Lawrence Driscoll

O Rose, thou art sick! (William Blake)[1]

Like all true gardeners I'm an optimist. (Derek Jarman)[2]

Whatever hope is yours,/Was my life also (Wilfred Owen)[3]

Much of the writing that addresses the work of Derek Jarman begins by assuming that his work is characteristically anti-Establishment, non-canonical and controversial. Simon Field points out that "Jarman is a troublesome case and appears to relish his role as a thorn in the official flesh of the British cinema...He is no less troublesome to the avant-garde".[4] Interestingly, both those who support Jarman's work and his adversaries agree in this respect. Both groups are correct, I suggest, but not in the way they might like to think. The image of Jarman as a controversial filmmaker has emerged not because he is an iconoclast of Britain's sacred institutions and values, but because he has chosen to speak for a very old British tradition, placing his faith in cultural values that are primarily aesthetic and historical. Jarman is perceived as radical because he worked in an environment in which this particular British tradition has been eroded both by the Left and by the Right. Given the failure of British postwar social and economic policies, Jarman is confronted with a cultural terrain torn between the failures of the Left and the inhumane alternatives of the Right. In order to provide Britain with an opportunity to re-establish a sense of community, history and culture, he returns to an older tradition, aligning himself with a strain of cultural criticism evident in medieval literature, as well as in Shakespeare, Blake, Ruskin and Larkin. Jarman strove to re-create a viable cultural base which would move Britain beyond the cultural, social and political impasse which the country confronted. His œuvre is thus best seen as a direct intervention, attempting to revitalize British culture by providing sustenance to its desiccated roots, enabling Britain to become once again "the rose revived".[5]

Jarman describes how his father, Lance (a New Zealander by birth), managed to preserve his integrity in the British Establishment:

he reflects that his father "joined them outwardly, but inwardly rejected them".[6] Jarman's work reverses his father's strategy and outwardly rejects the British Establishment, while inwardly feeling very much part of its history. This outward rejection has led many critics to see Jarman only as an iconoclast. This essay, however, is concerned to read Jarman beyond these surface rejections, by seeing them as inseparable from his desire to forge an alliance with a British tradition of middle-class dissent, a tradition which flickers consistently throughout British history but is commonly relegated to a subterranean and marginal existence.

Alan Sinfield points out that at the end of the 18th century the development of "enclosures, the factory system and urbanization helped to provoke the Romantic movement".[7] Jarman's critique of contemporary Britain emerges out of a felt alliance with the anti-industrial concerns of the Romantics, particularly Blake. Jarman, like Blake, saw himself as an artisan, working in relative poverty in London, receiving little or no national funding, and creating art at odds with both the demands of the market and the dominant ideology of the period. In *Imagining October* (1984), Jarman employs a black screen with white text to present reworked fragments from Blake's poem, "London", resurrecting England's blindness to its history:

> The harlot's cry in each high street
> Weaves old England's winding sheet
> Step Forward into the Past
> That is Not
> Into the Merrie Old Land of
> Was.[8]

Blake's poem, "The Garden of Love", also prefigures Jarman's critique of the policing of sexuality in *The Garden*:

> And I saw it was filled with graves,
> And tomb-stones where flowers should be;
> And Priests in black gowns were walking their rounds,
> And binding with briars my joys & desires.[9]

Reminiscing about the time that he strolled through Danesborough as a youth when visiting his aunt, Jarman quotes from his copy of Dorothy Wordsworth's journal, making explicit his identification with the Romantics:

> I too gathered worts on Danesborough, which she often climbed with Coleridge. We also 'sat a considerable time upon

the heath, its surface restless and glittering with the motion of the withered grasses...'[10]

The early opposition to industrialisation voiced by Blake and Wordsworth recurs throughout the 19th century: the period during which capital consolidated its hegemony. Ruskin, Morris and Wilde, heirs of Romanticism, went on to register "the ills of industrial capitalism",[11] and Jarman is part of this tradition. As Simon Watney points out, Jarman can be seen as the "Queer William Morris of the 90's".[12] Many 19th century social critiques emerged, like those of Jarman, from a desire to prevent what was perceived as an open attack on "beauty, elegance and sensitivity".[13] This tradition shares a notion of middle-class dissidence and a binding spirit which Tom Nairn believes is always "nostalgic".[14] Jarman, I believe, occupies a prominent position in the 20th century manifestation of this inheritance. Sinfield suggests that:

> Dissident middle-class intellectuals may be right-wing, left-wing or liberal: they may imagine a 'return' to traditional structures, attempt an alliance with the working class or other oppressed groups...The consistent feature is hostility to the hegemony of the principal part of the middle class – the businessmen, industrialists and empire-builders.[15]

Middle-class dissidence is marked by its insistence on "high" culture, and by the need to preserve the aesthetic aspects of British culture. E M Forster outlines the make-up of the tradition in *Howards End* (1910), in which the artistic, well-educated but economically weak Schlegels temper the destructive tendencies of the industrial and philistine Wilcoxes. What is of particular relevance to our understanding of Jarman's place in this tradition is that middle-class dissidents are associated with being – if not homosexual – effeminate and a threat to "masculine" values held by both the Left and the Right. For Sinfield, "[t]he idea that literature is 'effeminate' goes back to the Romantics...and broke through in the 1890s; Bloomsbury and the 1940s had only to keep it going".[16] Clause 28, by limiting the ability of public libraries to buy books by such authors as Marguerite Radclyffe Hall, Virginia Woolf, Wilde and Shakespeare – books which, in the opinion of the government, reveal a tendency to "promote homosexuality" – represents continued opposition to this dissident British tradition in the 1980s.[17] It is within this historical frame that we can understand Watney's notion of Jarman's "dissident national identity".[18]

Jarman's role within the British tradition is related to his view that history must be recuperated for use in the present. This places Jarman at odds with modernism's desire to minimise the role of history. While at the Slade School of Art, he pulled away from commercial art, choosing to mine an archaic form – landscape painting. Following the pastoral tradition of Blake and Samuel Palmer, Turner and Constable, Jarman saw his work as developing in opposition to modernism and its current manifestations in pop art. For the canonical modernists, the past is something to be escaped from. For Joyce's Stephen Daedalus, history was a "nightmare", and Conrad's Jim struggles to break free of his past actions, while the protagonist of Wells's *The Time Machine* (1895) only travels into the future. This modernist distrust of history permeated historical consciousness to such an extent that J H Plumb claimed in *The Death of the Past* (1969) that an industrial society "may simply no longer need the past".[19] In the tradition of modernism, pop art celebrates its separation from history – as Warhol said of his work, "[t]here's nothing behind it".[20] Jarman had no wish to work in a modernist tradition, choosing instead to take his influences from the Romantics and from contemporaries such as Hockney and Patrick Procktor.[21] Discussing his art of this early period, Jarman situates it in opposition to the pop art/modernism mainstream:

> I was painting landscapes, close to the red earth of north Somerset, the flowers, butterflies in the meadows...It was impossible to paint these landscapes at the Slade in 1964; everyone was falling over themselves for pop-art, we were focussed on Manhattan. The 'new' art was an urban art, the art of the glass-topped coffee table...the comic, the poster.[22]

As his colleagues left for America, Jarman notes that he could not be part of pop art: "I knew I couldn't fit in; I hadn't lost my passion for the Gregorian chant, so I kept my distance".[23] As with many middle-class dissidents before him, Jarman objected to pop art not only on aesthetic grounds, but also because of the links which the movement was forging with the bourgeoisie. As Jarman points out, his distance was provoked by a realisation that pop art "was tied to the apron strings of the very rich and the auction houses".[24]

This resistance to American capitalism comes across in *The Last of England* (1987), a film which positions itself firmly within the tradition of landscape painting. In the opening sections of the film, we see a young man (played by Jarman's friend, Spring) successively stomping on Caravaggio's painting, "Profane Love", shooting up heroin, and loitering around. While Spencer Leigh is attempting to clear the rubble around him, Spring simply sits and plays a set of pan pipes. Jarman points out that Spring is "in a cul-de-sac, adrift, his feet are not on the ground, he's a destructive force. Whenever you see him he is hell-bent on destroying...wrecking the landscape".[25] In the context of Jarman's relationship to pop art and American culture, it is significant that he notes how Spring had "rejected the ivory tower of my films, he loved adverts and fast food, Campbells soup, *Dallas*, James Dean".[26] Cut off from history, like the punks in *Jubilee* (1978), Spring represents a cultural dead end.

Jarman was born in 1942 and therefore grew up during a period that saw the introduction of the welfare state by the Labour Party in 1945 and its subsequent dismantling by the Conservative Party since 1979. British political historian Perry Anderson suggests that by 1978 (the year in which Jarman's *Jubilee* was released) both parties had failed to create an acceptable cultural milieu in which the British tradition could survive, let alone flourish. Anderson argues that the British political system has emerged from two legacies which combine to form a peculiar kind of ideological "fog": "[t]he two great chemical elements of this blanketing English fog are 'traditionalism' and 'empiricism': in it, visibility – of any social or historical reality – is always zero".[27] Anderson explains that while traditionalism "sanctions the present by deriving it from the past, empiricism binds the future by fastening it to the present. A comprehensive conservatism is the result, covering society with a pall of simultaneous philistinism (towards ideas) and mystagogy (towards institutions), for which Britain has justly won an international reputation".[28] In the face of this comprehensive conservatism from both Left and Right, Jarman's position as a middle-class dissident allowed him a space from which to see through the fog.

With the hardships of the 1930s and the suffering and hope of the 1940s still fresh in the cultural memory, Britain in 1945 was determined to change. In return for defeating Fascism, the working classes were provided with "full employment, a health service, universal full-time secondary education, nearly universal pension rights and public responsibility for housing".[29] A form of welfare capitalism was developed which aimed to protect the people from the worst excesses of *laissez-faire* capitalism. The postwar government thus developed a corporatism which facilitated a harmonious encounter between the needs of the people and the needs of capital. Yet, the emphasis on the former was soon lost as the Conservative governments of the 1950s redefined the "'good society' of welfare-capitalism in terms of individual striving and consumer goods".[30] The result was that after the consumption boom of the 1960s (and the influence of American culture), capitalism was liberated from "the fig-leaf decencies of old-style Toryism".[31] The outcome of this liberation laid the foundations upon which Thatcherism would build. The crisis that ushered in Thatcherism is signalled in Jarman's *Jubilee*, which focuses on the collapse of the postwar consensus. Early in the film, the protagonists decide to play a game of *Monopoly* to relieve their boredom. The game falls apart during an argument and the board is overturned. Throughout this scene the players are sitting in front of a newspaper headline, posted to the wall, that reads: "Healey's Budget Strategy In Ruins". The failure of Dennis Healey's 1976 Budget was to become the marker for the end of the postwar consensus – Healey, the Chancellor of the Exchequer, becoming the unlikely harbinger of punk. For Sinfield, the failure of the Healey Budget, as Jarman's *Monopoly* scene suggests, was "[t]he key economic crisis, the one that showed the game was up".[32]

The punk subculture emerged as part of this period of general discontent.[33] Jarman addresses this subculture in *Jubilee*, but does not celebrate punk's anti-Establishment position nor glorify its violent tendencies. The British Board of Film Censors attempted various cuts to the film, and it was cited in Parliament as an example of the controversial "video nasties". Punk subcultures felt that the film would be a testament to them, while the government assumed that it was an attack on decency. However, both groups were misreading Jarman's position. As he points out, "[f]or an audience who expected a punk music film, full of 'anarchy' and laughs at the end of the King's Road, it was difficult to swallow. They wanted action, not analysis".[34] In contrast to the government's perception of the film as a "video nasty", Jarman insists that all the violence in *Jubilee* is "seen negatively", suggesting that *Jubilee* had a "healing fiction [which] harked back to *Pearl* and *Piers Plowman*".[35]

At the beginning of *Jubilee*, Ariel says that the scenes of nihilism that he will show us are not supposed to be admired, for they represent "the shadow of this time". It is we, the audience, who live in the world of shadows and chaos, while the past is shown as a world of sympathy, culture and order. In contrast to the Elizabethan world order, the dislocation and violence of contemporary Britain have produced a generation cut off from History. Jarman considered the welfare state as a screen which protected the life of the country from being totally sapped by *laissez-faire* capital. In the absence of any restrictions on his economic behaviour, entrepreneur Borgia Ginz is free to exploit the situation in the same way that Malcolm McLaren, the salesman of punk, spoke unabashedly of making "cash from chaos".[36] In the dying moments of welfare capitalism, Ginz perceptively notes that "Heaven has been replaced by Progress". In this atmosphere, where Jarman feels "[v]alues and qualities cease to exist", we see him turning to the British tradition of middle-class dissent to solve the problems of the contemporary milieu.[37] Jarman upholds the role of the artist as a figure of hope when he states that in *Jubilee* it is "Viv, the artist, in many ways one of the most sympathetic characters of the film, [who] pleads for action".[38]

Ever since the English Civil War, middle-class dissidence has always turned away from the industrial middle-classes – the line from Cromwell leads straight to Thatcher – expressing a sympathy with the supposedly effete, effeminate and (from the bourgeoisie's point of view) decadent aristocracy. Given this situation, it is understandable that Jarman would locate a sympathetic voice in the House of Lords: "In the Lords of course [Lord Hutchinson said] we're not dealing with a democratic government any longer, we're dealing with an authoritarian government".[39] This link to the aristocracy is underlined when Jarman goes as far as to sympathise with the Queen (as he does with Elizabeth I in *Jubilee*): "I'm sure the Queen agrees with me. She looks desperate these days. I haven't seen her smile for years".[40]

In order to find a way out of the British "fog" of conservatism, Jarman turns to art and British history for his solutions. In his 1994 television interview, *Know What I Mean?*, Jarman recalls taking his parents to see *Jubilee*, and, as they were leaving the cinema, amid disturbance and disgust at the film, Jarman's mother, Elizabeth, told him that she found the film very accurate. Discussing the furore over *Jubilee*, Jarman continues:

> I think about people like Winston Churchill going mad about this film...because of course the film was the tradition, and my parents understood this, and Winston Churchill and that gang, those gangsters in Parliament are against all of this...one's father fought for the Welfare State, in a way, that's what they were all fighting for, and these people are dismantling it, so I represent the tradition, and these people are the wreckers. It's as simple as that. And so they doubly hate it. And in an odd sort of way I feel I can unmask that.[41]

After Britain celebrated the Silver Jubilee in 1977, the stage was set for the emergence of Thatcher. The period 1945-76 (the establishment of the welfare state to Healey's Budget crisis) was then perceived as a failure, and Thatcher was elected by promising openly to abandon any attempt at welfare-capitalism. As Sinfield notes, "[t]he old stories [had] failed".[42] After only nine years of Thatcherism, the image of a unified Britain was shattered by widespread rioting. At Tamworth, near Birmingham, in 1988 the Home Secretary, Douglas Hurd, attempting to smooth over a riot-torn community, suggested that what Britain needed was "'social cohesion alongside the creation of wealth through private enterprise: these are the two conditions of our future progress'".[43] Yet, as Sinfield points out, Thatcherism deliberately obscured the fact that "social cohesion" and "private enterprise" are "incompatible".[44] Despite a rhetoric of unity and cohesion, the Thatcher government "systematically assaulted institutions associated with welfare-capitalism, the labour movement and middle-class dissent".[45]

While these assaults continued, Jarman became increasingly vocal, seeing that the tradition he defended was now under open attack. Thatcherite ideology concerning the family and sexuality became focused in the Government's implementation of Clause 28 in 1988.[46] At this point Jarman says he knew, finally, that "one was dealing with criminal elements...that this government is criminal".[47] He points out that insofar as gay people start life within a heterosexual family, Clause 28 is "a direct attack on the family...This is the irony of the clause".[48] This reversal of margin/centre is relayed into Jarman's application of metaphors of disease to politics. He calls the Thatcher government the "virus" which "attacks creation", establishing a framework whereby monetarism and its followers are seen as eating away at the body politic.[49] Drawing upon Blake's symbolism in his poem, "The Sick Rose", we can suggest that Jarman and the tradition come to represent the rose, while Thatcherism and its attendant media become the maggot that "doth your life destroy". For Jarman, the prophylactic that can protect the Rose against the virus is located in the culture of the tradition: "The *Sonnets* and the *Symposium* are a cultural condom protecting us against the virus of the yellow press".[50]

Jarman describes Thatcherism as "a turning away",[51] and I think that we can read this act not only as a turning away from people's needs, but also as a rejection of the tradition of middle-class dissent. Whereas previous governments had tried to accommodate the dissenting tradition, Thatcher openly rejected its values. The desire to pull away from the British tradition was always present in British history but, for Jarman, Thatcherism represented "absolutely the worst in British tradition and British history...[t]here is absolutely nothing in Margaret Thatcher which is patriotic, intelligent or honourable".[52] In contrast, Jarman upholds these values. Jarman and the British tradition occupy a space that, although characterised historically as decadent and effeminate, is intelligent and honourably British. When asked if he was a patriot, Jarman replied affirmatively.[53]

While deploying a rhetoric of unity, family values and community, Thatcherism results in a society antagonistic to such goals. I want to reframe Thatcherism, proposing that, while the rhetoric appears *centripetal* at the level of ideology (a bringing together of self, history, culture and family), its economic and socio-political effects are *centrifugal* (decentralisation of public spending, dismantling of the

Greater London Council and the welfare state). In contrast, in Jarman's œuvre the surface rhetoric appears centrifugal (which accounts for the various misreadings of his work as radical and "alternative"), but has highly centripetal objectives. At a time when Thatcherism was pursuing a centrifugal path of social dismemberment and antipathy to history, Jarman's insistence on the historical unity of the British tradition was bound to anger the defenders of the Right. However, his position can also be lost or misread by making the assumption that the dissenting tradition is equated with ideology in the Marxist sense of mystification.[54] For Jarman, the middle-class dissident tradition is not to be confused with Thatcher's "fake patriotism", but it is what allows one to see through the mystification of (Thatcherite) ideology and into History.

The erasure of History, ushered in by modernism and continued by Thatcher, has created a group of writers who feel the need to return to History as a way of reinscribing British culture into an historical tradition from which it has strayed.[55] Affirming his role as nurturer, gardener, craftsman and the upholder of unity and form, Jarman states: "I am the pivot who gathers the communal threads and creates the pattern".[56] As he points out – sounding surprised that he has been so consistently misunderstood – "Shakespeare, the *Sonnets*, *Caravaggio*, Britten's *Requiem*, what more traditional subject matter could a film-maker take on?".[57] The same misunderstanding of his work occurred with *The Tempest* (1979). At the opening of British Film Year, Jarman was approached by a man who suggested that they "make an alternative festival for films like *The Tempest* at the NFT [National Film Theatre]", to which Jarman responds: "*The Tempest* alternative? Where do these people leave their minds? Try explaining to them that I don't make underground films, I have never made underground films".[58]

The Last of England, despite its implicit messages alerting us to the need to reconnect to an historical continuity, was again sorely misread by Jarman's critics *and* his fans. Responding to a sympathetic viewer who praised the film as a successful attack on England, Jarman disagreed:

It's a love story with England. It's not an attack. It's an attack on those things that I perceive personally as things without value. Things that have invaded the mainstream of British life. That's not an attack on England. It's the opposite.[59]

Another critic argued that the film is "very pessimistic", to which Jarman responded "[n]ot at all. The act of making the film is the opposite."[60] David Hirst also perceived the film as presenting the viewer with "very little hope",[61] to which Jarman replied: "They are the hope, the activity is the hope. I don't think I should project false hope if I don't feel it."[62] A series of images from the film can serve to illustrate Jarman's position. Black and white footage from the 1980s of city buildings burning and collapsing in the middle of a riot are intercut with a sequence in which Spencer Leigh, dressed in the pointed hat of the heretic, walks forwards holding up a lighted torch. Like the outspoken heretic who refuses to collaborate with mainstream ideological positions, Jarman is aiming to keep alight the cultural heritage during a period in which England runs the risk of losing its culture completely. Jarman suggests that "[w]ith *The Last of England*... I'm going back to my roots, to lay bare the contradictions"[63] and thereby to expose "the little white lies" which, as the voice-over tells us, have murdered Hope.

Jarman traces the dissident tradition as far back as Beowulf (widely perceived as one of the roots of Anglo-Saxon literature) as a way of explaining what he was doing in *The Last of England*:

> Think of the mead hall in *Beowulf*...Think of that mead hall full of the junk of our history, of memory and so on; there's a hurricane blowing outside, I open the doors and the hurricane blows through, everything is blown around, it's a cleansing, the whole film is a cleansing.[64]

Given the centrifugal pull of contemporary culture, Jarman speaks of the need for something around which to concentrate his centripetal energy: "I need a very firm anchor in that hurricane, the anchor is my inheritance, not my family inheritance, but a cultural one, which locates the film *in home*".[65] If *The Last of England* is to be seen in the tradition of landscape painting (Jarman links the colours of the film to Turner), the scenes of industrial wastelands and urban decay in London and Liverpool in the film signal the ways in which Englishness has been lost by allowing people to be cut off from the land. This rootlessness is symbolised by the images of Spencer Leigh's vainly attempting to clear away the rubble that surrounds him, and wandering hopeless – and homeless – amidst the ruined wasteland. Contrasted with these images are scenes of Tilda Swinton running through flowers and grass in sunshine, restoring our focus on the traditions that reside in nature and femininity. For Jarman, as for the contemporary London-based artists Gilbert and George, and, before them, Morris and Blake, Britishness is synonymous with landscape. As Jarman says, "Blake and William Morris...all of them look backward over their shoulders – to a Paradise on earth. And all of them at odds with the world around them. I feel this strongly".[66] Like Milton, Blake and Morris, and equipped with a camera, Jarman glances over his shoulder at "paradise lost". In many ways, Jarman's most important remark is "[l]ike all true gardeners, I'm an optimist",[67] for if Jarman communicates the destruction of the British countryside with the eyes of a painter, he feels it with the hands of a gardener, whose concern, above all, is growth.[68] In this light we can begin to understand the implication of Jarman's telling us that his films, like the natural growth of plants, always develop organically.[69]

In 1971, Philip Larkin wrote the poem, "Going, Going". His concern is that the landscape ("The shadows, the meadows, the lanes") will be destroyed by monetary interests.[70] Reading Jarman as radically queer and controversial precludes thinking of him as working alongside Larkin, or, as Simon Watney tells us, that Jarman could be friends with a conservative figure such as Sir John Betjeman.[71] However, History often produces figures who cut across the demarcations which we want to establish, and Jarman is a case in point. David Hirst compares Jarman's films to the work of Humphrey Jennings, whose films "merge landscapes with action in a very poetic evocation of England".[72] Jarman agrees, and says that he has seen the destruction of the British landscape "through commercialisation, a destruction so complete that fragments are preserved as if in a museum". In Rye, for example, Jarman notices how old English villages "have been made 'historical' – busily manufacturing themselves as picture postcards of their past". The same tragedy has befallen the destination of Chaucer's pilgrims: Canterbury, which is now a "'historic centre'...taken over by twee boutiques selling superfluous goods. The market town is dead...The city of pilgrims has become an empty 'theme park.'"[73] For Jarman, in short:

[D]estroying without purpose is endemic to our culture... Denying value to anything that can't be consumed...The valuable is so fragile...the environment, the hedgerows, a corner shop, something that you have grown accustomed to and need; suddenly its gone and you ask yourself why.[74]

Nostalgia for a vanished landscape, as Jarman says, lies "behind" *The Last of England*: "even if it's not really seen; it's lurking there".[75]

Jarman filmed on locations that are firmly rooted in British history.[76] Finding these locations, he says, is "crucial...you have to get stuck into one place".[77] For example, *The Tempest* was shot at Stoneleigh Abbey, while *The Angelic Conversation* (1985) takes place at Montacute House, "a very fine Elizabethan mansion".[78] In *The Garden* (1990), amidst all the intolerance and betrayal is the constant image of Jarman's garden at Prospect Cottage in Dungeness, providing, as Sean O'Hagan points out, "the still, spiritual centre of the film".[79] Some of Jarman's locations even overlap, providing the films with an intertextual cohesion. For example, Jarman relates how "*The Angelic Conversation* moves through the same landscape as *Jubilee*. Elizabeth and John Dee are wandering along the same cliffs, at Winspit, as Philip. The new film *The Last of England*, also ends there in the sunset".[80] Perry Anderson argues that Thatcherism was "calculated to reshape the British social landscape".[81] However, if recent changes to the landscape can be laid at the feet of Thatcherism, Jarman also feels that the Left fared no better in providing a decent home for Britain's people. He makes clear his irritation with the failure of the Labour Party to uphold the values which he sees as being central to British culture. For example, in *Jubilee*, Kid (Adam Ant) and Sphinx (Karl Johnson) are on the city rooftops looking down over London. Sphinx comments on the ways in which state intervention in the form of council housing (as well as modernist architecture) has failed to offer nourishment to any of the senses:

> Everything was regulated in that tower block, planned by the social planners to the lowest common denominator. Sight: concrete. Sound: the telly. Taste: plastic. Touch: plastic. The seasons regulated by a thermostat.[82]

The state can only offer a way of life which cuts people off from the natural cycles of the landscape. As a result of these political failures, Jarman feels trapped in a political system which is really one overarching "fog" of hegemony: "There is no longer any decency or consistency of vision in British politics, we are left in the tender hands of these loons of Right and Left".[83]

The loss of the landscape brings with it both a metaphorical and a literal loss of nourishment for Britain. For example, in *The Last of England* shots of a naked man eating a raw cauliflower are interspersed with shots of a businessman in callipers throwing away excess grain. Jarman remarks that "much of the land is desolate".[84] He is concerned, above all, with England's "roots". If the Labour governments of the 1970s failed to establish any firm cultural roots, under Thatcher the historical and cultural roots that had kept Britain alive for so long were finally dug up:

> Young bigots flaunting an excess of ignorance. *Little England* Criminal behaviour in the police force. *Little England.* Jingoism at Westminster, *Little England:* Small town folk gutted by ring roads. *Little England.* Distressed housing estates cosmeticised in historicism. *Little England.* The greedy destruction of the countryside. *Little England.*[85]

Jarman wonders what Pasolini would have thought of Little England, remarking that, while Pasolini's enemies saw him as a radical, "in fact he fought for traditional values".[86] Jarman reflects that Ezra Pound (the manly Fascist) and Pasolini (the homosexual Marxist) were, in fact, "allies". Both were protecting Italian civilisation from being destroyed by postwar democracy: "These corrupters [the Allies] lay waste the mental and physical landscape of dear Italy in a sea of rubbish".[87] Jarman sees himself operating in a similar vein, engaging in a strategy of radical conservatism by which to defend British culture against social and political erosion. In the face of this damage to Britain's roots, Jarman spent his last years living in Prospect Cottage in Dungeness in the shadow of the nuclear power station – a constant reminder of industry's desire to destroy nature in the pursuit of power. As Jarman notes, "[i]t's difficult to find a good vegetable garden...the supermarkets have wiped them out".[88] Considering Jarman's concern with a vanishing landscape it is significant that he tells us how Dungeness "has been declared a conservation area".[89] Jarman and the tradition which he represents are quite literally an endangered species.

Jarman died in February 1994, and the ways in which he approached his illness brought AIDS to the forefront of British culture. In the same way that he had worked to reappropriate the canonical British tradition and re-present it, Jarman – who tells us in *Blue* (1993) that "[t]he virus [has been] appropriated by the well"[90] – attempts in his later work and commentaries to reappropriate AIDS. While contemporary Britain has demarcated Thatcherite individualism and health on the one hand, and iconoclasm and illness on the other, Jarman weaves together patriotism and AIDS so that iconoclasm is a healthy activity, and Thatcherite individualism becomes a deadly illness. Jarman, by raging against the government's stupidity, and insensitivity to beauty and love, is – like his soldier father – fighting for his life and country. Jarman said that we should "take heart in being positive", but at a time when negation is in power, being (HIV) positive leads to attack from all sides.[91] In his treatment of his death, Jarman believes he is more British than those who mouth Thatcher's fake patriotism: like the soldiers of Brooke's and Owen's war poetry, Jarman was prepared to die for the country he believed in.[92] Jarman said that he was a pivot around which to weave the scattered threads of British culture, and his work can be seen as creating a space in which the supposedly "traditional" is exposed as the marginal, while the "marginal" is revealed as the traditional. By making the terms equivalent, Jarman then moves towards creating a cultural vision in which contrary positions can coexist, having been revealed as parts of one pre-existent tradition. It is this drive towards a larger cultural synthesis which helps to explain Jarman's comment that he is "not interested in political statements".[93] Jarman's vision has always been historical, not merely "political".[94]

While Jarman's posthumous film, *Glitterbug* (1994), is essentially a collection of home-movies, all his films are in fact "home" movies insofar as they are in search of a place where we can put down our roots.[95] For Eric Hobsbawm, the period from 1973 to the present constitutes "a sub-epoch of disintegration and disorientation".[96] In the midst of this, Jarman has been trying to locate somewhere for us all to live, to reorient us, to take us back home. As Jarman said, "[h]ome is where one should be...In all home movies is a longing for paradise".[97] By fighting for Blake's "Jerusalem" (as opposed to the public school/*Chariots of Fire* version appropriated by the Right), Jarman's life echoes that of the young man in Rupert Brooke's poem, "The Soldier": "A body of England's, breathing English air,/Washed by the rivers, blest by suns of home".[98] Despite the attempts of the government to turn Britain into a wasteland, Jarman always fought to make it a place where culture could take root and thrive. For Jarman, the British "garden" has the ability to accommodate a rich variety of difference, for it offers a plurality of identities, sexualities and histories. Jarman felt that it was his task to yoke together this culture of contradictions, enabling all of us to feel at home in a place which could once again be "forever England".

Notes

[1]   Geoffrey Keynes (ed), *Poetry and Prose of William Blake* (London: The Nonesuch Library, 1975): 71. For a discussion of England and Jarman, see Dick Hebdige, "Digging for Britain: An excavation in seven parts", in Dominic Strinati and Stephen Wagg (eds), *Come On Down?: Popular media culture in post-war Britain* (London; New York: Routledge, 1992): 366-371.

[2]   Derek Jarman, *The Last of England*, edited by David L Hirst (London: Constable, 1987): 151.

[3]   From the poem, "Strange Meeting". See *The Collected Poems of Wilfred Owen*, edited with an Introduction and Notes by C Day Lewis (London: Chatto & Windus, 1963): 35.

[4]   Simon Field, "The Garden of Earthly Delights", *The Face* 21 January 1993: 62.

[5]   The title is taken from the name of a public house near RAF Abingdon where Jarman's father was stationed during the war.

[6]   Jarman (1987): 118.

[7]   Alan Sinfield, *Literature, Politics and Culture in Postwar Britain* (Berkeley: University of California Press, 1989): 41.

[8] See Keynes (ed): 75.

[9] See ibid: 74. In Jarman's film this is rewritten as "I walk in this garden/ Holding the hands of dead friends/Winter came early for my frosted generation". The walls of the punks' room in *Jubilee* also carry Blake's words.

[10] Derek Jarman, *Modern Nature: The Journals of Derek Jarman* (London: Century, 1991): 68.

[11] Sinfield: 39-40.

[12] Simon Watney, "Derek Jarman 1942-94: A Political Death", *Artforum* May 1994: 119.

[13] Sinfield: 40.

[14] Ibid: 42.

[15] Ibid: 41.

[16] Ibid: 63.

[17] Clause 28 of the Local Government Act 1987-88 (Clause 28), which passed into law on 9 March 1988, outlined how local authorities would not be permitted to "intentionally promote homosexuality" nor would schools be allowed to teach homosexuality as a "pretended family relationship". See Ann-Marie Smith, "A Symptomology of an Authoritarian Discourse", *New Formations* 10 (spring 1990): 41-65.

[18] Watney: 85. Connections established in the popular mind equate homosexuality with art. In Jarman's *Blue* the narrator relates how an article in the paper revealed that one area felt that it didn't have to provide safe sex information because "they had no queers in their community" but that the Safe Sex organisations might try "district X – they have a theatre" (Derek Jarman, *Blue: Text of a film by Derek Jarman* [London: Channel 4 Television and BBC Radio 3, 1993]: 14).

[19] David Leon Higdon, *Shadows of the Past in Contemporary British Fiction* (Athens, OH: University of Georgia Press, 1985): 6.

[20] Quoted in Sinfield: 285.

[21] Jarman portrays Procktor in *Prick Up Your Ears* (1987), Stephen Frears's film of the life of gay British playwright, Joe Orton.

[22] Jarman (1987): 41.

[23] Ibid: 52.

[24] Ibid: 44.

[25] Ibid: 207.

[26] Ibid: 196. Emphasis in original.

[27] Perry Anderson, *English Questions* (London; New York: Verso, 1992): 31.

[28] Ibid.

[29] Sinfield: 15.

[30] Ibid: 279.

[31] Ibid.

[32] Sinfield: 282. In order for welfare-capital to work, the economy needs to maintain a level of productivity in order to raise the funds necessary to pay for social welfare. However, this balance was placed out of reach when, in 1973, OPEC doubled the price of oil. By August 1975 unemployment had exceeded 2 million. Having run out of money, the British government had no choice but to borrow from the International Monetary Fund (IMF). Such borrowing imposed severe restrictions on public spending and by 1976 Healey's Budget had collapsed.

[33] For more on punk's cultural/political significance, see Dick Hebdige, *Subculture: The Meaning of Style* (London; New York: Methuen, 1979): 62.

[34] Derek Jarman, *Dancing Ledge*, edited by Shaun Allen (London; New York: Quartet Books, 1984): 172.

[35] Jarman (1987): 188. The same recourse to the medieval English tradition occurs in *The Angelic Conversation*, which combines Shakespeare's Sonnets with the music of Coil. As Jarman states: "At the time I was thinking of the Anglo-Saxon poem *The Wanderer*" (Jarman [1987]: 133).

[36] See Jarman (1984): 170. For more on Malcolm McLaren, see Jon Savage, *England's Dreaming: Sex Pistols and punk rock* (New York: St Martin's Press, 1992).

[37] Jarman (1984): 177.

[38] Ibid: 179. For more analysis on the interpenetration of past and present in *Jubilee*, see the essays by Hawkes and Quinn-Meyler in this volume.

[39] Derek Jarman, *Know What I Mean?*, an interview preceding *A Night With Derek*. Channel 4 Televison, 16 July 1994.

[40] Ibid.

[41] Ibid.

[42] Sinfield: 282.

[43] Quoted in ibid: 296.

[44] Ibid.

[45] Ibid: 306.

[46] For more on Jarman and Clause 28, see my "Jarman/Burroughs: An Immanent Analysis", *The Spectator [Los Angeles]* 10: 2 (1990): 78-95.

[47] Jarman, *Know What I Mean?*.

[48] Ibid.

[49] Jarman (1987): 229.

[50] Jarman (1991): 163.

[51] Jarman (1987): 211.

[52] Jarman, *Know What I Mean?*.

[53] Jarman (1987): 211.

[54] For more on mystification, see Raymond Williams's chapter, "Ideology", in *Marxism and Literature* (Oxford: Oxford University Press, 1983): 55-71.

[55] On a popular level, this turn away from History was symbolised in the ideological image of the "yuppies" who, by a process of individualism, could climb free of their class roots. See Martin Amis's treatment of John Self in his novel, *Money* (1984).

[56] Jarman (1987): 197. Stanley Spencer also referred to painting as "his knitting". See Christopher Neve, *Unquiet Landscape: Places and Ideas in Twentieth-Century English Painting* (London; Boston: Faber and Faber, 1990): 40.

[57] Jarman (1991): 234.

[58] Jarman (1987): 136.

[59] Jarman, *Know What I Mean?*.

[60] Jarman (1987): 167.

[61] Ibid: 108.

[62] Ibid: 109.

[63] Ibid: 181.

[64] Ibid: 208-211.

[65] Ibid: 211. Emphasis in original.

[66] Jarman (1991): 25.

[67] Jarman (1987): 151.

[68] Christopher Neve, in his discussion of the British landscape painter, John Nash, outlines the connections between painting and gardening. He argues that both arts are concerned with "making something of beauty out of the

dark, from almost nothing" (Neve: 48).

[69] Jarman (1987): in particular, 197-199.

[70] See Philip Larkin, *Collected Poems*, edited with an introduction by Anthony Thwaite (London: The Manvell Press; Faber and Faber, 1988): 190.

[71] Watney: 119.

[72] Jarman (1987): 136. For an interesting analysis of nationalism and Humphrey Jennings, see David Finch, "The Idea of Britain", *Undercut* 19 (autumn 1990): 42-44.

[73] Jarman (1987): 138. For more on the heritage industry in Britain, see John Corner and Sylvia Harvey (eds), *Enterprise and Heritage: Crosscurrents of National Culture* (London: Routledge, 1991).

[74] Jarman (1987): 196.

[75] See the telephone interview with Jarman by Chris Lippard, reproduced in this volume (page 162).

[76] See Chris Lippard and Guy Johnson's essay on Jarman and the London Docklands, "Private Practice, Public Health: The Politics of Sickness and the Films of Derek Jarman", in Lester Friedman (ed), *Fires Were Started: British Cinema and Thatcherism* (Minneapolis: University of Minnesota Press, 1993): 278-293.

[77] Telephone interview with Jarman by Chris Lippard, reproduced in this volume (page 162).

[78] Jarman (1987): 143.

[79] Field: 63.

[80] Jarman (1987): 145.

[81] Anderson: 301.

[82] Quoted in Jarman (1984): 179.

[83] Jarman (1991): 163.

[84] Jarman (1987): 138.

[85] Ibid: 81. Emphases in original. Working in the tradition of Swift, Jarman says that the execution of Spencer Leigh in *The Last of England* occupies the same position as Gulliver in Lilliput, representing "like 'Gulliver'...a sacrifice to *little England*" (207). Emphasis in original.

[86] Ibid: 81.

[87] Ibid: 18.

[88] Jarman (1991): 23.

[89]   Ibid: 64.

[90]   Jarman (1993): 9.

[91]   Jarman (1987): 82.

[92]   For Raymond Williams, there are two types of nationalism. The first, shared by both the Left and the Right, reinforces the idea of the nation state. The second, to which I feel Jarman belonged, is a nationalism which "questions the whole basis of the unitary British state". See "Decentralism and the Politics of Place", in Robin Gable (ed), *Resources of Hope: Culture, Democracy, Socialism* (London; New York: Verso, 1989): 238.

[93]   Jarman: *Know What I Mean?*.

[94]   Gilbert and George have made the same arguments about their work, seeing it not as merely "political", but moral.

[95]   For more on the question of home-movies in Jarman, see Lippard and Johnson.

[96]   Quoted in Ross McKibbin, "The Age of Extremes", *The Times Literary Supplement* 4778 (28 October 1994): 4.

[97]   Jarman (1987): 54, 235.

[98]   *Rupert Brooke: The Complete Poems* (London: Sidgwick & Jackson, 1942): 150.

The process of Jarman's *War Requiem*: personal vision and the tradition of fusion of the arts

Joseph A Gomez

By the beginning of the 1990s, before his untimely death in 1994, Derek Jarman had emerged as Britain's most upfront and articulate advocate for homosexuality, and probably its most "in your face" critic of Thatcherite values – whether economic, political, social or aesthetic. Nevertheless, despite the aggressiveness of his public pronouncements and the political dimensions of his work, Jarman was first and foremost an artist: a painter, production designer, writer and, most notably, independent filmmaker, who may well come to be acknowledged as the "touchstone" British film director of this period.

Jarman's films are diverse and deeply rooted personal expressions that embody a sense of "tradition and history" and not the obscene, masturbatory flights of self-indulgence that his enemies have claimed. Indeed, Jarman's continuity with what might be called "the English tradition of radical imagination",[1] is essential to appreciating the multidimensions of both his ferocious attacks on the greed, repression and total self-interest of the British Establishment, and the less assertive, gentler manifestations of his muted romanticism.

In most of his films, Jarman attacked the present, mourned for the future, and, on occasion – despite acknowledging continuities of oppression – was obsessed about a past that could never be again. Although he could say that his was "the last generation that remembers what the countryside was like before mechanization totally intervened and destroyed everything",[2] he never tolerated nostalgia for fabricated images of England, such as those found in John Boorman's *Hope and Glory* (1987). Rather, like Bertrand Russell, who claimed that the 20th century had squandered the world's beauty, Jarman felt that the artist must warn the present about the destruction of the past in order to save anything for the future: "Surely, the task of the next century must be to protect what remains".[3] Wistfully, he may have yearned for the world of John Dee, Elizabeth I's magus, but Jarman was to be Elizabeth II's magus in the guise of apocalyptic artist. "As long as the music's loud enough, we won't hear the world falling apart", says Borgia Ginz, the manipulative media mogul in *Jubilee* (1978); but Jarman's films, with their razor-sharp edge, almost always made his audiences painfully aware of the world falling apart around them. Even his idiosyncratic cinematic adaptations of texts seemingly affirmative of so-called English ideals, such as Shakespeare's *The Tempest* (1979) and perhaps Benjamin Britten's *War Requiem* (1988), must be viewed not as anomalies, but as further examples of his genuinely subversive art.

War Requiem was probably the least acknowledged of Jarman's feature films when he was alive; despite the attention that his work has received since his death, this situation has hardly changed. For those who venerate him as the consummate outsider angrily railing against the British Film Establishment, *War Requiem* is his one film with restrictive mainstream ties. Much of the film's limited funding came from the BBC, but there were also commercial investors who wanted some bankable, recognisable names in the cast (Daniel Day-Lewis was slated to play Owen at one point, and Laurence Olivier appears briefly in the film, in what was to be his last role). Sympathetic producer Don Boyd even requested that Jarman "play down the relationship between OWEN and the UNKNOWN SOLDIER" in order to avoid alienating American investors.[4]

Over the years, Jarman himself expressed somewhat ambivalent feelings about his visualization of Britten's massive musical undertaking. In the 1991 preface to the reprinted edition of *Dancing Ledge*, he describes the film as an example of "the reclaiming of the Queer Past",[5] but later, in what turned out to be his final interview, he remarks to Richard Morrison that although "it was great to do the film", he does not think about it now: "You make a list of films you've made and I leave that off myself! It's funny. I think it got into a sort of trap with the people who owned it and promoted it. That's why it's so difficult to find anything to do with it".[6] Even the Britten-Pears Foundation, which had initially been supportive, seemed indifferent to the finished film, as did those investors who had pushed, during the pre-production stage, for more violence than Jarman's proposed screenplay indicated.

Part of the problem on another level may simply be that, while Jarman was rightly acknowledged as Britain's most personal and experimental independent filmmaker, there seems to be little that is genuinely personal and even less that is overtly experimental in *War Requiem*. Perhaps even the "reclaiming of the Queer Past" has more to do with presenting on film the work of an acknowledged homosexual (Britten) and a presumed one (Wilfred Owen) than with any direct visual representation of queer life – which is merely hinted at via fleeting homoerotic moments between the Wilfred Owen figure (Nathaniel Parker) and the Unknown Soldier (Owen Teale). Indeed, Jarman was more constrained with *War Requiem* than with any other film. *The Tempest* and *Edward II* (1991) were personal testaments rather than faithful adaptations of classic plays, and *The Last of England* (1987) was shot without a script. The situation with *War Requiem* was exactly the opposite: according to provisions set up by the Britten-Pears Foundation, the music could not be altered in any way for this "composed film" (a work in which the soundtrack already exists and images are shot to match it). In addition, the financial backers of the film expected a conventional narrative from a source that was a collage of Owen's poems and the Latin text of the Mass for the Dead, and from a director whose reputation was that of being "an enemy of narrative film".[7]

All Jarman's films are incomplete visions, altered by budgetary constrictions, improvisations and chance; this is the way he intended them to be – rough-edged, tentative and full of risk-taking. For Jarman – more than for any of his contemporaries – process was his most important product, and if that process was not exciting and fun, he did not want to make the film. From his earliest days of shooting Super 8 home-movies, Jarman indicates that, like Andy Warhol and Kenneth Anger, he was more interested in the people in his films and in what was going on than in the semantics of filmmaking.[8] As a result, there is a discernible amateur quality to Jarman's films, but the experience of watching his work is also unique – something comparable to a spellbinding ride through a bizarre, even apocalyptic, carnival funhouse. Despite the dominant repetitive, almost ritualistic patterns of his films, tone can shift without warning. Hostile and aggressive images which jolt and overwhelm are, on occasion, mingled with moments of surprising lyricism, and invariably there is an especially memorable sequence that initially appears strikingly inappropriate.

These are some of the very things, however, that seem missing from *War Requiem*. For example, there is nothing comparable to the unexpected flamboyant dancing of a hundred sailors and the show-stopping appearance of Elisabeth Welch as a goddess singing "Stormy Weather" in *The Tempest*. Nevertheless, *War Requiem* should not be slighted as a bland exercise in classical MTV, a respectful but dull visualization of what some music critics consider to be a 20th century choral masterpiece. Like a Renaissance sonneteer, Jarman works in a severely confined format in *War Requiem*, but nevertheless makes this film very much his own while also respecting the composer's form and much of his message. Finally, in addition to serving both Britten's and his own aesthetic and political purposes, Jarman attempts in *War Requiem* to fuse together the multiple arts (music, poetry, drama and film) that form the basis of this project.

Part of Jarman's approach to film derived from his interest and background in other art forms. He was trained initially as a painter and never retreated entirely from painting as a means of personal expression. In the late 1960s he also developed interests in other arts, most notably costume and set design, film and theatre production design, and Super 8 filmmaking. The early filmmaking ventures were initially fuelled by his literary interests: "I would write in poetry and try to bring that to life".[9] Given his various journals and autobiographical writings, one wishes that he had gone into specific detail, as Eisenstein did, about the interrelationship of the arts, and how, for example, his concerns with painterly textures and rhythms were manifested in his films. Occasionally, however, he does consider the interaction of other art forms with film. Discussing his adaptation of *The Tempest* in *Dancing Ledge*, he notes that settings in Shakespearian films are always in conflict with language. This observation, in turn, becomes a springboard for his generalisation that design is usually the key to a film:

> [W]hen design is integrated into the intentional structure, and forms part of the dialectic, the work begins to sing. *Ivan the Terrible* is the most perfect example. 'Epic' has had more than its fair share of icing, but Eisenstein reinforces the humanity and ambiguity of Ivan through *design*. This integration of design in a film is not only the preserve of 'high art'. *The Wizard of Oz* is another perfect example.[10]

For Jarman, therefore, film is "an alchemical conjunction" of light and matter, a fusion of multiple forms into a kind of magical synthesis.[11]

The idea of a synthesis of various arts dates back at least to ancient Greece, but probably the quest for artistic fusion was most widely attempted in Europe in the 19th century. Poets associated with the Romantic tradition began breaking down traditional genres and striving for a condition of synesthesia, and literary theorists of the period speculated as to how to achieve this goal. Gotthold Lessing, for example, wanted arts to respect each other's limitations but still supplement one another in some form of synthesis. Johann Herder wrote of the need for someone to overturn conventional forms of dramatic art and create "a cohesive lyric structure in which poetry, music, action, and decoration are all one".[12] The most notable experiments to achieve this goal came from Richard Wagner, who advocated *gesamtkunstwerk* or, as he preferred to call it, "the drama of the future", in which poetry, music and theatre were combined to create an invigorating and intoxicating experience, the essence of which was a blurring together of art forms to the point of fusion.[13]

The Russian composer Alexander Scriabin hailed the transforming role of art, and saw his grand purpose as unifying all art forms in a manner that communicated a primordial and spiritual power to those who experienced it. Scriabin told Rimsky-Korsakov that, upon hearing *Poem of Ecstasy*, he would "live with all sensations, with harmonies of sounds, harmonies of colors, harmonies of perfume!". Like Wagner, who came to feel that art is sterile when divorced from religion, Scriabin's aesthetics assumed monumental mystical dimensions. Against the backdrop of the beginning of the First World War and shortly before he died of blood-poisoning, Scriabin commenced work on *Mysterium*, a projected experience that would take seven days to perform: "after the assault on the senses of all the arts battering at man's psyche", man and nature would bring the world to a state of unity. Sexual polarization would vanish, and mankind would be consumed into an "ecstatic abyss of sunshine".[14]

On a more practical level, the multimedia nature of film has made it the ideal means for achieving a synthesis of poetry, music, movement and drama. Nevertheless, only a handful of filmmakers has attempted the kind of fusion of the arts sought by romantic extremists. Eisenstein, the most committed and articulate of these seekers, came the closest to this ideal with *Ivan grozny* (*Ivan the Terrible*, 1942-46). This sublime, grandiose and operatic film still frustrates conventional viewers' expectations, in that it foregrounds stylization at the expense of narrative, empathy, action and complex characterisation. Instead, with its music, elaborate art direction, artificial dialogue, chiaroscuro lighting, exaggerated make-up and kabuki theatre gestures, the film affects its audience primarily at the level of ritual.

At the other extreme, the great populariser of the concept of fusion of the arts was Walt Disney, who wanted audiences "to see music and hear pictures" in *Fantasia* (1940), "the ultimate entertainment". *Fantasia*, for Disney, was meant to be experienced more like a live concert than a mere film. Initial plans for widescreen, Fantasound, a possible 3-D section, and even scents for "The Nutcracker Suite" suggest that, in its way, Disney's conception of *Fantasia* was as grandiose as anything dreamed of by Wagner and Scriabin.[15] Nevertheless, Disney saw his enterprise to link high and mass culture primarily as a fun entertainment, and he had no problem allowing the visual images to overwhelm the music, or altering the music to accommodate his animators.

The English filmmaker most closely linked to film and fusion of the arts is Michael Powell, who directly influenced both Ken Russell and Jarman. From his early days in silent films, Powell believed that success in the cinema was achieved by bringing together the best in those arts (theatre, choreography, painting, etc.) that were necessary for the creation of a film. This idea remained constant with Powell, whether he proposed impossible schemes, such as getting together "a group of people – painters like Picasso and Sutherland, poets like Dylan Thomas – and offer[ing] twenty hours of entertainment in colour", or more practical ones, such as hiring painters to be production designers and composers to be music directors for the films that he made with writer, Emeric Pressburger.[16]

With *Black Narcissus* (1946), for example, he decided not to shoot the film on location in India but in the studio, in order to have complete control over how the atmosphere was built-up through colour, architecture, set design and music. Throughout his career, Powell's motto was "all arts are one", and with *Black Narcissus* he slowly began moving towards his goal of a "composed film" that would embody this conception. With Brian Easdale as his "musical collaborator", he constructed a ten-minute sequence at the climax of the film in which the music was composed first and thus dictated the movement of the characters, scene composition and editing. For Powell, the sequence became opera – "opera in the sense that music, emotion, image and voices all blended together into a new and splendid whole".[17]

The Red Shoes (1948) offered another "composed film" opportunity in the justly famous "Red Shoes" ballet sequence that Powell filmed not as ballet-theatre but as film-ballet. However, the ideal of fusion of multiple art forms that Powell was seeking in a "composed film" format was most notably achieved in *The Tales of Hoffmann* (1951), perhaps the wildest Expressionist film ever made in England. Shot to Sir Thomas Beecham's recording of the Offenbach opera, this film combines ballet, theatre and opera in almost equal portions, but it is Powell's cinematic techniques (gelled lenses, dramatic super-impositions, sweeping camera movements) that constantly amaze and magically dazzle the audience into the awareness that it is watching a film – a film that, for Powell, brings all arts into one.

Ken Russell not only revolutionized the nature of bio-pics during and after his years at the BBC, but also followed in Michael Powell's footsteps by attempting to employ the cinema as a means of bringing together multiple art forms. Even in some of his short television films for *Monitor* and, more notably, in the longer *Omnibus* works, such as *Isadora Duncan: The Biggest Dancer in the World* (1966) and *Dante's Inferno* (1967), Russell defined his subjects in terms of their respective arts, and incorporated music, dance and painting to externalize their internal states of being. Perhaps his greatest success in this area was *The Music Lovers* (1970), in which for lengthy sequences he matched Tchaikovsky's music to images, not only for the emotional context of the music, but also to further the narrative and to reveal the essence of the characters and the nature of his own attack on the decadence of Romanticism.

Even before making his popular "composed film" version of the rock-opera, *Tommy* (1975), Russell attempted to obtain funding for a *Fantasia*-like live-action history of classical music entitled *Music, Music, Music*. Instead, since then, his only other excursions into works using classical music as the basis for visual images are a kind of classical MTV version of Gustav Holst's *The Planets* and one of the ten arias from Don Boyd's *Aria* (1987). Russell's *The Planets* (1983) attempts – chiefly through a chain of disparate images that ignore the continuities of time and space – to characterise each planet visually. His editing patterns, like those of numerous rock videos, are generally frenetic. At their best, however, they effectively match the rhythms of the music, which is not surprising, since he first learned to edit by cutting shots to music.[18] In *The Planets*, Russell tries to use images as a means of generating further appreciation for the music, but much of the film is little more than obvious arrangements of stock footage to mirror the programmatic designations that Holst indicated for each planet. "Mars, the Bringer of War", for example, incorporates footage from *Triumph des Willens* (*Triumph of the Will*, 1934), Russian May Day parades, and military marching bands intercut with rocket blast-offs, exploding volcanoes and raging fires. Most of Russell's episode in *Aria*, on the other hand, is developed in a manner that foregrounds narrative structure, even though his story has nothing to do with the opera itself. Here the visuals easily overwhelm the music and become the primary source of information and pleasure – especially since the aria has no specific context in the film and is not even subtitled in English.

That Jarman belongs to the British non-realist tradition of visual excess fathered by Powell and further developed by Russell and Nicolas Roeg has been pointed out by numerous film critics. Ian Christie, for example, even claims that Jarman came to feel that his own project on *The Tempest* had in some special way been "inherited" from Powell.[19] Jarman himself also directly acknowledged his ties to these filmmakers, perhaps most succinctly in a 1980 interview with Timothy Hyman: "I couldn't think of a better mentor [than Ken Russell]; I prefer him to any other English filmmaker (with the exception of Michael Powell, who's my favourite)".[20]

Despite the fact that Powell and Russell were absolute directors, they often not only hired established artists (composers, designers and choreographers), but also allowed them the freedom to contribute their own ideas to film projects. Similarly, Jarman also established a kind of stock company of contributing artists whom he then orchestrated/directed in the making of his films, including *War Requiem*. Producer Don Boyd compares this approach to that frequently used by Italian painters in the Renaissance, and suggests

Caravaggio (1986)

Wittgenstein (1993)

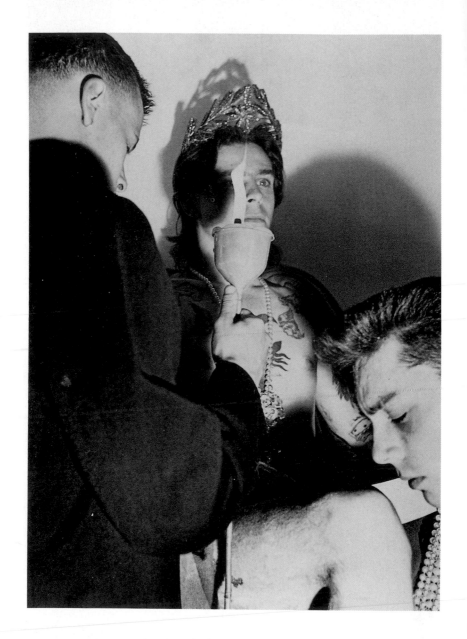

The Angelic Conversation (1985)

The Garden (1990)

War Requiem (1988)

The Tempest (1979)

The Last of England (1987)

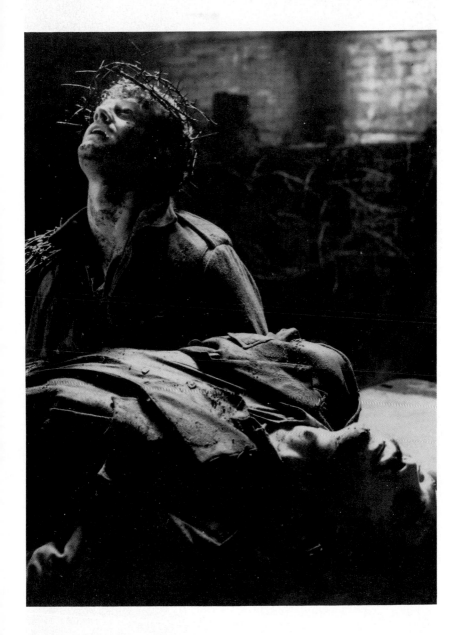

War Requiem (1988)

Sebastiane (1976)

The Garden (1990)

Edward II (1991)

The Tempest (1979)

Edward II (1991)

Jubilee (1978)

that, while each technician made unique contributions, Jarman always remained true to his particular vision and, as such, "ruthlessly" imposed his will on the project.[21] This is generally true in Jarman's films, but his diary for *War Requiem* reveals his anxieties about restrictions and obligations set up by the very nature of the project itself: "What place do I have in all of this? A conductor? An interpreter? A bridge to other audiences and other times?".[22]

Jarman admits that *War Requiem* was "the most difficult undertaking",[23] but it was his idea to seek funding for a composed film where his own role might be held in check for the sake of the music and the text. Jarman had worked in "composed film" situations before, directing music videos for Marianne Faithfull, Bryan Ferry, The Smiths and The Pet Shop Boys, as well as "Depuis le jour" in *Aria*. Nevertheless, for him, these were largely inconsequential efforts – especially the music videos, most of which were made to help finance his feature films. For Jarman, making music videos, or what he called "pop promos", was "a bit like being 17 always", and although he knew exactly how they were expected to be done ("eighty cuts per minute"),[24] he claimed that he was not very good at it because his mind did not work that way.

While Jarman may have seriously underrated some of his own pop promo work, perhaps most notably *The Queen is Dead* (1986), he worried sufficiently about not employing rapid cutting techniques in *War Requiem* that he reworked his first script out of consideration for what he feared would be the limited attention span of most audiences.[25] This lack of rapport with dominant music video techniques also probably accounts for *War Requiem*'s limited examples of footage edited primarily for the rhythms of the music, and for the fact that he shot so many alternative images to accompany the collage-like structure of Britten's score. Finally, Jarman's attitude towards his music video experiences should also help to dispel the notion that he conceived *War Requiem* as an exercise in classical music video.

That is probably how most of the ten directors conceived of their involvement in *Aria*, and why so much of the film failed. Jarman rightly understood, *post facto*, that little genuine fusion of art forms took place in *Aria* and that all of the directors, himself included, used the music merely as a backdrop for their own "arbitrary fantasies".[26] This was not to happen in *War Requiem*. From the beginning of the project, he was concerned with the relationship of text, music and image, so that the visuals would not rigidly determine the viewer's imagination and thus limit rather than expand interpretations of the music. Somehow he had to ensure that the visuals did not simply overwhelm audiences when, given the very nature of the film medium, images tend to dominate other sensory sources. His task, therefore, was to maintain a balance among all the various competing means of expression; at one point in his journal about the making of the film, Jarman indicates his apprehension about the entire enterprise: "Owen took on the war; Britten, Owen and the Mass; I'm taking on all three".[27]

Over the years, Jarman joked about possessing a kind of pragmatism, and perhaps it was his practicality, especially in the mixture of careful preplanning and the ability to alter his conception at a moment's notice, that allowed him to achieve the balance necessary not only to fuse together poetry, music and film, but also to do so in a manner in which Owen, Britten and Jarman himself are given almost equal voices. Of course, it helps that the three artists in question had similar attitudes of revulsion towards war and flagrant abuses of power, but Jarman was also especially attuned to nuances of difference between Owen and Britten and the degree to which he himself stood between them. Owen fought in the trenches and came to look askance at patriotic memorials and the Christian beliefs that dominated much of his youth. Britten, on the other hand, left England for America during most of the Second World War and, although a pacifist committed to specific socio-political beliefs, rarely publicly expressed his views on these topics. Instead, he remained, by and large, part of the English social and religious Establishment.

Indeed, there are moments of intense and profound conflict between the traditional liturgy of the Mass and Owen's poetry in *War Requiem*. The agnostic Jarman builds on these juxtapositions subtly to extend the oppositions found in Britten's work, and perhaps even to redress the balance between Owen and Britten by challenging the Christian synthesis achieved in the final section of the requiem. Despite Jarman's deep love for Britten's church music, which he knew as a child, it is his identification with the anger and pity emanating from Owen's poetry that most shaped his response to this work, which he dedicated in his heart "to all those cast out, like myself, from Christendom. To my friends who are dying in a moral climate created by a church with no compassion."[28] Jarman's personal vision, therefore, although not as obviously stated as in his other films, is as much a part of the total fabric of *War Requiem* as is his desire to meld together music, poetry and image into an experience which expands rather than limits Owen's poetry and Britten's music.

In order to discuss Jarman's success in remaining true to his personal vision and in fusing together art forms in his screen version of *War Requiem*, one must first briefly consider Britten's work in its own context. The origin of this Mass was a request in 1958 from the Coventry Arts Committee for a work to commemorate the new cathedral built to replace the medieval structure destroyed by Nazi bombers in the Second World War. Years before, Britten had considered writing a large-scale choral work in response to the dropping of the atomic bomb on Japan, as well as a requiem commemorating the death of Gandhi, and therefore he was able to respond quickly to the Coventry request with specific ideas about a work for chorus, soloists and orchestra. Some time after accepting the commission, Britten decided to structure the work around the Latin text of the Mass and nine poems by Wilfred Owen, who was killed in the last days of the First World War. In early 1961, after he had asked Dietrich Fischer-Dieskau to sing the baritone part alongside Peter Pears's tenor, he added the soprano soloist part (in Latin) for Galina Vishnevskaya. Thus there would be soloists from three of the major European nations involved in the Second World War singing in a work that Britten considered to be "a kind of reparation".[29]

Britten's *War Requiem* was first performed at Coventry Cathedral on 30 May 1962, and was immediately hailed as a watershed in his career. The critically acclaimed work also captured immediate public enthusiasm, probably because of the impact of Owen's emotionally charged poems set within the context of a requiem Mass. Placement of poems is at times for dramatic purposes, but even more effective and thought-provoking are the layers of irony created by juxtaposing the liturgy of the Mass or Britten's music with the poems. There is also a prophetic dimension to the work, signalled in part by Owen's words on the title page of the score: "My subject is War, and the pity of War./The Poetry is in the pity.../All a poet can do today is warn". Finally, despite the ironic and prophetic components, and the composer's outrage at the destruction of innocence, the ultimate purpose of this work was reconciliation.

As Hugh Ottaway and numerous other critics have noted,[30] the entire design of *War Requiem* depends on the intersection of distinct emotional, dramatic and musical planes. On one level, there is the tension between the personalised emotion of the English poems sung by the two male soloists, and the impersonal, ritualized liturgy in Latin sung by the female soloist, the chorus and boys' choir. Musically, there are three physical planes. In the foreground stand the soloists and chamber orchestra; in the middle ground are the full orchestra and chorus; and in the background, often far-removed from the stage, are the organ and boys' choir. Michael Kennedy even suggests that this physical placement helps to reinforce the dramatic and emotional aspects of the work, in that the boys' choir is almost totally depersonalised as if in some distant mystical realm; the soprano, chorus and orchestra "mourn humanity", and the male soloists and chamber orchestra become "the voices of the victims".[31]

The emotional and dramatic contrasts, in turn, are thus emphasised structurally and musically, with some sense of resolution present only in the conclusion of the "Libera me" section. Here, all the forces involved in the work finally come together as "Let us sleep now...", the last line of Owen's "Strange Meeting", is repeated several times and woven into the texture of the chorus's development of "In paradisum deducant te Angeli". The bells that began the work sound in the distance for the last time, and the chorus quietly intones "Requiescant in pace. Amen."

Jarman begins his visualization of *War Requiem* with credits over a close-up of a burning candle, his controlling visual metaphor. Throughout the film, a snuffed-out candle will serve both as a transition device and as a reminder of the numerous lives cast into darkness – and this is a film of much literal and symbolic darkness. Jarman's only addition to the Britten score is a "Prologue", depicting the Old Soldier (Laurence Olivier) being pushed in a invalid chair by a nurse (Tilda Swinton) with the auditory background of distant bells and Olivier's rendition of the first part of "Strange Meeting". By beginning and ending the film with this poem, Jarman emphasises its importance both thematically and structurally. The inserted documentary footage at key moments in the recitation indicates the method he will employ to depict the historical war, and the use of Tilda Swinton as the nurse here and in the loose narrative around Owen underscores the universality of the condition of war, as does the Old Soldier's Edwardian photo of a young nurse who resembles Tilda. The Old Soldier is a survivor, but one still marked by the war, and the last line of his recitation, "The pity of war, the pity war distilled", allows the "Prologue" to serve as a visual counterpart to Owen's inscription at the top of Britten's score.

The visuals to the first half of the "Requiem aeternam" section establish another of Jarman's key methods in approaching this cinematic adaptation. He begins with images of Owen's corpse via close-ups and a *mise en scène* derived from Charles Sargeant Jagger's Hyde Park memorial. What at first seems a painterly but conventional introduction takes on additional ironic nuances if one becomes conscious of the relationship between the images and the Latin text. The line, "et lux perpetua luceat eis" ("and let light eternal shine upon them"), for example, is undermined by the painful close-up of the Nurse silently screaming while holding her fingers over her eyes. A few moments later, she will offer up Owen's helmet like the host in the "Offertorium". Such reverse religious icons appear throughout the film to counter the false patriotic-religious rhetoric used to justify wars, but these images also serve to undercut the genuine Christian overtones of Britten's work.

Riveting close-ups dominate this film, in part as a result of its low budget, but also because they disturbingly evoke the claustrophobia associated with trench warfare and intensify the internal landscape of the characters. Like many of the images in Owen's poems, this concentration on close-ups – especially on the individual agony of Owen, the Nurse, the Unknown Soldier and the German soldier – creates emotional attachments to these characters as victims. In addition, close-ups emphasise the part for the whole and the central figures as microcosms. This sense of universality is, in turn, further reinforced by the film's many visual motifs: the candle, feet, boots (perhaps an allusion to the film version of *All Quiet On the Western Front* [1930]) and multiple references to blindness. In other instances, this relationship between the individual and the general is more direct, as when the Nurse (presumably Owen's sister) picks up the crumbled paper containing his poem, "Anthem for Doomed Youth", and the word "Nation" is seen scrawled in the upper right-hand corner above the title. For Jarman, Owen's poem is not only an ironic hymn about young men sent to the front to die, but also a dirge for the entire country – a country whose false values have allowed these men to be sacrificed.

The images for this poem do not attempt a literalisation of the text. There are no specific shots of cattle, for example, to visualize the poem's central metaphor of young men being led to slaughter. Rather, we encounter a near surreal scene with recruits being trained in a courtyard, while three horses are being groomed on a first-floor balcony surrounding the courtyard. The "Kyrie" in this section returns us to the bier, now a conventional altar, as Owen places his "bible" – a volume of Keats's poems – on the steps. In the muted colours and lyrical soft focus of Super 8, which Jarman uses chiefly for Owen's memories, the poet is seen breaking bread with his sister in a brief series of shots that, together with many of the film's domestic images from the past, sacramentalize the secular.

The visuals which accompany the mounting apprehension of the "Dies irae" section of the Mass again rely chiefly on irony for impact. Crisp colour footage of soldiers digging in the rain in a chalk pit is juxtaposed with black and white images of a choir in front of murky stock footage of battle scenes. The ominous brass fanfares of Britten's setting of the "Dies irae", however, often accompany nothing more dramatic than the digging of slurry cut to the music, and this visual deflation of musical crescendos weakens some of the abstract religious significance of the liturgy's announcement of the Last Judgment.

Jarman's world is essentially physical, a world where delight derives from nature, human companionship and objects. Most of his films, despite constant limitations of budget and location, and a style totally at odds with social realism, convey a palpable sense of physical environment and the importance of physical things. In his diary of the making of *War Requiem*, he indicates that he has "developed an intense feeling for what, I think, is mistaken as the 'object' world. I hope this can be seen in my films."[32] This emphasis on things tangible and concrete means, for example, that he is much more intent on emphasising the literal bugle mentioned in the "Bugles Sang" poem than that of the symbolic trumpet of the "Dies irae".

Likewise, the home-movie-like Super 8 footage, with its warm colours, soft edges, sacramental images of domestic life, and sense of spirit of place, resonates with the sad innocence and beauty of a physical past that has been irrevocably lost – in this context through ideologies that spawn and bless devastating nationalistic wars. Some of this romanticized footage, often of flowers, country landscapes and treasured moments (the hanging of sheets by the Owen family and the sacrificial burning of the teddy bear by the three children) is later metaphorphosed into frightening images (the death shroud and the sacrifice of Isaac by Abraham) that carry much of the film's anger and anguish.

Because Jarman edits so little to the rhythm of the music (the notable exception being "Libera me"), and because most of the film is not a literal visualization of the poems or of the liturgy, it is easy to understand how he could insist that he kept the making of the film fluid, and that alternative visuals for most sequences were always possible. What Jarman did decide to include in the film, however, like much of Britten's music, creates structural patterns through parallelism, variations and repetitions. In what he calls the "Lady of the Lamp" sequence, which accompanies the soprano and chorus rendering "Liber scriptus", Jarman parallels the humane caring actions of the nurse with those of Owen to his men in the trenches: concrete manifestations of human mercy to parallel words about pleading for divine mercy on Judgment Day.

The side-drum of the chamber orchestra becomes the ironic transition from "Salva me, fons pietatis" ("Fount of pity, then befriend us") to one of Owen's few upbeat poems, "The Next War", which offers a kind of cheerful willingness to sacrifice oneself for a just cause. Jarman reinforces the irony of Britten's particular placement of this poem by presenting images of a fantasy charade, a vaudeville entertainment in which Owen (as a child) beats a tin drum to the antics of soldiers in cancan dress, while a fat Britannia in drag laughs, and businessmen with scythes look on approvingly. Intercut with this stage act is footage of nurses playing blind man's buff. The metaphorical implications are clear: too many of us are blind to the reckless swagger of false patriotic sentiments instilled in us since childhood. The ultimate result of this propaganda is senseless killings, microcosmically depicted in the wrenching visuals that serve as a prelude to the pathos delineated in the "Futility" sequence, where a snowball fight between a German and a British soldier ends in their senseless deaths. The narrative here is perhaps the most accessible in the film, but many of the sequence's more complex images derive from personal allusions (Caravaggio's "The Raising of Lazarus" and Cocteau's *Le Sang d'un poète* [*The Blood of a Poet*, 1930]), and key visual motifs (the washing of the Unknown Soldier's feet, and the placement of his body in crucified fashion on barbed wire) further undercut any hope of divine intercession.

Musically, the richest ironies in Britten's work occur during the "Offertorium", where we are told that the Archangel Michael will lead the faithful into light – "quam olim Abrahae promisisti, et semini ejus" ("which of old, Thou didst promise/unto Abraham and his seed"). At this point, Britten quotes from one of his most beautiful and moving compositions, "Canticle II: Abraham and Isaac" (1952). This line and the borrowed melody become the transition to Owen's "The Parable of the Old Man and the Young", in which his Abraham refuses the offer of a ram to sacrifice and, instead, "slew his son,/And half the seed of Europe, one by one". Jarman ironically depicts Michael's "holy light" as fires from bombs and has Owen imagine himself as Isaac and a Christian bishop (Nigel Terry) as Abraham. In this instance, Jarman largely follows the literal narrative of the poem but in the style of Victorian melodrama, adding only caricatures of businessmen, who wildly applaud this sacrifice performed by the Church and sanctioned by the state (as represented by footage of George V and members of the General Staff). This section is one of the best examples of how Jarman meshes attitudes similar to his own by complementing the ironies and philosophical vision of the music and poetry through visuals. Indeed, the emotional and intellectual impact here depends on how the music, poetry and images all reinforce one another; as such, the sequence stands out as the film's most chilling metaphorical statement.

Britten follows tradition and sets the "Sanctus" apart musically from the rest of the Mass. There is no expression of grief and no depiction of war here, but rather, as Anthony Milner suggests, an "acclamation" of God.[33] It is only after the liturgical text is finished without interruption that Britten turns, with his most daring juxtaposition, to Owen's "The End", a poem full of despair that questions the possibility of life after death and everything else expressed in the preceding liturgy. Jarman also depicts the "Sanctus" in a visual manner totally different from any other section of the film – a single almost seven-minute take of the Nurse in close-up and medium shot expressing a myriad of emotions as she sits in front of the altar/bier, braids her hair, and rhythmically sways her body to some kind of internal music. Despite seeming moments of rapture, her dominant feeling is one of uncontrollable grief, and this single shot ruthlessly juxtaposes the praises to God that aurally shimmer on the soundtrack. Jarman understood the power of the sequence and feared that it would dwarf the visuals that immediately followed.[34] It certainly does that, but paradoxically – because of the intense visual concentration on a single individual – it also evokes a universality missing from the slow-motion montage of conventional documentary footage that accompanies "The End". Much of the impact of this "part for the whole" example comes not only from the cinematically effective long take, but also from Tilda Swinton's performance before an unflinching camera that captures all her facial twitches and each of her subtle gestures.

The "Agnus Dei" is the shortest and most simply constructed section of the entire requiem, but, as both Kennedy and Milner suggest, it may also be the musical and emotional "summing up of the work's central message".[35] In any case, the "Agnus Dei" is Britten's reply to the questions raised at the end of the "Sanctus". The Owen poem, "At a Calvary near the Ancre", sung here is decidedly anti-clerical and an illustration of Owen's claim that patriotism is incompatible with pure Christianity. Britten, however, merges the poem's final words, "But they who love the greater love/Lay down their life; they do not hate", not only with the chorus's "dona eis requiem sempiternam" ("grant them eternal rest"), but also with the tenor's final "Dona nobis pacem" ("grant them peace"), which he added to the liturgy probably as a statement of his own belief that redemption is possible only through the sacrifice of Jesus Christ.

Jarman, of course, has full sympathy with Owen's views about the failure of a Christianity that sends its priests to the trenches to watch soldiers "being crucified" in a religious-sanctioned war. Thus, these suffering soldiers, largely abandoned by religion, become the true suffering Christ-figures. The motif of the crown of thorns (perhaps the most potent symbol of suffering in the Passion story) dominates the iconography of this section, not only via the crowned Unknown Soldier wrapped around the martyred Owen in a garland of thorns, but also even with the mourning Nurse who holds a crown of thorns in her hands as an offering to heaven – a heaven which, unlike Britten's, will grant neither rest nor peace.

From the metaphorical Golgotha ("the place of the skull") of Owen's poem, Jarman takes us to its literal counterpart in the opening and closing of "Libera me". Musically, although closely related through similar themes and a faltering march to "Dies irae", this section, at least for its first half, is the darkest and most frightening in the entire work.

Terror also reverberates from Jarman's visuals, which are the most graphic and visceral in the film: images from all the wars of this century, but especially those since this very Mass was first performed; images (firing guns, dragging wounded or dead bodies) of the same actions repeated over and over again in different wars; images of ripped, shot, burned and decayed bodies; and images of multiple explosions culminating in the mushroom cloud of the atomic bomb over Japan. The rhythmic editing and near subliminal superimpositions of these last shots are close to that of conventional music videos, but the content of the images so overwhelms the viewer that these techniques seem entirely appropriate to this montage of horror.[36]

Jarman's visuals for the last poem, "Strange Meeting", follow a largely literal treatment as Owen descends through a nearly endless corridor into a hell-like cavern where he encounters anonymous, dust-covered bodies and the German soldier he bayoneted to death. Key motifs reappear (most notably the broken trumpet and the soldier as Christ figure), but the theme of resurrection, expressed by the text of the Mass and the visual evocation of Piero della Francesca's "Resurrection", remains muted, as the film's final moments return us to grieving women and to a literal and metaphorical darkness.

The fact that Jarman had so many alternative images for sections of the *War Requiem* should not mislead one into thinking that his approach to the film was arbitrary. The visuals employed to complement the music and text of this work mirror some of the methods employed by both the poet and the composer; the visualization is totally in keeping with the work's elegiac yet deeply unsettling tone, which exists despite the ostensible purpose of reconciliation. As an artist, all Britten could do – to quote the Owen poem prefaced to the score – "is warn"; *War Requiem* does that, together with expressing a sense of hope in the midst of outrage. Jarman's juxtapositions, his subtle and clever ironies, his mirroring of the complex structure of both text and music, and his low-key, unglamorised presentation of the war itself indicate that he successfully took on the war, Owen and Britten.

Jarman lacks the hope of Britten's Christian vision; given that this was his first film after announcing that he was HIV+, he surely found obvious parallels between the treatment of men for canon fodder and those suffering with AIDS in present-day Britain. This latter instance is yet another example of innocence dismissed and destroyed by a society and a religion that, in Jarman's mind, always says "no" to love: "So many friends dead or dying – since autumn: Terry, Robert, David, Ken, Paul, Howard. All the brightest and the best trampled to death – surely even the Great War brought no more loss into one life in just twelve months, and all this as we made love not war".[37] Indeed, it is remarkable, given his aggressive stance and often brutal directness, that Jarman remained as faithful as he did to the themes and style of his original source. Of course, this does not mean that he was false to his own vision. His personal attitudes emerge in the film, but in a manner in keeping with the role that he set up for himself in this project.

Jarman successfully merged his images with Owen's poetry, the text of the Mass and Britten's music to create an integrated film of intellectual complexity and emotional impact. Yet, he probably will not be recognised for this accomplishment because, in order to achieve his goal, he had to keep his images restrained. For the most part, films that successfully merge multiple art forms do so through a kind of visual excess that matches the epic or overblownly romantic dimensions of their subjects. Even Jarman's own *The Angelic Conversation* (1985), with its low budget and minimalist approach to incorporating Shakespeare's Sonnets and original music by Coil, exhibits sufficient stop-action camera techniques and visual flair to generate a haunting, near-mythic atmosphere. With *War Requiem*, however, Jarman grimly focuses on the stasis and claustrophobia of trench warfare in the First World War. The only images of beauty and warmth in the film are those of the lost past – images shot on grainy Super 8 and full of sacramental depictions of everyday life that further accentuate the sense of loss. Indeed, in this film there is not the slightest visual glorification of battle. There is no false epic scope, and there are no adrenalin rushes (which can even be found in classic anti-war films such as *All Quiet On the Western Front*). Jarman's reserved, low-key approach is right for this project, both in terms of his fusing various art forms, and reflecting his own pessimistic vision; as a result, however, the film is demanding in ways that may alienate both new audiences and those familiar with his previous work.

Alas, Derek Jarman's films will never be widely screened, but perhaps he would appreciate the irony that *War Requiem*, the one film most closely linked to the British Film Establishment, may turn out to be the one least seen and least acknowledged by friend and foe alike.

Notes

[1] Michael O'Pray, "Britannia on Trial", *Monthly Film Bulletin* 53: 627 (April 1986): 101.

[2] Katherine Dieckmann, "Dancing Among the Ruins", *Village Voice* 24 January 1989: 59.

[3] Derek Jarman, *War Requiem* (London; Boston: Faber and Faber, 1989): 15.

4   Ibid: 40.

5   Derek Jarman, *Dancing Ledge*, edited by Shaun Allen (London; New York: Quartet Books, 1984): 7.

6   Richard Morrison, "Derek Jarman, The Final Interview", *Art & Understanding* 3: 1 (April 1994): 21. In another interview, Jarman commented: "I don't know why I did *War Requiem*. I'm sort of muddled about it." See Jonathan Hacker and David Price, *Take Ten: Contemporary British Film Directors* (Oxford: Clarendon Press, 1991): 259.

7   Jarman (1989): xi.

8   Michael O'Pray, "News from Home: Super-8, video and home movies: Derek Jarman discusses 'real' film-making with Michael O'Pray", *Monthly Film Bulletin* 51: 605 (June 1984): 189.

9   Ibid: 190.

10   Jarman (1984): 186. Emphasis in original.

11   Ibid: 188.

12   Jack M Stein, *Richard Wagner & The Synthesis of the Arts* (Westport, CT: Greenwood Press, 1973): 4.

13   Ibid: 12-16.

14   See Faubion Bowers, *The New Scriabin: Enigma and Answers* (New York: St Martins Press, 1973): 69 and 125-126.

15   Leonard Maltin, *The Disney Films* (New York: Crown Publishers, 1973): 43-44. See also John Culhane, *Walt Disney's Fantasia* (New York: Harry N Abrams, 1983): 8-32.

16   Ian Christie (ed), *Powell, Pressburger and Others* (London: British Film Institute, 1978): 42.

17   Michael Powell, *A Life in Movies: An Autobiography* (New York: Alfred Knopf, 1987): 583.

18   Joseph A Gomez, *Ken Russell: The Adaptor as Creator* (London: Frederick Muller, 1976): 28-30.

19   Ian Christie, *Arrows of Desire: The films of Michael Powell and Emeric Pressburger* (London: Waterstone, 1985): 116.

20   Timothy Hyman, "Cinema: Talking to Derek Jarman", *London Magazine* 20: 7 (October 1980): 73.

21   See Don Boyd's "Introduction" to Jarman (1989): vii.

22   Ibid: 10.

23   Ibid: 1.

[24] Dieckmann: 59, and O'Pray (1984): 189.

[25] Jarman (1989): 1. For an analysis of *The Queen Is Dead* as "one of the most striking films ever to come out of the much-maligned British Avant Garde", see Julian Stringer, "Serendipity into Style *The Queen Is Dead*", *Millennium Film Journal* 27 (winter 1993-94): 3-14.

[26] Jarman (1989): xi.

[27] Ibid: 11.

[28] Ibid: 35.

[29] Humphrey Carpenter, *Benjamin Britten: A Biography* (New York: Charles Scribner's Sons, 1992): 395-407.

[30] See Hugh Ottaway's notes to the EMI LP recording of *War Requiem* (Angel DSB-3949).

[31] Michael Kennedy, *Britten* (London: J M Dent & Sons, 1981): 223-224.

[32] Jarman (1989): 15.

[33] Anthony Milner, "The Choral Music", in Christopher Palmer (ed), *The Britten Companion* (London; Boston: Faber and Faber, 1984): 342.

[34] Jarman (1989): 37-38.

[35] Milner: 343.

[36] See Chris Lippard and Guy Johnson, "Private Practice, Public Health: The Politics of Sickness and the Films of Derek Jarman", in Lester Friedman (ed), *Fires Were Started: British Cinema and Thatcherism* (Minneapolis: University of Minnesota Press, 1993): 278-293, for a detailed discussion of the depiction of "suffering male bodies" in Jarman's films.

[37] Derek Jarman, *Modern Nature: The Journals of Derek Jarman* (London: Century, 1991): 56.

"The shadow of this time": the Renaissance cinema of Derek Jarman

David Hawkes

I.

The two definitive motifs of Derek Jarman's films are his burning desire to undermine the normative sexuality assumed by the classical Hollywood cinema, and his fascination with the historical era and art of the Renaissance. What is the connection between these two motifs? I believe that the answer can be found in Renaissance literature's concern with the construction of gender roles, and with the influence of sexual orientation on the individual personality or "subject". The school of literary criticism known as the "New Historicism" suggests that modern notions of subjectivity and sexuality were moulded into their present form during the Renaissance, or "early modern" period. Works such as Greenblatt's *Renaissance Self-fashioning* and Jonathan Goldberg's *James I and the Politics of Literature* make a convincing case that the modern conception of the individual, which is often presented as self-evident and unchanging, is, in fact, produced through a laborious historical process of "construction". By means of close analysis of literary texts, they argue that this "self-fashioning" can be perceived most clearly in the artistic legacy of the European Renaissance.

The English theatre of the Elizabethan and Jacobean reigns seems to give an especially clear vantage of the germination of modern subjectivity. In particular, the stage seems to have offered an opportunity to study and interrogate the ambiguities of gender and the delineations of sexuality. The plays of Shakespeare and his contemporaries show a persistent delight in blurring and manipulating sexual identities. Until the Restoration, female roles in the theatre were played by boys, and this initial confusion of identity was frequently compounded by plot devices involving cross-dressing and various forms of disguise. To the consternation of generations of critics, many plays of the early modern period also brazenly examine the dynamics of homoeroticism. Clearly, this is their most obvious attraction for Jarman. There is also, however, a more formal explanation for his interest. In the early modern theatre we can discern the emergence of the mode of storytelling known as "narrative realism". During the 16th and 17th centuries, the convention that a story should be a transparent representation of a realistic, linear sequence of events gradually displaced older emblematic and allegorical aesthetic techniques. This process is very marked in the theatre, where emblematic techniques are used alongside realistic ones, and where the pleasures of spectacle are juxtaposed with the demands of plot development. In literature, narrative realism culminates in the 19th century novel; in cinema, it reaches its apotheosis in the still-dominant classical Hollywood tradition. Recent film theory often suggests that this generic convention inculcates certain assumptions about sexuality and gender identity. Jarman dedicated his career to undermining those assumptions. In order to do so, he had recourse to the genre and period when they first took shape: the English theatre of the early modern period.

II.

In her canonical account of the Hollywood cinema's representation of desire, "Visual Pleasure and Narrative Cinema", Laura Mulvey argues that classical narrative cinema assumes a heterosexual, male viewer. It constructs the subject-position from which it is to be viewed by soliciting a narcissistic identification with the male protagonist, and this involves a corresponding objectification of the female characters:

> An active/passive heterosexual division of labour has... controlled narrative structure. According to the principles of the ruling ideology and the psychical structures that back it up, the male figure cannot bear the burden of sexual objectification... Hence the split between spectacle and narrative supports the man's role as the active one of forwarding the story, making things happen.[1]

According to Mulvey, therefore, narrative cinema operates by means of a binary heterosexual opposition between the active male ego-ideal who drives the narrative forward, and the passive female who, by providing an alluring but static spectacle, tends to retard the progress of the narrative. Mulvey claims that this objectified woman suggests the possibility of castration, and that Hollywood movies defuse this anxiety in one of two ways. Either they fetishize the woman, turning her into a pure spectacle, which impedes the narrative flow; or, where such an impediment is inconvenient, the story contrives a way of judging the woman, finding her guilty or punishing her. In contrast to the static effect of fetishization, Mulvey writes:

> This sadistic side fits in well with narrative. Sadism demands a story, depends on making something happen, forcing a change

in another person, a battle of will and strength, victory/defeat, all occurring in a linear time with a beginning and an end.[2]

Classical cinematic storytelling is thus characterised by a dialectical struggle between a sadistic diegetic impulse to narration (figured as male) and a fetishized spectacle which freezes the forward movement of the narrative (and which is represented as female). In a later essay, Mulvey qualifies her earlier position by noting that the identification of masculinity with activity, and of femininity with passivity, which she draws from Freud, is originally metaphorical.[3] It does, of course, achieve a certain empirical verity, in everyday life as in the narrative structure of cinema. But this does not mean that the roles must always be assigned according to biological sex. There is, Mulvey comes to believe, no reason why the protagonist should always be male, or the fetishized figures of spectacle female.

It may be true, as Mulvey says, that "[t]he presence of woman is an indispensable element of spectacle in normal narrative film, yet her visual presence tends to work against the development of a story line, to freeze the flow of action in moments of erotic contemplation".[4] However, as critics such as Judith Mayne, E Ann Kaplan and Teresa de Lauretis have pointed out, exactly who fills the role of erotic spectacle depends at least partly on the viewer, and a female or gay viewer may well fetishize and identify with different figures than would be chosen by a heterosexual man.[5] Furthermore, Tom Gunning has shown how the orientation of early silent movies towards spectacle rather than diegesis – what he calls "the cinema of attraction" – does not simply disappear once narrative becomes the dominant mode. Rather, it "goes underground, both into certain avant-garde practices and as a component of narrative films, more evident in some genres (e.g., the musical) than in others".[6]

In Jarman's films, the spectacle re-emerges from the underground to disrupt and complicate the assumptions of narrative realism, and, in doing so, it challenges the definitions of sexuality and gender roles which have defined classical cinema. In Jarman's work, the fetishized body is always male. His films offer a telling example of what Fabienne Worth has in mind when she suggests that:

> gay men's interrogation of psychoanalysis provides not only the hidden trump card of the psychoanalytic puzzle, i.e. the mapping of the construction of male heterosexuality, but more importantly, the key to unlocking the feminist impasse regarding psychoanalysis, the impasse that keeps us reverting to some variant of the gendered opposition between passive and active.[7]

This "gendered opposition" is not, in other words, natural or eternal, despite the difficulty of getting beyond it, either in psychoanalysis or in the cinema. Nor are the aesthetic tenets of narrative realism the only possible way of organising a story-line. These are the two essential points of departure for Jarman's "Renaissance" films.

Jarman's treatments of Marlowe's *Edward II* and Shakespeare's *The Tempest* call attention to these plays' meditations on identity, sexuality and history. He also employs these themes as vehicles for his critique of the narrative conventions and gender constructions inculcated by the cinema. This juxtaposition of the Renaissance with the late 20th century – also found in *Caravaggio* (1986) and *The Angelic Conversation* (1985) – is a recurrent feature of Jarman's work. His most explicit use of the early modern period as a commentary on the postmodern era is *Jubilee* (1978). This is Jarman's bleakest work, portraying contemporary Britain as a burnt-out wasteland populated by psychopathically nihilistic punk rockers. An apocalyptic aura hangs heavy in the air, and we are constantly reminded that we are witnessing the death of a civilisation. The idea that history is a narrative of linear progress is thus ridiculed, and the entire film is presented as a horrifying prophetic vision, conjured up and exhibited to an aghast Queen Elizabeth I by her court magician, John Dee. Dee accomplishes this feat with the aid of the spirit, Ariel, who greets his master with words from *The Tempest*, "All hail, great master! grave sir, hail!" (I, ii, 189), before assuring the Queen that "I will reveal to thee the shadow of this time". The desolate, post-industrial landscape presented in the remainder of the film thus represents the lengthening "shadow" cast by the Elizabethan era.

The Queen, accompanied by Dee and Ariel, wanders perplexedly through the world of Kid and Amyl Nitrite, observing that "a great chill embraceth this place", and lamenting over the dead body of the drag queen, Wayne County (playing Lounge Lizard). Her poignant question to Dee, "Is God dead?", is answered by the ironic gloat of the evil impresario, Borgia Ginz, that "progress has taken the place of heaven", while the horrific condition of the second Elizabeth's England clearly demonstrates not progress, but terminal degeneration. Occasionally we are reminded that the action is narrated for Her Majesty's benefit by close-ups of Ariel staring into the camera, or standing with arms folded and a flashing mirror on his crotch. We are thus kept aware that what appears to be a conventionally diegetic narrative is, in fact, one long flashforward that has evidently been composed and arranged by a figure living 400 years earlier.

Through techniques such as this, and Amyl Nitrite's memorably grotesque travesty of "Rule Britannia", Jarman suggests that the first and second Elizabethan reigns represent, respectively, the beginning and the end of the "modern" epoch. The characteristics of that epoch are indicated by their conspicuous absence from the world portrayed in *Jubilee*; they include the belief that life has some ultimate end or meaning, that history is progress, and that the self is a stable, conscious entity. The disappearance of these ideas is not altogether mourned, however. *Jubilee* looks with indulgence and admiration on the androgyny of the late 20th century characters, and their perverse sexuality is constantly accentuated. The film's only heterosexual coupling is mocked and ridiculed by the punks standing by, and it culminates dramatically in the murder of the male protagonist. Jarman thus signals his implacable hostility to the compulsory heterosexuality of modernity, and this hostility accounts for his preoccupation with the Renaissance period – the dawn, or cusp, of the modern age.

The irony of Borgia Ginz's faith in "progress", therefore, emerges out of his situation in an obviously decadent society, and Jarman emphasises the corruption of modern Britain by presenting it through the innocent eyes of Elizabeth I. This gesture also has the effect of disrupting the narrative realism of the film, as Elizabeth and her courtiers keep anachronistically popping up in the post-punk environment. Jarman thus questions the modern idea that history is a teleological narrative of progress, and he links this idea to the classical Hollywood cinema's preoccupation with diegetic narrative. His revulsion from this latter convention is unsurprising, given the investment of traditional cinematic diegesis in heterosexuality. The Elizabethan references which crowd Jarman's work serve as a means by which he can deconstruct teleological narrative in its historical and cinematic forms, and, in doing so, attack the heterosexual, patriarchal presuppositions which such narratives support.

III.

Jarman's treatment of *The Tempest* (1979) exemplifies his view of the connections between the early modern theatre and the postmodern cinema. By drawing out those aspects of the play – its homoeroticism, its overall concern with sexual dynamics and power relations, and its juxtaposition of narrative with spectacle – which are also pertinent concerns of the cinema, Jarman affirms a kinship between his own work and the early modern theatre, and thus distances the audience from the conventions of narrative cinema. Of course, Shakespeare's play is also concerned with the nature of narrative, and Prospero, the magician who orchestrates and narrates the action, is usually portrayed as an archetypal figure of benign patriarchal authority. By presenting Prospero as an overtly sadistic tyrant, Jarman thus alludes to the connections between the diegetic force driving the narrative forward and sadistic, patriarchal sexuality.

In Shakespeare, Prospero is at once the author of the action, and the authoritative, patriarchal ruler of the island: father to Miranda, master of Ariel and Caliban. Traditionally, critics have viewed his rule as kindly and well-intentioned. In Jarman's film, however, a quite different picture emerges. Prospero storms and threatens, stamping on the hand of the squirming Caliban, and mercilessly humiliating his subordinates. We are shown the tortures of which he reminds Ariel in hideous detail, and the latter spirit, usually played as a joyous, willing servant, is here an exhausted and resentful serf. We see him obsessively rehearsing his plea to be released from his servitude – "Let me remember thee what thou hast promis'd,/Which is not yet perform'd me" (I, ii, 243-244) – in front of the mirror, and his defeated agreement to carry out Prospero's commands "to th' syllable" is delivered with extreme fatigue and bitter irony. In Prospero's enslavement of the naked Ferdinand, sadism is given an explicitly sexual dimension ("Come, I'll manacle thy hands together"), and Jarman has Caliban present at the torture, exclaiming "Beat him enough; after a little time, I'll beat him too" (III, ii, 81) – a line which is spoken in an entirely different context in Shakespeare's play.

In Jarman's film, therefore, the figure who controls the diegetic narrative is portrayed as a monster of sadism. This precludes any sympathetic identification with Prospero, and complicates the classical narrative form, which generally presents the male protagonist as an ego-ideal for the viewer. This disruption is emphasised by the fact that the figure who is fetishized, as in all Jarman's work, is male. From the moment Ferdinand (David Meyer) staggers naked from the ocean, the camera lingers lovingly on his generally unclad form with the kind of drooling lust traditionally reserved for female figures. His female counterpart, Toyah Willcox's punky Miranda, is, by contrast, an aggressive, active figure, poking her tongue out at the camera, bathing in a brusque, matter-of-fact fashion, and chasing away the lecherous Caliban. This latter grotesque functions as a caricature of heterosexual male desire, helplessly slavering over the inaccessible Miranda, alternatively contemplating rape and shrinking back in cowardly terror.

Through the repellant portrayal of Prospero, therefore, Jarman disengages himself from the diegetic narrative mode, and indicates that abandoning this technique makes it possible to re-imagine the roles which cinema has traditionally assigned to the feminine and the masculine. As in the play, the narrative movement towards the closure of the final wedding is repeatedly disrupted by *tableaux vivants* and other forms of spectacle. Ultimately, the heterosexual union of Ferdinand and Miranda, which would conventionally represent the moment of narrative closure and resolution, takes place within an absurdist parody of Shakespeare's masque. Miranda speaks the line "O, brave new world that hath such people in it" as she beholds a bevy of camp sailors in modern dress performing an unorthodox hornpipe, and the scene is rendered even more surreal by the sudden appearance of Elisabeth Welch crooning "Stormy Weather". The moment of traditional narrative closure – the union of active hero and passive heroine – is thus subverted by a farcical intrusion of spectacle and anachronism.

IV.

Jarman's other Elizabethan source, Christopher Marlowe, performs a similar operation on the narrative form of his own medium in *Edward II*. Marlowe uses the King's homosexuality as a way of criticising a particular understanding of history which developed at the dawn of modernity. He questions Machiavelli's notion that a teleological narrative of history is produced by a conflict between an active, dominating male principle and a female figure that must be conquered. Jarman's film version of *Edward II* (1991) facilitates such a reading of the play by emphasising the homoerotic elements in Marlowe. Like *The Tempest*, this film renders glaringly apparent a thematic pattern which is often missed or occluded in critical interpretations of the play, and Jarman once again uses the homoerotic aspects of the Elizabethan theatre to disrupt the classical Hollywood cinema's dependence on heterosexual diegesis.

In his production notes, published together with diary entries and acerbic asides as *Queer Edward II*, Jarman offers an indignant comment on the media reception of his project. He complains that, in their ignorance, critics have accused him of overemphasising the play's homoerotic connotations, and of imposing on Marlowe an anachronistic queer political agenda:

> The paper today accuses me of making a 'Gay version of Edward II'. They really shouldn't write about things they don't understand. Could Marlowe's poetry describe an ordinary friendship? Has anyone who writes for or reads these papers actually read the play?[8]

Jarman does not name the newspapers he has in mind, but this reading of his work was not limited to the conservative or homophobic press. J Hoberman believed that:

> [T]he British director reworks Christopher Marlowe's 400 year-old play to emphasize the obsessional gay love story *latent* in the text, as well as identify the deposed Edward...with militant queer activism.[9]

Jarman feels that such interpretations betray a misreading of the play. His film succeeds precisely because it assumes that homosexuality is central to Marlowe's account, for Jarman is then able to utilise this "gay love story" in order to comment on the conventions of his own medium.

It is true, however, that in addition to Edward's transgressive sexuality, Marlowe's play also examines the violation of other social conventions. The evil uncle and nephew Mortimer actually discount the sexual love between the King and Gaveston as a motive for rebellion. "Leave now to oppose thyself against the king" (I, iv, 389), Mortimer senior counsels his nephew:

> Thou seest by nature he is mild and calm;
> And, seeing his mind so dotes on Gaveston,
> Let him without controlment have his will.
> The mightiest kings have had their minions; (I, iv, 390-393)

And he goes on, as Jarman puts it, to "open the classical closet", listing the homosexual affairs of heroes and philosophers. In response, the younger Mortimer explains that his enmity for Gaveston springs from a quite different source:

> Uncle, his wanton humour grieves not me;
> But this I scorn, that one so basely born
> Should by his sovereign's favour grow so pert,
> And riot it with the treasure of the realm. (I, iv, 404-407)

In fact, the historical Gaveston was not at all "basely born"; he was a scion of Gascon nobility. Marlowe's decision to introduce this element into the story thus suggests that we are to regard Gaveston's transgression of class boundaries, rather than his sexual relations with the King, as the reason for his downfall. Significantly, Jarman omits these lines from his film, and gives Mortimer senior's "outing" speech to Edward's brother, Kent. There thus appears to be some validity to the criticism that the film bestows on Edward and Gaveston's homosexual love a fundamental importance which is warranted neither by the historical nor by the literary context of Marlowe's play. Moreover, the film lingers far longer than does the play on what might be termed the "hyper-heterosexuality" displayed by Mortimer and Isabella. It seems that Jarman is intent on emphasising the opposition between heteroeroticism and homoeroticism. Thus, we first meet Gaveston in bed with two boys; we first see Mortimer in bed with two girls. We are shown Edward and Gaveston being entertained by male strippers, boys in the gym, and a naked rugby scrum; Mortimer fulminates about Edward's salacious reputation while himself deeply engrossed in a heterosexual S&M scene. We hear nothing of Edward's intention to marry Gaveston to the Earl of Gloucester's heiress, and nothing of subsidiary explanations for the barons' displeasure, such as the defeat at Bannockburn. In direct contrast to the play, Mortimer is presented as overtly homophobic – as he beats Spencer, he calls him "girlboy" (a line not found in Marlowe, but apparently coined by the actor, Nigel Terry).[10]

Jarman also explicitly locates the motive for Isabella's hostility to Edward in her heterosexuality – more than one reviewer has found the film misogynist – and the correlation between the Queen's malice and her sexuality is undeniable, although, to be fair, the same can be said of Mortimer. Nevertheless, there is a bedroom scene in which Isabella attempts to seduce Edward and is repulsed; she is shown embracing not only Mortimer, but also the torturer Lightborn; she speaks several cruel and scornful lines which Marlowe gives to the barons; and, most memorably, she murders Kent with a sensual bite to the jugular. Jarman thus makes it clear that a mutual antagonism between heterosexuals and homosexuals is the driving force behind the overthrow of Edward II.

We might pause briefly here to consider Gregory Bredbeck's reading of Marlowe's *Edward II*. Bredbeck demonstrates how Mortimer exploits the King's homosexuality as a kind of synecdoche for unnatural and unorthodox behaviour in general, and is thus able to use it as a means to separate his attacks on Edward the man from rebellion against the abstract and atemporal "body" of the King. Once again, however, this reading tends to downplay the role in the play of homoeroticism as such, and thus – by extension – to endorse the criticism of Jarman's film as overly concerned with literal and explicit male-to-male sex.[11]

V.

The question remains: what is it in the play which allows or even encourages Jarman's impulse to view the story predominantly through the lens of sexuality? I believe that the answer lies in the fact that the Renaissance political theory to which Marlowe alludes in this play – and, indeed, in all his others – was always inherently gendered, both tropologically and conceptually. Marlowe's work as a whole betrays a fascination with the political theories of Niccolò Machiavelli. His heroes – Tamburlaine, the Duke of Guise, Faustus, Barabas and, of course, Mortimer – are investigations into different aspects of the machiavellian character. Of these, Mortimer most closely approximates to the portrayal of the modern or "new" prince described in *Il principe* (*The Prince*, 1513) and the *Discorso* (*Discourses*, 1531). Mortimer paraphrases a famous passage from *The Prince* when he is at the height of his power: "Fear'd am I more than lov'd; – let me be fear'd" (V, iv, 50), and he consistently interprets events through the machiavellian idiom. In particular, he makes several references to the qualities of *virtù* and *fortuna*, applying them so as to make sense of his own career. For example, when Edward briefly captures Mortimer in the third act, the rebel exclaims:

> What, Mortimer! can ragged stony walls
> Immure thy virtue that aspires to heaven?
> No, Edward, England's scourge, it may not be;
> Mortimer's hope surmounts his fortune far. (III, iii, 73-76)

Here we can discern the nature of the relation between power and sexuality that Jarman emphasises in his interpretation.[12] In the civic humanism of Renaissance Florence, and especially in the works of Machiavelli, two things happen to the ancient polarity of *virtù* and *fortuna*: it is politicized, and it is gendered. In early chapters of *The Prince*, Machiavelli is particularly concerned to describe and explain the careers of usurpers. Hereditary monarchs, he remarks, can easily demonstrate the legitimacy of their rule through reference to custom. Usurpers, on the other hand, must actively disrupt custom; they impose their own will on history and shape it to their ends. Whereas in Boethius this imposition of form on history took place only in the mind, Machiavelli investigates the implications and consequences of an external, political *virtù*. Pre-eminent among these is the fact that the usurping prince is locked in a dialectical struggle between his own will, or virtue, and the flux of often recalcitrant events, or fortune. In order to expound the character of this opposition, Machiavelli has recourse to a notorious metaphor:

> I am of the opinion that it is better to be rash than over-cautious, because Fortune is a woman and, if you wish to keep her down, you must beat her and pound her. It is evident that she allows herself to be overcome by men who treat her in that way rather than by those who proceed coldly. For that reason, like a woman, she is always the friend of young men, because they are less cautious, and more courageous, and command her with more boldness.[13]

Machiavelli thus conceives of the opposition between active will and passive history through the trope of a heterosexual union between an active, masculine principle and a passive, feminine figure. This opposition describes the process by which human beings take control

112

of events, and impose on them a narrative form and a teleological significance. Machiavelli clearly views the relationship between *virtù* and *fortuna* as sadistic in nature. Referring to the careers of Caesar and Alexander, he writes:

> From this example plainly may be seen how much he pleases Fortune and how acceptable to her he is who strikes her, who thrusts her aside, who hunts her down.[14]

In her book on Machiavelli, Hanna Fenichel Pitkin asks: "Why is it that so many of the theorists of republican or participatory politics appeal specifically to patriarchal values and are fearful of and hostile towards the 'feminine'?"[15] In Machiavelli, however, this opposition is given a new inflection:

> The conception of fortune as responsive to human effort, the revival of virtu as symbolizing that effort, and the specific interpretation of that symbol in terms of virility were widespread in the Renaissance. But it is Machiavelli who presents man's relationship to the outcomes of human action in terms of sexual conquest – less violent than rape but more forceful than seduction. Thereby he not only anthropomorphizes and sexualizes the givens and the outcomes of human action in history but invests them with the specific desires, fears, and attitudes his male readers already bear toward woman – as unreliable nurturer, as sexual object, as 'other'.[16]

In Marlowe's play, it thus makes thematic sense for Mortimer, the would-be usurper who must ravish *fortuna*, to become the lover of Edward's wife – just as it follows that Edward, the hereditary ruler who does not need to become embroiled in the *virtù/fortuna* dialectic, should show no interest in women. At the end of the play, however, Mortimer comes to realise the hubris of believing that one can force one's will on history, and he submits once more to fortune, admitting that the pattern formed by events is not a linear narrative, but a *cyclical* process:

> Base Fortune, now I see, that in thy wheel
> There is a point, to which when men aspire,
> They tumble headlong down: that point I touch'd,
> And, seeing there was no place to mount up higher,
> Why shall I grieve at my declining fall? (V, vi, 59-63)

The narrative mode, which imposes a teleology on film, thus bears some resemblance to the narrative imposed on history through Machiavelli's opposition of *virtù* to *fortuna*, and to his injunction that the latter, being a woman, will respond favourably to violent treatment. And just as Marlowe's play uses Edward's homosexuality to problematise Machiavelli's gendered dichotomy, so Jarman's film disrupts the formal narrative conventions of classical Hollywood cinema in order to deconstruct the heterosexual active/passive oppositions which such narrative demands.

The most obvious technique Jarman uses to disrupt narrative is the flashback. The published script of the film, *Queer Edward II*, opens with the death of Edward I, which took place before the play's action begins, while the film itself begins with a scene from the very end of the play – Edward and Lightborn alone in the dungeon. The entire film thus takes place in flashback, and Jarman emphasises this by frequent and regular cuts back to the dungeon scene. The editing is abrupt and highly visible, and the use of modern costume for the unsympathetic characters further disrupts the viewer's sense of chronology, while obviating any attempt at realism. As we might expect, this disruption of narrative removes the necessity to objectify the female protagonist. The sexual spectacle in this film is provided exclusively by the male body – the stripper with the snake, the nude rugby scrum, and many other homoerotic *tableaux*. But this is not a "buddy" movie, in which the active/passive dichotomy is acted out between a homoerotically linked pair of male protagonists. On the contrary, in the film, as in the play, Edward and Gaveston are both presented in passive roles. The active function is assumed by Mortimer and Isabella, both of whom are portrayed as overtly sadistic, and, as with Prospero, this prevents any sympathetic identification by the audience. In contrast to the woman's role in narrative cinema, Isabella is not "castrated", but phallic, as is indicated by her sexual aggression, her wielding of a crossbow, and her symbolic castration of Kent.

In fact, the only significant character to be fetishized in this film is Lightborn, played by Jarman's real-life companion, Keith Collins, whose physical beauty is surely intended as a stark contrast to the feral Gaveston and the Heseltinesque Edward. We hear Gaveston's rhapsodic speech about the "lovely boy in Dian's shape,/With hair that gilds the water as it glides" (I, i, 61-62) in a voice-over, as we join Edward in watching Lightborn undress and bathe in the dungeon. As he describes his expertise in murder, Lightborn kneels before Isabella, and she kisses him repeatedly. His Geordie accent and pet polecat – neither of which appear in Marlowe – also serve to fix his image in the viewer's mind. The viewer knows, however, that Lightborn is about to murder Edward in a gruesome parody of the sexual act. By presenting the torturer as the film's central object of lust, Jarman is thus fetishizing and objectifying the supposedly active principle of sadism itself.

We should recall here that, according to Mulvey, sadism is the impulse which drives the classical cinema narrative along, while fetishization is the manœuvre by which the linear narrative is impeded. By fetishizing sadism, therefore, Jarman achieves the ultimate triumph over the classical narrative mode, and thus renders obsolete the heterosexual active/passive binary constructed by that mode.

The nature of this triumph is revealed by the film's "double ending". Jarman has Edward dream, or fantasize, about being murdered by Lightborn in the prescribed manner. In the following shot, we see Lightborn apparently about to carry out the murder in earnest, when he suddenly throws his poker into the water, kneels down by Edward and kisses him. A surprise happy ending thus depicts homoeroticism triumphant over the sadistic active/passive dichotomy implicit in traditional narrative. And, in order to stress the deconstructive power of androgyny, the final scene shows Prince Edward, the heir to the throne, in earrings and make-up, dancing on top of a cage which contains the calcified bodies of Mortimer and Isabella. The dual achievement of *Edward II*, as of all Jarman's "Renaissance" films, is thus to bring out the subversive homoeroticism lurking behind early modern constructions of gender, while simultaneously using that homoeroticism as a weapon against the oppressive sexuality implicit in his own medium and age.

Notes

[1]   Laura Mulvey, "Visual Pleasure and Narrative Cinema", in Gerald Mast, Marshall Cohen and Leo Braudy (eds), *Film Theory and Criticism: Introductory Readings*, fourth edition (New York; Oxford: Oxford University Press, 1992): 751.

[2]   Ibid: 753.

[3]   Laura Mulvey, "Afterthoughts on 'Visual Pleasure and Narrative Cinema' inspired by *Duel in the Sun*", in Constance Penley (ed), *Feminism and Film Theory* (New York: Routledge, 1988): 69-79.

[4]   Mulvey (1992): 750.

[5]   See Judith Mayne, *The Woman at the Keyhole: Feminism and Women's Cinema* (Bloomington, IN: Indiana University Press, 1990); E Ann Kaplan, *Women and Film: Both Sides of the Camera* (New York: Methuen, 1983); Teresa de Lauretis, *Alice Doesn't: Feminism, Semiotics, Cinema* (Bloomington, IN: Indiana University Press, 1984).

[6] Tom Gunning, "The Cinema of Attraction: Early Film, Its Spectator and the Avant-Garde", *Wide Angle* 8: 3-4 (1986): 64.

[7] Fabienne Worth, "Of Gayzes and Bodies: A Bibliographical Essay on Queer Theory, Psychoanalysis and Archaeology", *Quarterly Review of Film and Video* 15: 1 (1993): 8.

[8] Derek Jarman, *Queer Edward II* (London: British Film Institute, 1991): 70.

[9] J Hoberman, "Prisoners of Sex", *Village Voice* 24 March 1992. Emphasis added.

[10] See Jarman: 142.

[11] See Gregory W Bredbeck, *Sodomy and Interpretation: Marlowe to Milton* (Ithaca: Cornell University Press, 1991).

[12] As J G A Pocock has pointed out, the treatment of the binary opposition between *virtù* and *fortuna* that most influenced Machiavelli is found in Boethius's *De Consolatione Philosophiae* (*The Consolation of Philosophy*, 524). In that work, the author is in prison awaiting execution, and struggling to comprehend the cruel fate which has brought him to this pass. He ultimately achieves consolation through the conviction that what appears to him as blind chance must in fact be part of a larger, divine plan. He thus imposes a narrative form on the apparently random events of his life – that is to say, he converts fortune into *providence*. Boethius refers to the exercise of faith which enabled him to perceive the hidden hand of the Almighty behind the chaos of human experience as Christian *virtù*. The *Consolation of Philosophy* thus lays the foundation for one of the defining projects of the Enlightenment: it argues that history has an end, a telos. In order to perceive this meaning, the Christian must impose his virtue on the seemingly meaningless flow of fortune. The Providential narrative of history is thus produced out of a binary opposition between an active *virtù* and a passive *fortuna*. See J G A Pocock, *The Machiavellian Moment: Florentine Political Thought and the Atlantic Republican Tradition* (London: Princeton University Press, 1975).

[13] Niccolò Machiavelli, *The Prince*, translated by Allan H Gilbert (Chicago: Packard and Company, 1941): 176. Subsequent references are to this edition.

[14] Ibid: 215.

[15] Hanna Fenichel Pitkin, *Fortune is a Woman: Gender and Politics in the Thought of Niccolò Machiavelli* (Berkeley: University of California Press, 1984): 5.

[16] Ibid: 292.

Opposing "Heterosoc": Derek Jarman's counter-hegemonic activism

Martin Quinn-Meyler

Sexuality colours my politics – I distrust all figures of authority, including the artist. Homosexuals have such a struggle to define themselves against the order of things, an equivocal process involving the desire to be both 'inside' and 'outside'...I distrust those with blueprints for our salvation.[1]

Driven by the "in-your-face" militancy of the punk movement, *Jubilee* (1978) is Derek Jarman's first explicitly political film, and it marks the beginning of his sustained critique of contemporary British society. In the words of Viv, the artist-figure in *Jubilee*, one can discern Jarman's gradual linking of art with his rising political activism:

[Artists] become blood donors – their life blood drips away until they're bled dry. And the people who control the world make it as inaccessible as possible by driving the artists into corners...Our only hope is to recreate ourselves as artists...and release the energy for all.

Yet, for all her good intentions, Viv remains unable to combine her hope in the utopian promise of the vanguard artist with the bleak reality of her own situation: her call to action is confined to the sterile walls of her empty black room. Unlike his isolated and ineffectual character, however, Jarman sought to expand the transformative potential of the artist by developing in his own filmmaking a politically determined and often reckless analysis of the world in which he lived.[2] While making *Jubilee*, Jarman declared there were "now no amusing stories to tell"[3] after his first, orgiastic feature, *Sebastiane* (1976), and his early, experimental Super 8 shorts, such as *The Art of Mirrors* (1973) and *In the Shadow of the Sun* (1980).

From the apocalyptic visions of Dr Dee (Richard O'Brien) to Amyl Nitrite's (Jordan) grotesque rendition of "Rule Britannia", *Jubilee* challenged conventional notions of British nationalism by exposing the oppressive nature of the state and its demands for conformity to existing social, political and sexual norms. Throughout the next decade, Jarman refined his analysis and began to focus his attention specifically on the state and civil oppression of the queer minority. This essay examines the development of Jarman's notion of Heterosoc as a useful means of assessing the asymmetrical power relations between the queer and heterosexist components of society, as well as his formulation of a sexual politics which challenged the imperatives of hetero-domination. In particular, because of its political subject-matter and its emphasis on the nature of hetero-oppression, Jarman's *Edward II* (1991) will be discussed in detail, in order to trace the ongoing conflict of an oppositional queer subculture and the oppressive Heterosoc majority.

Jarman described the 1980s as "the time when all that was rotten bubbled to the surface",[4] and his films, personal writings and interviews of the period exhibit an increasingly radical response to the AIDS pandemic, as well as to the oppressive social policies of Margaret Thatcher and the New Right. It is important, however, to emphasise from the outset that Jarman's indictment of the existing political structure cannot be limited to his opposition to the reactionary platform of the far Right. In light of the state's uniform intolerance of sexual difference, Jarman does not make a distinction between liberal and conservative politics in what he maintains is an active and pervasive anti-queer sentiment throughout Great Britain. He holds that this bias has historically cut across party lines and continues to characterise contemporary politics:

> When it comes to sexual politics left and right never meant much – witness Peter [Tatchell]'s ejection from the Labour Party and their inability to take our call for equal rights on board. In these matters Britain is so far behind the rest of Europe. It's always a relief to get out of this place, people relate to you so much better on any other street in the world.[5]

The state's ability to define and punish what it deems deviant – from the "liberal" recommendations of the Wolfenden Report (1957), to the "legalising" of consensual homosexual acts between adults (1967), through to the open persecution of sexual difference by the British government under Thatcher – has continued unabated, even as forces opposed to hetero-oppression have gained increasing influence. Considering Jarman's refusal to align himself with established political organisations, and his dismissal of attempts to reform the existing political system from within,[6] one must move beyond a simple or reductive examination of the state in order to understand the full scope and intent of Jarman's disapprobation.

In his development of the concept of "Heterosoc", Jarman incorporates a discussion of civil society as a central component of his analysis. While Jarman never consolidated his ideas in a formal sense, it is possible to glean the principle characteristics of Heterosoc from his frequent writings on the nature of heterosexist oppression. Heterosoc is Jarman's term for the systematic domination of the queer subculture by the hetero-oppressive majority that continues to control the offices of the state and institutions of civil society. Heterosoc emerges as a sexual component within an encompassing hegemonic impetus to social and political homogeneity, and promulgates its ascendancy relatively unimpeded by atomistic class, ethnic, generational, gendered or regional interests. Although advancing an ideology of individual freedom, particularly in the private domain of consensual adult relations, Heterosoc is, in fact, predicated upon a strict, unquestioning adherence to naturalised conceptions of licit heterosexual desire and affection.

Jarman's isolation of sexuality as a distinctly identifiable component within the development of socio-political hegemony is consistent with formulations of hegemony which developed in the Marxist tradition. According to Stuart Hall, hegemony may be defined as the culminating moment in an ongoing "process of the coordination of the interests of a dominant group with the general interests of other groups and the life of the state as a whole...[within] a particular historic bloc".[7] In other words, the notion of hegemony refers to an unstable solidarity as a result of alliances and compromises within and between different classes temporarily to serve the specific interests of the dominant class. As in the Marxist formulation of hegemony, Jarman's concept of Heterosoc identifies a sexual hegemony – which must constantly be reinscribed in order to ensure the continuation of the rights and priorities of the heterosexist majority. However, unlike the conceptualization of hegemony as a temporary moment of general consensus, Jarman maintains that the sexual hegemony of Heterosoc constitutes an historical constant which continues to persist.

Heterosoc's insistence that monogamous, opposite-sex attraction forms the cornerstone of "natural", "healthy" or "legitimate" relationships limits the human capacity for self-transformation. The devastating impact of living within the confines of Heterosoc is vividly depicted in Jarman's account of his own life-experiences:

For the first twenty-five years of my life, I lived as a criminal, and the next twenty-five were spent as a second-class citizen, deprived of equality and human rights. No right to adopt children – and if I had children, I could be declared an unfit parent; illegal in the military; an age of consent of twenty-one; no right of inheritance; no right of access to a loved one; no right to public affection; no right to an unbiased education; no legal sanction of my relationships and no right to marry. These restrictions subtly deprived me of my freedom. It seemed unthinkable it could be any other way, so we all accepted this.[8]

Like other queer men of his generation, Jarman was forced to choose between the rubrics of criminality and inferiority through which Heterosoc characterised his sexuality: imagining a queer alternative to the domination of Heterosoc proved to be a lifelong challenge for him. At least the former classification of queersex as criminal was more forthright: those who are outlawed are not formally entitled to the same range of freedoms. Since the legal reforms of the 1960s, however, the state's policing of queer desire has focused on the containment of sexual difference, rather than on its prohibition. By seeking to eliminate queer visibility in every area of the public arena – by refusing to legitimate queer partnerships through legal sanction; by raising the age of consent for queersex above heterosex; by denying the ability of queers to serve as parents or in the military; and by prohibiting queers from openly expressing their desire – Heterosoc has endeavoured to (re)inforce the isolation of the closet in all aspects of public life.

Jarman's resistance to the imperatives of Heterosoc, and his advocacy of an emergent, counter-hegemonic queer sexuality, are rooted in the intense struggle between the queer subculture and hetero-oppression. The expression of queer desire, whether in everyday life or on the screen, constitutes a physical and symbolic affront to the continuation of hetero-dominance. The result of this volatile conflict is frequently violent, and Jarman's cinematic representation of queersex speaks to the social reality from which it arose. His depiction of queer lovemaking is often militaristic and physically aggressive; it is difficult at times to decide if the men are embracing out of passion or if they are locked in battle. Jarman's connection of queer sexuality to violence can be traced in several of his films,[9] from the sadomasochistic slaying of the Roman solider in *Sebastiane*, to the terrorist who fucks a man draped over the British flag in *The Last of England* (1987), and to the brutal torture and crucifixion of a queer couple in *The Garden* (1990). Jarman's portrayal of violent queersex suggests that queer love – even when it is privately performed – is always an act of subversion with the potential to destabilize the control of Heterosoc.

Representation of the physicality of this intense and aggressive struggle also underlies Jarman's 1985 film, *The Angelic Conversation*. Harking back stylistically to his earlier Super 8 films, *The Angelic Conversation*'s non-narrative form is loosely held together by Judi

Dench's reading of fourteen sonnets which Shakespeare intended for his mysterious "young man", while three handsome, youthful men search aimlessly for one another across a barren landscape. Jarman supplements the seeming randomness of the men's wandering by combining the slow, almost plodding tempo of stop-action photography with the atonal, industrial soundtrack of Coil to produce a sombre, meditative quality for the film. The men are overburdened by huge weights they carry on their backs as they trudge along, isolated and alone. Even for the comparatively brief time the actors come into each other's presence, the burdens they carry, the brute ruggedness of the sand and stone they walk across, and the indulgently languid pace of the film all serve to emphasise the men's difficulty in finding one another, rather than celebrating their transitory union. Jarman exposes the oppression of Heterosoc in *The Angelic Conversation* by rendering visible the tangible effects of a system which seeks to exclude, silence and ultimately eliminate queer desire: if Jarman's men appear to be better fighters than lovers, it is a direct result of Jarman's identification of an oppositional dimension inherent in queersex.

Together with his visual representation of a counter-hegemonic, militarised queersex, Jarman also challenges established, heterocentric interpretations of canonical literary and artistic figures. As suggested by his use of Shakespeare's Sonnets, Jarman is primarily interested in Renaissance authors, although his use of works from this period is more than merely a product of his "neoromanticism";[10] rather, his choice is determined by his commitment to reclaiming works of queer artists whose sexuality has been downplayed, misrepresented and/or ignored within the Heterosoc tradition:

> Most of our biography is located in fiction...The sexuality of so many men was not loved in the history books. No-one could be Queer and celebrated; Michelangelo, Leonardo, Shakespeare were all neutered. Hollywood invented heterosexual affairs for Michelangelo in *The Agony and the Ecstasy* and took forty years to reinstate Queer Caesar in *Spartacus*. This is why Hollywood is contemptible. Its ecstasy was exclusively heterosexual.[11]

Jarman's focus on queer figures from the past, while partially reconstructing the "biography" of queer men, never attempts to re-create or recapture that past. Jarman rejected the purported historical realism of "costume drama", calling such recreations "delusion[s] based on a collective amnesia, ignorance and furnishing fabrics".[12] His use of Renaissance texts and historical figures enables him to recast the familiarity of contemporary events in an unfamiliar fashion; his focus always remains on the events of his own time.

Jarman's merger of the queer literary/artistic past with the concerns of the queer subculture in contemporary Britain was perhaps most effective in *Edward II*. The source is Christopher Marlowe's Renaissance play of the same name, first published in 1594. With his typical candour, Jarman says of his choice to stage Marlowe's text:

> How to make a film of a gay love affair and get it commissioned. Find a dusty old play and violate it...Marlowe outs the past – why don't we out the present? That's really the only message this play has. Fuck poetry.[13]

Jarman's outing of the present is clearly visible from the outset: the film opens with "two hustlers in bed, naked...[who] fuck without a blush",[14] as Gaveston (Andrew Tiernan) learns that his lover, the newly-crowned Edward II (Steven Waddington), has recalled him from exile to share his throne. While some critics have insisted that Marlowe's play is primarily concerned with Edward's political, rather than sexual, transgressions,[15] Jarman's film ensures that Edward's oppositional sexuality remains central: Isabella (Tilda Swinton) and the "chorus" of earls claim that their move to re-exile Gaveston is motivated solely by his "undue influence" over the King, but Gaveston's influence is meaningless independent of his identification as Edward's lover.

Forced to choose between his love for Gaveston and the crown, Edward repeatedly cries out, "Was ever a king so overruled as I?", and Jarman couples the response of the established Church and nobility to the crisis of Edward's sexuality with the oppression queers continue to face from religious institutions and the state. The Bishop of Winchester (Dudley Sutton) – as apparently unrelenting as the current Archbishop Carey of Canterbury[16] – was initially responsible for Gaveston's exile during the reign of Edward's father. After being brutally humiliated when Gaveston returns from France, Winchester spearheads the campaign to have Gaveston permanently banished. Led by the soldierly Mortimer (Nigel Terry), and angered that Edward has chosen a "base peasant" to receive his favour, the Chorus of Nobility is quick to comply with the Bishop's request. Outfitted in business suits and bow-blouses, the earls' attire resembles that of the politicians of the New Right. The visual parallels are made unambiguously clear when the earls meet to sign the proclamation of Gaveston's exile:

Christopher [Hobbs]'s design for the form of Gaveston's exile has the House of Common's logo. The green blotters acted as reflectors giving the conspirators a sickish look...The table was a copy of the cabinet table...We don't want to undermine the opposition in the mind of the audience. If they are dangerous they must appear so. And they are.[17]

Jarman ensures that there are no questions in the minds of the audience regarding the connection of the earls with the New Right: the long-standing alliance of conservative politics with the political agenda of the Church has repeatedly protected and enforced the claims of Heterosoc. The combined support of the Church and nobility is too much for the young King Edward to suppress. With the earls' unanimous support, and under penalty of "discharg[ing] the Lords/Of duty and allegiance",[18] the Bishop forces Edward to sign the form of Gaveston's exile, and the exiled Gaveston is made to run the gauntlet between two lines of savagely expectorating clergy.

The pivotal, mediating figure in this alliance of the Church and state, however, is Queen Isabella. In an effort to regain (sexual) access to her husband, she aligns herself with the most powerful members of the Church and nobility. Isabella presents herself as an unjustly wronged wife to ensure the sympathy and support of the Church and the earls. She solidifies her relationship with Mortimer, the most politically expedient of the earls, by serving as his confidant and eventually as his lover. Isabella complains to Mortimer that Gaveston "wears a Lord's revenue on his back/And Midas-like he jets it in the court",[19] although depleting the royal treasury does not appear to have been an issue until the King's lover is doing the spending: the Queen is clothed in exquisite couture, while Jarman's Gaveston is customarily depicted wearing a T-shirt and jeans. If Gaveston has managed to oust Isabella from Edward's bed, she is determined not to let him also upstage her at court. Moreover, in her desperate gamble to be rid of Gaveston and regain Edward's love, Isabella proposes the repeal of Gaveston's exile – only to demand his death upon his return to England.

Jarman's treatment of Isabella does nothing to mitigate the overt misogyny of Marlowe's original text. Isabella is presented as a woman of uncontrollable sexuality who quite literally threatens to consume every man with whom she comes into contact. She is so starved of affection that she cannot resist Gaveston's temptations, even as she despises him. When Isabella succumbs to the lure of his kiss, Gaveston mocks and belittles her, yet in a parallel scene where Isabella attempts a similar seduction of the executioner Lightborn (Keith Collins), he refuses her efforts: queer men are given the power to resist and sexually manipulate Isabella, while she is unable to exert similar control. Jarman's Isabella can only be controlled through the sexual domination of a man.[20] In her role as a rebellious queen, however, Isabella's voracious sexual appetites will destroy any male who does not satisfy her lust.

Isabella's systematic destruction of both Gaveston and Edward highlights the precarious yet central position of queers within Heterosoc. Edward's repeated rejection of Isabella fuels her desire for revenge after the King's forces are defeated in a bloody civil war. With a snippet of her hair as a fraudulent token of her love, Isabella sends Lightborn to execute Edward. Broken by the murder of Gaveston, Edward has been locked away deep in the bowels of the castle, held in isolation while located at the foundation of the entire structure. He awaits his torturous death, buried deeply under the very centre of power; Edward's deviant sexuality is paradoxically placed at the heart of culture, yet remains totally circumscribed. Through Isabella's systematic destruction of Gaveston and Edward, the oppression of Heterosoc finds its logical conclusion: the virtual eradication of the queer presence.

While Jarman's connection of the Bishop and the earls to the New Right movement is unambiguously clear, the queenly Isabella's contemporary cognate is difficult to discern at first glance. However, in her role as a powerful mediator and authority within the alliance of Church and state, Isabella's function as a central figurehead in Heterosoc domination brings her historical counterpart into sharper focus: Margaret Thatcher certainly shares her convictions and her determination to eliminate queer opposition. In her closing speech to the Conservative Party Conference in 1987, then Prime Minister Thatcher announced the terms of her assault: "Children who need to be taught to respect traditional values are being taught that they have an inalienable right to be gay".[21] Her remarks at this conference led to an amendment to the committee stage of the Local Government Bill which, with slight modification, eventually became Clause 28 of the Local Government Act in 1988.[22]

Jarman dedicates *Edward II* to "the repeal of all anti-gay laws, particularly Section 28",[23] and the opposition to Clause 28 resulted in the largest queer demonstrations ever seen in Europe – more than 25 000 people over the course of several months protested at the proposed amendment. Jarman's response to Clause 28's designation to "protect children" from exposure to representations of queer life can be read through his treatment of Edward and Isabella's only child, Prince Edward (Jody Graber). Whereas the future Edward III appears only at the close of Marlowe's play to announce the downfall of Isabella and Mortimer, Jarman employs Prince Edward to cut to the heart of the controversy surrounding children, education and the formation of sexual identity in contemporary Britain. Prince Edward is Jarman's "eye in the castle", moving between Edward and Isabella's respective camps, and serves as a witness to his uncle's execution at the hands – literally, the mouth – of his mother.

When Prince Edward is first presented in the film, he appears as a "normal" little boy, dressed in a loose black suit and casual white shirt; there is nothing about his apparel or behaviour that does not conform to Heterosoc's stereotyped expectations of appropriate gender roles. Yet, in the course of the film, he begins to experiment with cross-dressing: initially, he wears his mother's clip-on earrings and, as the film progresses, adds her lipstick, make-up and summer hat. His increasingly unorthodox behaviour moves him completely outside the established masculine conventions of Heterosoc. The process of his coming out culminates in his shuffling two-step on Isabella and Mortimer's cage to the tune of queer Tchaikovsky's "Dance of the Sugar Plum Fairy", during which Prince Edward completes the transformation of his attire through the addition of Isabella's stiletto heels.

While Prince Edward's observation of the events of the palace certainly influences his maturation, Jarman is far from correlating children's cross-dressing and queer identity. Even if his father's example is shaping Prince Edward's emergent queer sexuality, cross-dressing is not one of the skills he acquires from the King. Prince Edward does not appear in his father's presence while in drag, nor does King Edward appear in drag in the film. Additionally, with the exception of two scenes – Edward's bestowal of the title "Lord of Man" (I, i, 156) upon Gaveston, and his holding of his son as Gaveston goes into exile – Prince Edward is under Isabella's care and the brutally hypermasculine attentions of Mortimer.

Prince Edward's development may be also be charted through an examination of the toys with which he plays. The prince is first seen grasping an enormous, sheathed sword while he and Gaveston mimic the sound of a machine-gun. Gradually, his toys become even more militaristic and mechanised. He plays with a flashing mechanised robot while Isabella puts on her show of grief for the earls; by the time Isabella completes her alliance with Mortimer, the prince wears camouflage gear and a terrorist face-mask, and sports a realistic toy machine-gun. Prince Edward seems to follow a pattern of queer militarisation observable in several of Jarman's films: the more the prince is queer-identified within Heterosoc, the more the conflict of his oppositional sexuality is expressed through metaphors of violence. While Prince Edward is not educated in any formal sense – he has no tutors, nor direct instruction from his parents – the informal education he receives is central to understanding that what is at stake in the education debates is not an individual identity, but the continuation and replication of a hetero-dominant system of power.[24]

Jarman's Prince Edward is an emergent, oppositional queer who suggests that existing efforts at compulsory heterosexist education are not only unacceptable, but also ultimately futile. Although the passage of Clause 28 marked the retrenchment of Heterosoc's endeavour to "protect" children from homosexuality, its insistent heterosexualization denies queer youth the guidance many desperately seek:

Silence puts the young in peril...In 1990, over 14,000 calls were made to the National AIDS Helpline by lesbian, gay or bisexual children under the age of sixteen. A further 38,000 came from lesbian, gay or bisexual young adults between the ages of sixteen and twenty-one. If these figures show a degree of anxiety amongst young adults and children what about the fears of children that are left unrecorded? There is little discussion or even less research about Homosexuality in childhood.[25]

Even without direct guidance or encouragement, Prince Edward still manages to negotiate the complex and contradictory spaces of the queer minority while positioned within the realm of Heterosoc. Jarman's young prince challenges the universalization of heterosexual desire by underlining the fluidity of sexual desire, intimating that everyone is capable of making the transition from heterosex to queersex. Jarman's universalizing of queer desire contradicts the biologism of essentialist notions of sexual desire: the number of queer individuals is not limited to the genetic make-up of a deviant few. This pluralization of queer desire appears to be consistent with Jarman's own desire to love men rather, than the particulars of any one man:

My life had fluidity and possibility...What was so exciting was meeting new people with new ideas while Heterosoc felt that all we were doing was putting cocks in each other's mouths. Before those cocks got into our mouths we were exchanging ideas...Heterosoc, imprisoned by monogamy in the ruins of romantic love, is quite dumbfounded when faced with our plurality.[26]

A major impediment to Heterosoc's comprehension of queer love is that sex – the physical act presumed to define sexual orientation – for many queers is not restricted to the exchange of semen; as a life-orientation (rather than merely life-style), sexual exchange can also facilitate the dissemination of revolutionary ideas. As every male is a Gaveston or an Edward, every male is potentially a different version of the same oppositional sexuality. Jarman overturns the presumed universality of heterosexual attraction and posits an omnipresent homosexuality to take its place.[27]

The promise of a "Queersoc", however, remains unattainable while queers continue to be destroyed by the state-sanctioned and institutionally sanctioned bigotry of Heterosoc. Nowhere else has the full import of Heterosoc oppression over queer lives been as painfully evident as in its disastrous response to the AIDS crisis, where policing queersex remains more important than providing necessary funding for developing research and new strategies for treatment. Jarman is adamant about queer sexual autonomy, especially in the face of the AIDS pandemic:

> Understand that if we decide to have sex whether safe, safer, or unsafe, it is our decision and you have no rights in our lovemaking...[The pandemic] has changed my perspective radically. I'd always been under the impression that Heterosoc was pretty dim. Now I know that I was right. Actively or through indifference they murdered us.[28]

Jarman tested positive for the HIV virus in December 1986, and the AIDS crisis forms a central underlying theme in most of his later films. In *Edward II*, he uses colour symbolism and the omnipresence of bodily fluids to address the pandemic. Red is one of the dominant colours in the film: it is picked up in Isabella's dresses, in Gaveston's shirt, in the blanket on the hospital bed, and in the lighting during the poker scene. Jarman employs a rich, saturated crimson-red that is consistent with the predominance of blood throughout the film. The Bishop is assaulted until his head oozes blood; Edward strikes his forehead against the wall until it bleeds; Gaveston and Spencer are beaten to a bloody pulp before they are murdered; Edward and Spencer coat themselves from head to toe in an orgy of blood when they execute Gaveston's murderer.[29] Moving beyond the military metaphors which Jarman employs for the clash of queers and Heterosoc, the blood metaphors suggest not only the violence of the conflict, but also the violent disease that the resulting bloodshed can transmit.

Jarman's use of blood metaphors, however, is part of a larger cultural movement to liberate body fluids from the spectre of AIDS. From this standpoint, Isabella's execution of Kent by biting out his jugular vein is not merely a horror cliché, nor is it simple sensationalism: vampirism has traditionally been connected with mysterious, often incurable epidemics and plagues. In a society terrorised by AIDS, Isabella's action is the supreme transgression of a sexual taboo inseparable from queer sexuality. While vampire stories predate AIDS by hundreds of years, the current obsession with blood-sucking directly corresponds to the re-emergence of an incurable disease transferred by the blood. The link between homosexuality, AIDS and vampirism has not been lost on those who oppose queer rights:

> Vampire-like slurs against gays have been standard ammunition for the religious right for quite a while. Consider Anita Bryant's charming assertion that 'the male homosexual eats another man's sperm. Sperm is the most concentrated form of blood. The homosexual is eating life.' Tangled blood themes run beneath the surface of gay clashes with the Catholic Church over AIDS issues. It was somehow appropriate that the 1989 demonstration at St. Patrick's Cathedral specifically disrupted the communion service – the purest ritual sublimation of the blood drinking, 'life-eating' impulse in Western civilization.[30]

Underlying the assertion that those who consume blood/semen are consuming life is the unspoken assumption that they are partaking of death as well. Jarman's visual representation of vampirism affords his audience an unparalleled indulgence, a glimpse at an unattainable "supernaturalized sexuality that survives and thrives in a world of death".[31] When Prince Edward dips his finger in Kent's wound and sucks on his blood, he experiences a naïve taste of "first blood" that corresponds to the terror and fascination surrounding the dangerous potential of (contaminated) blood. It is not coincidental that there is a parallel photograph in the published screenplay where Jarman is seen tasting the blood of the dead Kent. The blood that flows so freely through Jarman's film represents an attempt to surmount the horrors of his "world of death", localised at the height of his career in the slow debilitation of his body by the AIDS virus:

> I am the man who kissed in that *Guardian* photograph which was captioned '*Kiss of death?*'...I kissed him. He said 'Suck my cock – you have the dick of death'. 'Let me fuck you' 'O.K.' *Death Fuck* – What a great splash for the tabloids.[32]

Death Fuck: two inseparable words which encapsulate the state of queersex, the impossibility of love's escape from the pervasive spectre of death. Struggling, bound, and pinned to a stone table, a deep blood-rush colours the ruddy face of the screaming Edward as

Lightborn thrusts a red-hot poker up his arse. The death fuck of Edward serves as a fitting metaphor for how Heterosoc perceives his crime, and graphically represents the ultimate consequence of hetero-domination. The eroticization of the destruction of the queer body excises the homoerotic tension that is always present in Heterosoc; the physical and visual depiction of Edward's execution enables Heterosoc to consummate its erotic attraction to queer Edward by anally penetrating him, while at the same time it destroys the object of its desire by torturing Edward to death. The meaning is intrinsically clear: those who take it up the arse – unnatural, perverse, unmanly, less-than-human – deserve the violence of their death. The death sentence is self-fulfilling; if not as a victim of bashing, then the internal violence of AIDS will also serve the designs of Heterosoc: *Actively or through indifference they murdered us...*

At the end of *Edward II*, Jarman presents an alternative to this apocalyptic vision of a triumphant Heterosoc. Isabella and Mortimer are covered in a thick, brittle white paste and sit in a large cage under the feet of Edward III. And there they will remain, safely imprisoned in the ruins of romantic love. Queer Edward III ignores his mother's outstretched hand, and Mortimer bemoans his "declining fall" from the fickle wheel of base fortune. While Edward expects Lightborn to fulfil the vision of his execution he has had in his dream, Lightborn instead throws the poker into a pool and gently kisses Edward. Thus, the kiss of death is transformed back into the kiss of life: one can hope that Edward escaped with his life, as one of Jarman's 15th century sources suggests.[33]

With his deteriorating health, however, the possibility of Jarman finding an escape from his illness looked increasingly bleak. Yet, the last image in the screenplay depicts a resilient Jarman with Edward's crown placed squarely on his head, one raised fist clenched in a sign of victory, and the other flung campily to the side. It is the pose of a man who refuses to acknowledge defeat: his eyes are focused with determination, and his face, although tired, bears more than a trace of a smile. Edward's fight has become Jarman's own, and the outcome of their fight for survival appears to be irreversibly conjoined. In theory, Edward and Jarman may survive their impending death, and the verses which close the film refer as much to Jarman as to Edward:

But what are Kings, when regiment is gone,
But perfect shadows in a sunshine day?
I know not, but of this I am assured,
That death ends all, and I can die but once.
Come death, and with thy fingers close my eyes,
Or if I live let me forget myself.[34]

These lines are spoken as the King's army huddles outside the castle, silently mourning their vanquished King; the last scene is an OutRage memorial service for those who have died of AIDS. Contrary to the commentary in the screenplay, Edward is never seen again on his throne. Perhaps prefiguring his own death, the screen gradually fades to black; the voice of Edward is heard reciting the last lines in complete darkness. For Jarman, there was no possibility of living and forgetting. Soon, Jarman's eyes closed, and Death's fingers followed closely behind.

*   *   *

I would like to thank Paula Massood and Gayatri Patniak for their help and encouragement in preparing this essay, and Timothy, whose love and support makes everything worthwhile.

Notes

1   Derek Jarman, *Dancing Ledge*, edited by Shaun Allen (London: Quartet Books, 1984): 241.

2   Ibid: 176. In *Jubilee*, the political concerns of Jarman's immediate historical situation merge with the fictional narrative of his film. Jarman writes of the making of *Jubilee*: "The source of the film was often autobiographical, the locations were the streets and warehouses in which I had lived during the previous ten years...Whereas in *Sebastiane* we lived in a world outside the film, in *Jubilee* our world became the film. A first note to myself makes the position quite clear – JUBILEE is a fantasy documentary fabricated so that documentary and fictional forms are confused and coalesce" (176-177). For an account of the making and content of his early Super 8 films, see 124-132.

3   Ibid: 176.

4   Derek Jarman, *At Your Own Risk: A Saint's Testament* (London: Hutchinson, 1992): 83.

5   Derek Jarman, *Queer Edward II* (London: British Film Institute, 1991): 126. The openly queer Peter Tatchell lost the Bermondsey by-election in 1983 due to a vitriolic slur campaign. Tatchell recounts his perspective of the election in *The Battle for Bermondsey* (London: Heretic Books, 1983). For more on Jarman's opposition to both Left and Right, especially on aesthetic grounds, see Lawrence Driscoll's essay in this volume.

6   Jarman scathingly condemns the efforts of "Establishment" queer men who work within the confines of Heterosoc to reform the system, and the closeted queers who refuse to work for political change: "[Ian] McKellen's knighthood is more shocking; wining and dining in the erroneous belief that his honour improves our situation. There are many gay men with Tory

hearts who believe in this honour. I don't. It was brave of Ian to come out – but that is all he had to do" (Jarman [1991]: 106). He later restates his frustration in *At Your Own Risk*: "[Closeted queers] took everything and did nothing, sat in their interior decoration, attended the opera and did fuck all to help change; their minds as starched as their shirts...Stonewall – the self-elected and self-congratulating parliamentry [sic] lobby group – have made more than enough compromise with convention. Did those who rioted at the Stonewall bar fight so that we could so easily be co-opted by a gay establishment?...Part of the con was to steal the name Stonewall and turn *our* riot into *their* tea party. We are now to be integrated into the worst form of British hetero politic – the closed room, the gentlemen's club – where decisions are made undemocratically for an ignorant population which enjoys its emasculation." (59-60). Emphasis in original.

7   Stuart Hall, "Gramsci's Relevance for the Study of Race and Ethnicity", *Journal of Communication: Inquiry* 10 (summer 1986): 5-27. The development and refinement of the concept of hegemony within the Marxist tradition is far too broad to recount here, although Gramsci's original formulation of hegemony contained in Quintin Hoare and Geoffrey Nowell Smith (eds), *Selections from the Prison Notebooks of Antonio Gramsci* (London: Lawrence and Wishart, 1971), and Raymond Williams's more recent explication in *Marxism and Literature* (London: Oxford University Press, 1977), are indispensable to a basic understanding of hegemony. My own understanding of hegemony, and particularly of its usefulness in discussing Thatcherism, comes from the work of Stuart Hall. See especially Stuart Hall, Bob Lumley and Gregor McLennan, "Politics and Ideology: Gramsci", in *Working Papers in Cultural Studies* 10 (1977): 45-76, and Stuart Hall and Martin Jacques (eds), *The Politics of Thatcherism* (London: Lawrence and Wishart, in association with *Marxism Today*, 1983).

8   Jarman (1992): 4. For more on Jarman as "criminal", see David Gardner's essay in this volume.

9   See Chris Lippard and Guy Johnson's discussion of the other side of Jarman's representation of queer violence, the suffering male body, in "Private Practice, Public Health: The Politics of Sickness and the Films of Derek Jarman", in Lester Friedman (ed), *Fires Were Started: British Cinema and Thatcherism* (Minneapolis: University of Minnesota Press, 1993): 282.

10   Peter Wollen, "The Last New Wave: Modernism in the British Films of the Thatcher Era", in Lester Friedman (ed): 46. After accounting for the influence of "neoromanticism" on Jarman's filmmaking, Wollen concludes that he remains outside the "romantic mainstream", subverting rather than promoting myths of consolidated British nationalism. For a thorough analysis of Jarman's attitudes and interpretation of the Renaissance, see David Hawkes's essay in this volume.

11   Jarman (1992): 72.

12   Jarman (1991): 86.

13   Ibid: frontispiece.

[14]   Ibid: 6. The sexual frankness of this scene is not repeated elsewhere in the film, perhaps because of the heterosexual orientation of the leading men, and the monitoring influence of the BBC.

[15]   See, for example, Leo Kirschbaum, *The Plays of Christopher Marlowe* (New York: Meridian, 1962): 7-156. Most critics traditionally appeared to be incapable of accepting the notion that a queer subject-matter could lead to a literary masterpiece. Typically, this dilemma is solved by labelling *Edward II* as an inferior play, or, as in Kirschbaum's case, so strongly emphasising the political aspects of the drama as to effectively nullify the importance of Edward's sexuality. See also John Bakeless, *Christopher Marlowe: The Man in his Times* (New York: Washington Square Press, 1964), and A L Rowse, *Christopher Marlowe: A Biography* (London: Macmillan & Co., 1964). Note, however, Jarman's observation that: "On 'The Media Show' A. L. Rowse said Shakespeare was a conservative, Marlowe much more radical. Shakespeare's wilful misinterpretation of the 15th century to bolster Tudor dynastic claims has blighted our past" (Jarman: [1991]: 112).

[16]   It is hard to encapsulate Jarman's disdain for Archbishop Carey, although these quotations from *Queer Edward II* provide an accurate summation of its depth: "'Gay men are unfit to be ordained as priests' Ugly Archbishop Carey" (32); "Bishop Carey's pronouncement that our sexuality cannot be condoned, only forgiven, by his church, adds fuel to the fire. Unnatural, not part of nature; hence the reason for the new book's title, 'Modern Nature'" (104); "'Peace-loving' Archbishop Carey had SAS marksmen all over Canterbury Cathedral for his enthronement. Blood. Kensington Gore. Max Factor Massacre. Claret. Morag's SPECIAL MIX." (128).

[17]   Jarman (1991): 56.

[18]   Ibid: 60.

[19]   Ibid: 54.

[20]   While female roles are seldom of major importance in Jarman's films, the ancient women and Tilda-as-feminine-godhead form the moral core of *The Garden*. However, most of Jarman's women are merely ancillary in the predominantly male space of his films. In his comments on shooting the bedroom scene where Isabella attempts to seduce Edward (sequence 10), Jarman notes that Swinton herself was concerned with the implicit misogyny of her role: "An unsatisfactory bedroom scene with Tilda and Steven – she thought it might be misogynist, I thought the audience would have some sympathy for her, even if she plays it hard" (Ibid: 20).

[21]   Stephen Jeffery-Poulter, *Peers, Queers, and Commons: The struggle for gay law reform from 1950 to the present* (London; New York: Routledge, 1991): 218. Although Jeffery-Poulter's book tends to be politically conservative, it remains the most thorough account of contemporary gay legal reform in Great Britain.

[22]   Jarman provides the exact wording of Section 28 and a brief synopsis of queer efforts to oppose it under the heading, "How The Kiss Of Death

Became The Kiss Of Life", in Jarman (1992): 113. Section 28 reads as follows: "1) A local authority shall not: a) Intentionally promote homosexuality or publish material with the intention of promoting homosexuality. b) Promote the teaching in any maintained school of the acceptability of homosexuality as a pretended family relationship. 2) Nothing in subsection 1 shall be taken to prohibit the doing of anything for the purpose of treating or preventing the spread of disease. 3) In any proceedings in connection with the application of this section a court shall draw such inferences as to the intention of the local authority as may reasonably be drawn from the evidence before it."

23   Jarman (1991): frontispiece.

24   Several of Jarman's later films also treat the oppressiveness of Heterosoc education. In *The Garden*, groups of old men taunt Jody Graber, pounding their pointers in military time, while *Wittgenstein* (1993) underscores the violence and repression of the British system. During the period Jarman was filming *Edward II*, the controversy surrounding a film made for a British education series, *The Two of Us*, shows the relevance of Jarman's cinematic critique. The film deals with the problems of two teenage queer boys who fall in love with each another. The film was designed to promote a better understanding of the difficulties of gay youth: gradually, members of the boys' peer group come to accept their relationship. Yet, because the two boys briefly kiss, the film was pulled from the BBC. When it was eventually aired, it was shown at 11.30 pm – not an opportune time to reach its intended audience. See also Melanie McFayean, "When the Kissing Has to Stop", *Manchester Guardian* 19 January 1990: 20.

25   Jarman (1992): 37. Jarman points out that the denial of children's sexual activity may have disastrous effects: "So many kids lie about their age...A scenario for disaster! As a twelve year old you become HIV+, and then you fuck the whole school! The epidemic is potentially uncontrollable. The only solution is discussion rather than censure." (25). Simon Watney's work is invaluable to any discussion of the battles over education and of the impact of AIDS on youth in Great Britain. See "School's Out", in Diana Fuss (ed), *Inside/Out: Lesbian Theories, Gay Theories* (New York; London: Routledge, 1991): 387-401, and *Policing Desire: Pornography, AIDS and the Media*, second edition (Minneapolis; London: University of Minnesota Press, 1989), especially "Moral panics": 38-57.

26   Jarman (1992): 4-57.

27   Throughout this essay, I have purposely chosen to use the word "queer" as a sign of commitment to a unified movement of sexual difference including lesbians, gays, bisexuals and transgendered. However, as this passage indicates, Jarman's politics do not appear to be so encompassing, particularly with regard to lesbians. Jarman does occasionally mention the contribution and significance of lesbians in his account of the struggle to oppose Heterosoc, but only in a cursory manner. Jarman's androcentric focus on the experience of gay men is perhaps best illustrated in the battle sequences of *Edward II*: Edward's forces are composed of members of OutRage, and the only visible lesbian presence is among the victims of the

firing squad.

[28] Jarman (1992): 6-101.

[29] In his review of *Edward II*, "Blank Verse and Body Fluids", Francis Spufford also draws attention to the bloodiness of the film. See *Times Literary Supplement* 4624 (15 November 1991): 19.

[30] David Skal, "Blood Borne Monster", *Out* January 1993: 34.

[31] Ibid: 33-34.

[32] Jarman (1992): 6. Emphasis in original.

[33] "We've adopted the conspiracy theory for the end of the film. Manuel Fieschi, writing to Edward III, told him that his father had escaped from Berkeley Castle, to Corfe, and from there to Avignon, where he was received by Pope Urban XXII, and from there he made his way to North Italy, to become a hermit living a life of prayer" (Jarman [1991]: 158).

[34] Ibid: 166.

Language games and aesthetic attitudes: style and ideology in Jarman's late films

Richard Porton

Derek Jarman's early films delight in excess, and embrace a self-consciously baroque style, while his later work reveals an austere, frequently elegiac sensibility. Although Jarman is unquestionably stripping his later films of extraneous ornamentation, *Edward II* (1991), *Wittgenstein* (1993) and *Blue* (1993) are not prototypical "late works" made by an artist approaching death. Despite their surface restraint, they are not mellow rejoinders to the more obviously incendiary early films. The austere late films fuse an aesthetic strategy with a serious, but never solemn, political agenda. *Edward II*, *Blue* and, in a more subtle manner, *Wittgenstein*, are simultaneously lyrical and politically engaged, and convey a distinctive mixture of melancholy and anger. In Jarman's work it is impossible to separate cinematic style from a decidedly undidactic political fervour; formal choices are simultaneously political choices. Yet, unlike practitioners of traditional political cinema, Jarman always filtered his political outrage through an intensely personal and frequently autobiographical perspective.

Jarman's films resist facile classification. His work could easily find a niche within any of the "five faces of modernity" cited by critic Matei Calinescu – modernism, the avant-garde, decadence, kitsch and postmodernism.[1] Whether we view Jarman as a modernist, postmodernist or unregenerate Romantic, it is clear that he was never wedded to monolithic assumptions concerning visual style or narrative structure. Jarman's aesthetic strategies are not influenced by a predetermined agenda, but emerge pragmatically from specific contexts. His stylistic flexibility implicitly affirms Ludwig Wittgenstein's belief that it is impossible to arrive at a comprehensive definition of art, or at a "set of conditions necessary and sufficient to works of art".[2]

Although Jarman never subscribed to essentialist notions concerning the nature of art, he also never minced words when detailing both his idiosyncratic aesthetic preferences and his cinematic *bêtes noires*. An unswerving hostility to naturalism – particularly British postwar naturalism – is discernible in his films and published writings. Jarman's personal pantheon has no room for directors such as Tony Richardson, Karel Reisz or Lindsay Anderson. On the other hand, his work often evokes memories of such disparate figures as Kenneth Anger, Stan Brakhage, Michael Powell, Jean Cocteau and Pier Paolo Pasolini.[3] All these directors are united by their hostility to mainstream naturalism and their radical individualism – an individualism that does not foreclose the cultivation of collective, but non-dogmatic, radical hopes.

While *Wittgenstein* and *Blue* are the culmination of Jarman's gradual rejection of stylistic excess, both his early and his late works are preoccupied with asserting the political importance of sexual dissidence. "Sexual Anarchy" – a phrase first used pejoratively by novelist George Gissing to stigmatize the late 19th century's new-found fascination with concerns once considered "deviant", particularly women's emancipation and homosexuality – is unabashedly celebrated in all Jarman's films.[4] His abandonment of calculated flamboyance enabled him to tone down his preferred "overripeness"[5] and eventually to adopt a more self-effacing style.

Jarman's deceptively simple film on Wittgenstein is arguably the pivotal late work. This biographical study is a fascinating meld of asceticism and whimsy, emulating the philosopher's own moral rigour while poking gentle fun at his sometimes humourless cerebration. "I have much of Ludwig in me", confessed Jarman, although he qualified this surprising confession with an even odder admission – "Not in my work, but in my life".[6] Yet, once one goes beyond the simple incongruity of an unabashedly gay and ebullient filmmaker claiming an affinity with the famously closeted, introverted philosopher, a rationale emerges for Jarman's idiosyncratic kinship with Wittgenstein.

There are tangible, if subtle, elective affinities between the aesthetic creed embraced by Wittgenstein, termed one of the century's leading "gay modernists",[7] and the "bare bones" style of Jarman's late work. As Allan Janik and Stephen Toulmin demonstrate, turn-of-the-century Viennese architect Adolf Loos's extreme distaste for excess ornamentation precedes and influences Wittgenstein's assault on metaphysics. Loos believed that the distinction between *objets d'art* and utilitarian household objects was an explicitly *moral* differentiation.[8] Wittgenstein's *Tractatus Logico-Philosophicus* (1921) converted this hatred of architectural *bric-à-brac* into the century's most important critique of metaphysical clutter. Paradoxically but not uncharacteristically, Wittgenstein's youthful philosophical masterpiece is concerned more with what cannot be said and with what must be "passed over in silence",[9] than with affirmative verities.

It might seem initially nonsensical to align Jarman's work with this kind of modernist asceticism. The playful provocation of *Jubilee* (1978) and *The Tempest* (1979) is obviously more influenced by the flamboyant aestheticism of Oscar Wilde, and has little in common with

Wittgenstein's sombre denunciation of art for art's sake. Yet, the image of Wilde as nothing more than a frivolous aesthete[10] is as one-dimensional as the traditional portrait of Wittgenstein as a humourless philosophical hair-splitter. It is necessary only to peruse Wilde's *The Soul of Man under Socialism* (1891) to learn that his aestheticism had roots in a social and political critique, and a quick glance at Wittgenstein's *Philosophical Investigations* (1953) makes one aware that his dismantling of philosophical essentialism is more ludic than lugubrious. Jarman's late works effectively unite, however unwittingly, Wilde's belief in "the truth of masks" with Wittgenstein's contempt for aesthetic clutter. A sparer style replaces the frenetic camera movement, disjunctive editing, and fondness for non-synchronous sound found in *The Last of England* (1987) and *The Garden* (1990). However, Jarman never completely abandoned the Wildean penchant for carefully orchestrated artifice. Wilde believed that "art anticipates life"[11] and, despite the implicit "aestheticism" of his assertion, this playful inversion of received wisdom has much in common with Wittgenstein's belief that art, as a form of life, is an intersubjective practice. For both Wittgenstein and Wilde, "beauty" is a sterile abstraction, meaningless without the knowledge of how specific individuals and groups formulate aesthetic concepts that never remain static. Similarly, Jarman's films undermine traditional distinctions between aestheticism and sociological critique – films such as *The Last of England* and *Edward II* demonstrate that political cinema can be formally adventurous and need not ape the conventions of "kitchen sink" naturalism.

On another level, Wittgenstein's conception of human activity as a series of "language games", one of the century's most influential refutations of philosophical idealism, can help us evaluate the varied, if interrelated, panoply of stylistic approaches employed by Jarman during his film career. Although Wittgenstein believed that *all* aesthetic activity was the product of "ensembles of linguistic and non-linguistic activities", as well as of the "institutions, practices and the meanings 'incorporated' in them",[12] it is experimental artists such as Jarman who most self-consciously immerse themselves in often labyrinthine language games. Wittgenstein's definition of these "language games" is notoriously fluid, alternately referring to language acquisition on the one hand, and an interconnected web of social practices – within Wittgenstein's schema linguistic activity inevitably becomes embedded in "forms of life" – on the other. Wittgenstein's corpus always forces us to examine specific cultural practices, since he insists that linguistic meaning is always linked to specific uses generated by specific social contexts. Wittgenstein's antimetaphysical and anti-ontological bias teaches us that even the deeply submerged vicissitudes of the self are tied to a social nexus. One of the most celebrated sections of the *Philosophical Investigations* debunks the notion of a "private language",[13] since language is invariably linked to social interaction and is never merely solipsistic. Jarman's allegiance to sexual libertarianism and gay militancy has little relationship to Wittgenstein's own quietistic – even masochistic – sexual ethos.

Nevertheless, films as disparate as *Sebastiane* (1976) and *Blue* are aesthetic experiments that share the provisional quality of the *Philosophical Investigations* and partake of the Wittgensteinian desire to infuse private experience with a public resonance. Wittgenstein was fond of comparing language to a "tool-box",[14] and Jarman shares the belief that art's reception and assimilation by actual viewers, readers and listeners are of more interest than abstract notions of beauty. Wittgenstein denounces aesthetic idealism, whether derived from Plato, Hegel or Kant, believing that aesthetic activity immerses us "into a new group of confusions...There is constant surprise at the new tricks language plays on us when we get into a new field".[15] Jarman's films are open-ended and inspire interpretations that are subject to constant revision; he reflexively examines the sometimes frustrating and often edifying confusions that language games engender. In a famous passage, Wittgenstein argued that there is not necessarily one attribute that unites all language games; they are united by a network of "family resemblances...a complicated network of similarities and relationships overlapping and criss-crossing".[16] If Jarman's œuvre is viewed in its entirety, family resemblances between disparate narrative and stylistic strategies become apparent. The baroque early work, and the stylistically antithetical late films are equally determined to undermine the ideological solidity of what Jarman terms "Heterosoc",[17] and to herald the emergence of a new gay subculture.

From this perspective, it is possible to view Jarman's *The Tempest* and *Edward II* as distillations of Renaissance "language games", *Jubilee* as an exploration of the punk language game, and *Caravaggio* (1986) and *Wittgenstein* as good-natured travesties of the usual biographical games played by more mainstream directors. Jarman's reinvention of the conventional bio-pic in *Wittgenstein* is particularly congruent with a Wittgensteinian modernism, since the narrative clichés and constrained visual style of Hollywood biographies are discarded for a more elliptical cinematic strategy.

A recent critical study of the Hollywood bio-pic argues that this genre implies that, despite the "unusual gifts" of famous individuals, "most of the greats are normal, just like you and me".[18] If Hollywood bio-pics tended to normalise even the most eccentric scientists, composers and statesmen, Jarman's cinematic portrait of Wittgenstein relishes and, in fact, flaunts the unalloyed oddness of this bumbling philosopher. Old-style Hollywood bio-pics such as *The Life of Emile Zola* (1937) or *Dr Ehrlich's Magic Bullet* (1940) present intellectual endeavour as a series of contrived epiphanic interludes. The obvious limitations of such an approach become clear when faced with the life of a philosopher who revels in ambiguity. Steadfastly opposed to mere hagiography, Jarman fragments Wittgenstein's life into a series of prismatic moments which combine philosophical vaudeville and a bemused critique of academic mores.

Wittgenstein's brilliance resides in Jarman's ability to transform philosophical debates into fodder for brittle comic exchanges. While Hollywood bio-pics invariably transformed their heroes into extroverted "regular guys", Jarman's film emphasises the protagonist's recalcitrant solitude. Much of the film's comic brio derives from the cognitive dissonance that ensues when we realise that Wittgenstein, a solitary, abrasive figure whose obstreperous manner tries the patience of all his colleagues, devotes his life to demolishing a time-honoured philosophical shibboleth – the isolated, thinking subject. The choice of a stark *mise en scène* with austere black backdrops may have been influenced by budgetary considerations; nevertheless, the unadorned visual style focuses attention on the paradoxes of highlighting the inner life of a man who spurned inwardness. The restrained use of vivid colours (occasionally augmented by a flashy costume), the minimal use of camera movement, and the predominance of close-ups and medium close-ups all reinforce Jarman's playful interrogation of Wittgenstein's often sullen isolation. *Wittgenstein* envisions the mature Ludwig as a philosopher who, despite his interest in communal forms of life, suffers from a myopic propensity thoroughly to misunderstand other individuals' needs and desires. Perhaps the most succinct example is a flashback to Wittgenstein's inglorious career as a provincial Austrian schoolteacher. Jarman includes a brief but devastating thumbnail sketch of Ludwig's imperious approach to pedagogy. The short-tempered instructor chides a young girl for committing the same philosophical mistakes he discerns, and now abhors, in his early work, while in the background a school blackboard is festooned with quotations from the *Tractatus Logico-Philosophicus*.

The film insists that Wittgenstein's self-loathing and sudden bursts of aggression are inextricable from his palpable sexual alienation. Near the end of the film, Jarman includes a shot of a brooding Wittgenstein crouching in a suspended bird cage. His loneliness assuaged only by a green parrot confined to his own cage, Wittgenstein delivers an anguished speech that is perhaps the most poignant evidence of Jarman's active identification with his tortured protagonist:

Philosophy is a sickness of the mind. I mustn't infect too many young men. How unique and irreplaceable Johnny is. And yet how little I realise this when I am with him. That's always been a problem. But living in a world where such a love is illegal and trying to live openly and honestly is a complete contradiction.[19]

For Jarman, there is an obvious kinship between Wittgenstein's epigrammatic, often gnomic approach to philosophy and his own, less opaque, gay aesthetic. Jarman's seemingly incongruous sense of solidarity with the priggish philosopher enables *Wittgenstein* to share a family resemblance with his less cerebral bio-pic, *Caravaggio*. Although Caravaggio's more brazen "transgressiveness" has little in common with the philosopher's quieter heterodoxy, Wittgenstein's well-documented life as a tortured denizen of the closet proved as deeply poignant for Jarman. Given Jarman's disdain for the institutionalization and "epistemology of the closet", a bio-pic based on the life of, for example, Jean Genet might have been a more likely project for a director long considered in the vanguard of gay liberation. Clearly, Jarman was attracted to Wittgenstein's multivalent ironies and fascinated by his chaotic inner life. Jarman's autobiography, *Dancing Ledge* (1984), chronicles his own gradual coming to terms with his sexual identity – a process that had initially, despite the evidence of some of the films, more in common with Wittgenstein's ambivalent view of his homosexuality than with Genet's unabashed outrageousness. In addition, Wittgenstein's philosophy was gaining popularity in the 1960s art world during Jarman's early art school apprenticeship. Jasper Johns's early work,[20] for example, was heavily influenced by his reading of Wittgenstein's *Philosophical Investigations*. In addition, Jarman's posthumously published *Chroma* is convincing evidence of the filmmaker's assiduous perusal of the *Investigations*.[21]

Jarman's decision to align his own aesthetic agenda with Wittgenstein's idiosyncratic – and obliquely gay – modernism enabled him to construct a work of fiction that functions as both idiosyncratic *homage* and thinly veiled autobiography. Consequently, Jarman's bio-pic is both scrupulously accurate and extremely selective. Since he is more interested in "reclaiming a whole history for gay people"[22] than in detailed historical exegesis, it makes sense that *Wittgenstein* freely scrambles chronology, passes over its eponymous hero's youthful friendship with the older philosopher, G E Moore, and consolidates several ardent young men who were smitten with Wittgenstein into a composite surrogate known as "Johnny". Occasionally, a crucial component of Wittgenstein's background will be compressed into one economically-composed shot. A good example is a brief close-up of the young Wittgenstein standing before a blackboard covered with chalk renderings of the Star of David. This offhand allusion avoids a protracted sequence explaining the philosopher's Jewish self-hatred without letting him off the hook. The pithiness of the shot is richly suggestive, however, and brings to mind Eve Kosofsky Sedgwick's observation that the "epistemological distinctiveness of gay identity" is comparable to "ethnic/cultural/oppressions such as anti-Semitism... the stigmatized individual has at least notionally some discretion...over other people's knowledge of her or his membership in the group".[23] Jarman was undoubtedly interested in the fact that Wittgenstein never forgave himself for concealing his "non-Aryan" heritage at a time when Nazi Germany had become a palpable threat. There is no question that Wittgenstein's furtive homosexuality and concealed Judaism fuelled a compulsive, self-lacerating gloom.

Long before Jarman's *Wittgenstein*, Thomas Bernhard's novel, *Korrektur* (*Correction*, 1975), and Tom Stoppard's play, *Jumpers* (1972), offered imaginative re-creations of Wittgenstein's life and legacy. Yet, Jarman's film has little in common with Bernhard's Beckett-like stream-of-consciousness novel or with Stoppard's buoyant *jeu d'esprit*.[24] Obviously, Wittgenstein's sexual hibernation was bound to prove unappealing for a proponent of unfettered sexual liberation. *Wittgenstein* synthesizes Brechtian distance with Wildean insouciance, and the putative hero's tendency to remain, in Jarman's words, "locked up by denial"[25] is treated with amused detachment. Jarman does not naïvely reinvent Wittgenstein as – to use Ray Monk's succinct phrase "the Joe Orton of philosophy".[26] Instead of anachronistically idealising Wittgenstein as a gay liberationist *avant la lettre*, Jarman introduces a Caliban-like Martian – "Mr Green" – who poses uncomfortable, if fanciful, philosophical questions to the young Wittgenstein. The impish Martian subtly illustrates the gap between Jarman's own lack of sexual inhibition and Wittgenstein's repressed and frequently lugubrious solemnity.

Jarman's decision to see Wittgenstein as a modern – and modernist – gay is both polemical and self-reflexive. As in many of Jarman's films, *Wittgenstein*'s antic spirit is commingled with an undogmatic form of political intervention. Colin MacCabe has observed that "Jarman stresses the focus on a black background against which the colours and Mr Green blaze – illuminating a queer life".[27] Wittgenstein is decidedly strange, although not precisely "queer" in the contemporary sense promoted by the postmodern Left. Jarman acknowledges Wittgenstein's strangeness by portraying the philosopher as a somewhat tragic figure who avoids hubris through an awareness of his own ridiculousness, a process facilitated by the

Martian's resourcefulness. Jarman's desire to recast Wittgenstein's life as "queer" is an aesthetic leap of faith, his version of the Wittgensteinian concept of *seeing as*, outlined in *Philosophical Investigations*. A simple drawing of a "duck-rabbit", Wittgenstein notes, can, depending on one's vantage point, be perceived as either animal.[28] The notion of the shape-shifting duck-rabbit elegantly demonstrates the indeterminacy of everyday perceptions, and speaks to the instability of our most fundamental aesthetic attitudes.

The film's ruse of bifurcating its hero into two personae – an astonishingly mature child and a child-like adult – reflects Jarman's propensity for both self-referential rhetoric and measured empathy. An early shot of the young Wittgenstein, innocently resplendent in Roman garb, is interestingly emblematic. Jarman opined that "Vienna at that time must have been like the end of the Roman empire",[29] but the budding genius's unlikely choice of finery might also be viewed as a self-parodic reference to Jarman's first film, *Sebastiane*. This film's unabashed celebration of the body, as well as the implicit effort to recapture a lost homosexual paradise, reveals Jarman as a radical Edwardian in modern dress. Similarly, the spontaneity of young Wittgenstein recalls Jarman's reminiscences in *Modern Nature* of cavorting with a friend – "clambering onto each other's beds like the heroes of Edwardian picture books". A childhood of "strange tribal initiations. Warmth and giggles" is evoked.[30] The primal sexuality of *Sebastiane*, as well as the more innocent childhood high jinks chronicled in Jarman's journals, are 20th century variants of the late Victorian essayist Walter Pater's nostalgia for a "universal pagan sentiment, a paganism which existed before the Greek religion, and has lingered far onward into the Christian world, ineradicable, like some persistent vegetable growth".[31] Jarman's Wittgenstein is reluctant to take advantage of his more pagan intuitions, and this reticence probably accounts for Jarman's ambivalent view of his protagonist. Shots of the adult Wittgenstein donning kite wings and brandishing lawn-sprinklers transform the dour philosopher into a bumbling Icarus. On a literal level, these shots refer to the actual biographical desire of Wittgenstein to become an aviator in England. More profoundly, the sequence accentuates a tormented intellectual's inability to take flight and fully discover the pleasures of the flesh – a failing that Jarman found both disheartening and understandable.

Wittgenstein's contempt for his own body, coupled with a feverish introspection and self-loathing, inspired him to lead a near-monastic existence. Appropriately, the philosopher's ascetic ideal is reflected in *Wittgenstein*'s stylistic restraint. Moreover, Jarman's decision to disregard chronology, by fusing quotations from Wittgenstein's early work with fragments from the radically different later philosophy, does not simplify a complex intellectual legacy. This compression accurately captures Wittgenstein's overweening asceticism, since, according to Geoffrey Galt Harpham, both phases of his career betray a yearning for an "unworldly mode of being, a radical dissociation from social customs, norms, habits". When Wittgenstein turns from asserting that the limits of language merely circumscribe the limits of our world to a consideration of language games grounded in social institutions as well as the self, Harpham maintains that, like more moderate Christian ascetics, he "accepts certain worldlinesses...and tries to perfect them".[32] Despite the later Wittgenstein's contempt for solipsism, he could never entirely transcend his own self-absorption.

Jarman dramatises Wittgenstein's ascetic intransigence by envisioning a climactic confrontation between the dying protagonist and John Maynard Keynes. The more worldly Keynes, a bisexual economist who conducted an affair with the painter Duncan Grant and eventually married the Russian dancer, Lydia Lopokova, essentially shares Jarman's own perspective – a blend of empathy and baffled detachment. Lytton Strachey's biographer emphasises Wittgenstein's lack of interest in the conversational repartee cherished by Bloomsbury luminaries such as Keynes, Moore and Strachey. Wittgenstein thought that the Cambridge Apostles'[33] banter was a waste of time: ethical issues could only be resolved through "self-communion".[34] This stance could either be regarded as ridiculously inflexible or lauded as a product of exemplary integrity. A parable narrated by Keynes to the terminally ill Wittgenstein illustrates the journey taken from the rigid asceticism of the *Tractatus Logico-Philosophicus* to the modified self-abnegation of the *Investigations*:

> There was once a young man who dreamed of reducing the world to pure logic. Because he was a very clever young man, he actually managed to do it. And when he'd finished his work, he stood back and admired it. It was beautiful. A world purged of imperfection and indeterminacy. Countless acres of gleaming ice stretching to the horizon...The ice was smooth and level and stainless, but you couldn't walk there...as he grew into a wise old man, he came to understand that roughness and ambiguity aren't imperfections...And the words and things scattered upon this ground were all battered and tarnished...But something in him was still homesick for the ice, where everything was radiant and absolute and relentless.[35]

Wittgenstein's late work is devoted to a consideration of public discourse – language games that offer a glimpse of a world which is far from perfect. *Wittgenstein* emphasises the fact that his interest in this messy intersubjective realm was still animated by a yearning for an unattainable purity. For Jarman, a problematic oscillation between guilty desire and morose introspection comes to the fore in a sequence in which Keynes chides Wittgenstein for behaving like a "true Protestant". When Keynes assures him that "there's nothing in the world like the warmth of a sated body", Wittgenstein can only wail that he feels "burnt by a freezing wind", while berating himself for "infecting" young men.

Keynes once wrote to Wittgenstein that he alternated between "loving and enjoying" his company, and having his "nerves worn to death" by his eccentricities.[36] Something of this annoyance with Wittgenstein's frequent perversity is evident in the scripts of both Jarman and Eagleton; Eagleton has little patience for Wittgenstein's political dilettantism, while Jarman is obviously unhappy with Ludwig's sexual reticence. Unsurprisingly, a stormy contretemps between Jarman and Eagleton influenced the shape and tone of the final film. The feud, however, pinpoints vital issues engendered by divergent political and social perspectives. Eagleton's original screenplay, rejected by Jarman as unfilmable, constructed a linear narrative out of the emigré philosopher's frequently belligerent conflicts with his Cambridge cohorts, primarily Bertrand Russell and G E Moore. (Moore is referred to in Jarman's film, but does not appear as a protagonist.) Eagleton is also preoccupied with the contradictions of a wealthy thinker of aristocratic lineage preaching ascetic self-sacrifice to young disciples. Despite the fact that Eagleton's script is enlivened by intermittent wit, it often resembles a wooden variant of a Brechtian *Lehrstück* ("learning play"). Brecht's *Die Massnahme* (*The Measures Taken*, 1930), for example, unravels an untenable political argument – in this case, an implicit apologia for Stalinist ethics – with a beautifully austere style.[37] Eagleton subscribes to a more libertarian form of Leninism – a nuanced variety of Trotskyism – but his *Lehrstück* inspired by Wittgensteinian themes lacks the limpid clarity of Brecht's best work.

In an essay on Wittgenstein published nearly ten years before his commission to write a script based on the reclusive philosopher's life, Eagleton claimed that Wittgenstein's superficially radical attack on the metaphysical tradition contained elements that were reactionary and, in fact, covertly metaphysical.[38] While Eagleton's unusually restrained script lacks his usual penchant for ideological evisceration, it is far-removed from Jarman's depiction of the Cambridge milieu as a combination of fretful pillow talk and academic backbiting. Eagleton faulted Jarman's transmutation of his script for falling prey to what he deemed an inveterately English predilection for "character". He maintained that Jarman had converted his sober study of an archetypal modernist intellectual into a film in which "hunky young men for whom Spinoza is probably a kind of pasta shamble around ineptly disguised as philosophers".[39] Tongue-in-cheek colloquy between Bertrand Russell and his hairdresser probably did not sit well with the original scriptwriter, whose draft focused on the protagonist's "patrician" detachment.[40] Jarman's light-hearted approach to Wittgenstein's naïve attempts at political commitment, moreover, might well have been calculated to annoy Eagleton – a literary theorist whose work, despite expressing a grudging respect for the author of the *Investigations*, castigates him as a man who "returns us exactly to where we are, leaving the whole structure of everydayness comfortingly in place".[41] Yet, for both Jarman and Wittgenstein, a separation between serious intellectual activity and the "forms of life" that sustain this activity is unacceptably artificial.

Perry Anderson, although even less sympathetic to Wittgenstein's philosophical stance than Eagleton, expressed his objections in a manner that provides a key to the effectiveness of Jarman's playful biographical study. Anderson considers the British infatuation with Wittgenstein a by-product of an ingrained philistinism, and bemoans the fact that a man who resembled a philosophical guru was ignorant of "economic and sociological thought" and subscribed to a "vague moralism and naive religiosity".[42] It is not necessary to accept this inordinately harsh judgment in order to acknowledge the fact that Jarman's affectionately ironic detachment from his protagonist enabled him to capture the insularity and pettiness of the milieu that enshrined Wittgenstein as a prophet. The film, which appropriates an ample number of quotations from the philosopher's work as dialogue, allows us to assess Wittgenstein's charm, as well as his limited intellectual purview. A hairdresser's shocked observation that Wittgenstein "has never read Aristotle", for example, more cogently evokes the contradictions elucidated by Anderson than does Eagleton's schematic original script.

Surprisingly, Eagleton's script neglects Wittgenstein's brief but bizarre flirtation with the Soviet Union, while Jarman devotes a lengthy sequence to this incident. In Jarman's film, Wittgenstein's vaguely Tolstoyan desire to settle in the Soviet Union during the darkest days of Stalinism is handled efficiently in a sequence highlighting both his altruism and his contingent ignorance of political realities. Wittgenstein's political *crise de conscience* takes the form of a comic vignette in which the dreamy intellectual is interviewed by a humourless Soviet *apparatchik* named Sophia. Jarman again emphasises Wittgenstein's physical and emotional isolation. Two shots that bracket the sequence offer us glimpses of Ludwig and his comically doctrinaire interlocutor, before and after their energetic verbal jousting. Otherwise, close-ups of Sophia striking a preposterously jaunty pose in front of a red banner alternate with similarly tight shots of Wittgenstein announcing his distaste for Hegel and expressing a desire to work as a manual labourer on a collective farm. The extent of Ludwig's naïvety becomes evident when he inserts a favourable reference to Trotsky's manifesto on revolutionary art into the conversation. The irreverent tone of the protagonists' banter seems designed to irritate incorrigible Leninists, and the spirit of this sequence is close to the Situationist fusion of Surrealism and anti-Leninist Marxism discernible also in Jarman's early homage to punk, *Jubilee*. The Situationist injunction to transmute desire into reality is more congruent with Jarman's aesthetic and political creed than are sanctimonious testimonies to work and self-sacrifice. In certain respects, many of Jarman's films resemble quasi-Situationist acts of *détournement*. During the brief heyday of Situationist activism, *détournement* – which might be approximately translated as "subversion" – was a strategy designed to disrupt the equilibrium of "spectacular" society. The practice of *détournement* encompassed the defacement of billboards with graffiti, the anarchic defilement of second-rate paintings, and an overall negation of bureaucratic discourse summarized by Sadie Plant as a "gigantic turning around of the existing social world".[43] *Wittgenstein* treats both the self-contained world of Cambridge and the bureaucratic state Socialism of the Soviet Union with a strategic flippancy that never deteriorates into mere frivolousness. If Jarman lacks the militant wherewithal to subject academia and pseudo-Socialist ideology to fully-fledged *détournement*, he is certainly closer to the Situationists' anarchic subversion than to Eagleton's more orthodox political posturing.

Wittgenstein's weakness for kitschy American movies also inspires satirical digressions with autobiographical implications. Jarman punctuates his irreverent account of philosophical heterodoxy with several shots of his hero enjoying the much-derided films of Betty Hutton and Carmen Miranda. When the young Wittgenstein attends a matinee decked out in 3-D glasses while nonchalantly sucking on an "ice blue lolly", he observes that "film felt like a shower bath, washing away the lecture". The philosopher's distaste for philosophy corresponds to the filmmaker's irreverent view of filmmaking. Jarman is quite determined to make us aware of this parallel. In some epigrammatic remarks included in the published screenplay, cinéphilia is the farthest thing from his mind: "Who cares about film. Well I never did. I feel for film the same as Ludwig felt about philosophy. There are more pressing things."[44]

Although Jarman does not celebrate high art, he refuses to simplistically spurn canonical works, or hail pop culture as unproblematically emancipatory. His autobiographical writing nevertheless oscillates between nostalgic evocations of happy cinematic memories and barbed commentaries on films and actors. In fact, Jarman's jaundiced view of cinema has little to do with traditional distinctions between high culture and popular art. In *Dancing Ledge*, art is pronounced "dead, especially modern art". Jarman invokes Duchamp's Dadaist contempt for institutionalized art and proclaims that "[o]nly when art is demoted to the ranks again, treated as nothing remarkable, will our culture start to breathe".[45] On the other hand, *Modern Nature* playfully juxtaposes a discussion of Shakespeare's Sonnets and Plato's *Symposium* with a homage to male nudes culled from the pages of *Physique* magazine.[46] The productive tension embedded in all these passages is profoundly Wittgensteinian. Jarman's focus is on the specific *uses* of art, not on facile, essentialist distinctions. The contempt for "dead art" encourages an appreciation of truly vibrant art, whether canonically blessed films, literature and visual art, or ephemera traditionally reviled as schlock. In short, aesthetic valuation is nurtured by a linguistic community and its shared language games. Abstract notions of beauty muddy the waters; aesthetic judgments can only be formed with the help of specific criteria. A particular political or social impetus can lead to an appreciation of either Betty Hutton's films or Plato's *Symposium*. An appeal to causal explanations of beauty only leads to what Wittgenstein labels "aesthetic puzzlement".

Wittgenstein believed that the decipherment of aesthetic puzzles is inevitably a public, communal process. Never interested in mere textual narcissism, Jarman always sought to provoke public debate through his work. His later films, particularly *Edward II* and *Blue*, disentangle the moral and political aporias of the AIDS crisis through a critique of the political rhetoric responsible for stigmatizing AIDS sufferers and trivializing their plight. Jarman's late films – *The Garden* no less than *Edward II* – risked alienating his obvious constituency by confronting the virulence of AIDS obliquely and, more often than not, allegorically. The reinvention of Marlowe's *Edward II* includes explicit allusions to AIDS activism, but an advocacy of grass roots resistance is filtered through a surprisingly faithful rendering of Marlowe's Renaissance tragedy. Agitprop clichés are avoided, and the saccharine platitudes of narrative films devoted to the AIDS scourge are adeptly eschewed. Jarman's refusal unduly to manipulate his audience spawned *Edward II*'s two-pronged strategy: a revisionist examination of an Elizabethan play, zestfully accentuating the contemporary pertinence of its sexual politics, and the deployment of Marlowe's tragedy as a critique of Thatcherite insensitivity to the AIDS crisis. Although *Edward II* has a tighter political focus than Jarman's earlier

Elizabethan forays, *The Tempest* and *The Angelic Conversation* (1985), the film's equation of the repressive backlash against "queer Edward II" with Margaret Thatcher's anti-gay political agenda shares the gleeful love of anachronism found in the earlier films. Like *Wittgenstein*, *Edward II* employs a restrained visual style and relatively conventional editing strategies; the protagonist's tragic hedonism is rendered with unfettered simplicity.

The subtle militancy of *Edward II* stands in stark opposition to the bloated verisimilitude of many, often well-intentioned, narrative films which ineptly explicate the AIDS crisis to a wider public. Many of these banal cinematic narratives – "AIDS films" constitute a particularly ghoulish subgenre – are both aesthetic and political failures. Films such as Angela Pope's BBC film, *Sweet As You Are* (1988), Cyril Collard's *Les Nuits fauves* (*Savage Nights*, 1992) and Jonathan Demme's *Philadelphia* (1993) epitomize the phenomenon labelled the "spectacle of AIDS" by Simon Watney. Watney argues that this variant of specular moralism "reduces the 'social' to the scale of 'the family'", thus disavowing "all aspects of consensual sexual diversity".[47] Watney's critique sheds a great deal of light on the liberal melodramas of Demme and Pope, films ultimately tethered to idealised, if "progressive", family values. Similarly, despite *Savage Nights*'s pseudo-subversive veneer, Collard's film ultimately proves more conformist than liberatory.[48] Neither suburban morality plays nor hymns to self-immolation can adequately convey the nuanced view of the AIDS pandemic that Jarman provides in *Blue*.

Blue, Jarman's penultimate film (the posthumously released *Glitterbug* [1994], a retrospective inventory of out-takes and home-movies, is technically his final work) is also his most far-ranging cinematic contribution to the discourse of AIDS. *Blue* encourages a certain amount of salutary communal bafflement, since the film traverses conventional generic boundaries. *Blue* features a constant monochromatic sky-blue screen, accompanied by Jarman's text (which might be described as an autobiographical prose poem) recounting his experience with AIDS. A mixture of formal rigour and political rage, the film contains elements of both confessional cinema and the "structural film" pioneered by experimental filmmakers during the 1970s.[49] In some respects, Jarman's progression from a cluttered baroque style to a restrained minimalism resembles the path taken by the American avant-garde. Jack Smith and the Kuchar Brothers' aggressive appropriation of kitsch is not unlike the camp androgyny of *Jubilee* and *The Tempest*, while *Blue* also shares some of the preoccupation with stasis and thoroughgoing abandonment of narrative associated with the work of Hollis Frampton and Michael Snow. Nevertheless, *Blue*'s hybrid aesthetic resists this type of taxonomy; the film's language game bears only a family resemblance to superficially analogous precursors.

Blue provides an impeccable object-lesson in the indivisibility of form and content. Although it is possible to appreciate *Blue*'s soundtrack without the accompaniment of an incessant blue screen (the BBC, in fact, once broadcast the audio-track on the radio), the film's juxtaposition of a never-changing image and unobtrusive voice-over is an important component of Jarman's aesthetic strategy.[50] The complex interdependence of sound and image fuses modernist detachment with a compulsion to convert personal testimony into political practice. Much of the critical writing on modernist art celebrates its self-referentiality,[51] as well as its transcendent aspirations. Critics often discern spiritual motifs in the monochromatic canvasses of Mark Rothko, Barnet Newman, and especially Yves Klein,[52] the painter whose ultramarine paintings provided the formal impetus for *Blue*'s leap into the "wine-dark" void. Jarman's austere artistry de-spiritualizes this aspect of modernist ideology. It is impossible for the viewer to fetishize Jarman's film as pure, transcendent form.

Meyer Schapiro observes that modern artists want to be "free creators, unconfined by any goal external to art; but they wish to participate in the most advanced consciousness of their society and to influence it by their work".[53] While partially indebted to modernist tradition, *Blue* is more obviously an example of "committed art" than are the paintings of Klein, Rothko or Newman. After all, the film's monochromatic screen evokes Jarman's AIDS-induced failed eyesight more than it does some ahistorical existential void. Yet, as Schapiro demonstrates in an important essay on abstract art, modernist painting "is deeply rooted...in the self and its relation to the surrounding world".[54] From Schapiro's position, the work of Newman or Rothko is not particularly spiritual. Rather than celebrating the autonomy of the artist, he claims that "the fragility of the self" in a society that has become increasingly impersonal and governed by economic concerns "intensifies the desire of the artist to create forms that will manifest liberty in a striking way". This desire unites formal concerns and the ability "to reach out into common life". With a final – and perhaps overly optimistic – utopian flourish, Schapiro claims that modernist art can then become "a possession of everyone...related to everyday experience". Jarman's choice of a non-representational background for his mixture of lyrical reflection and often sardonic anger merges the impersonality of the best abstract art with this yearning to "reach out to common life", and to a wide public that Schapiro celebrates as the social impetus underlying the modern fondness for abstraction.

Schapiro's explanation of abstract art's significance is implicitly Wittgensteinian. Although canvasses suffused with solid blocks of colour would have seemed absurd in previous centuries, Schapiro explains how a new language game is best understood *contextually*. Mark Rothko's and Yves Klein's stark paintings speak directly to the reified nature of contemporary life. Despite radically divergent aesthetic approaches, both *Wittgenstein* and *Blue* delineate the contours of a modernist, permeable self. Wittgenstein's conviction that "[e]thics and aesthetics are one and the same"[55] seems partially designed to alleviate the alienation and sheer confusion endemic to modern life. *Blue*'s rejection of artifice is an aesthetic decision inspired by specific political and ethical criteria: a determination to bypass the "spectacle of AIDS" by avoiding melodramatic contrivance.

The typically modernist avoidance of narrative contrivance is often infused with what P Adams Sitney terms "the antinomy of vision". Sitney believes that "[m]odernist literary and cinematic works stress vision as a privileged mode of perception, even of revelation, while at the same time cultivating opacity and questioning the primacy of the visible world".[56] Jarman's film is an archetypal example of this schism, despite the fact that *Blue* is not as unadulterated in its modernism as the works by Mallarmé, Stein and Blanchot discussed by Sitney. *Blue* alternates between secular illumination – the blue screen as a collective shroud[57] capable of conveying the particularity of one community's experience – and a despairing "cultivation of opacity". Colour itself – the almost inexhaustible connotations of the colour blue – becomes the vehicle for both reverie and melancholy. Jarman's meditations on colour in *Chroma* demonstrate how the filmmaker was fascinated both by the Proustian mnemonics of colour, and by the more philosophical issues raised by works such as Goethe's *Zur Farbenlehre* (*Theory of Colours*, 1810) and Wittgenstein's *Bemerkungen über die Farben* (*Remarks on Colour*, 1951).

Wittgenstein believed that the language used to describe our understanding of colour was "essentially anthropocentric, and the existence of a colour language depends upon agreement in response to paradigms".[58] Inventively taking advantage of our deeply entrenched colour paradigms, the novelist William Gass's *On Being Blue: A Philosophical Inquiry* (1976) wittily assembles the hoariest clichéd emotions aligned with our experience of the colour blue. Gass's playful treatise regales us with both the erotic and melancholy sensations engendered by feeling blue.[59] Yet, Jarman's *Blue*, despite a limited indebtedness to modernist detachment, is not fuelled by the same dispassionate sensibility – an above-the-fray mandarinism – underlying Gass's tribute to Picasso's "blue period" and Wallace Stevens's "The Man With the Blue Guitar".

Blue's soundtrack also defies easy categorisation. It does not as much augment the image as offer another variety of "blueness" in the form of noise, music and voice-over narration. Simon Fisher Turner's music, a haunting mixture of tinkling glockenspiel, choral interludes and poignant silence, is not "commentative" or supplementary. The music calls little attention to itself, and occasionally is mixed with additional ambient sounds. Although the text is written by Jarman, his own voice alternates with the voices of fellow narrators, Nigel Terry, John Quentin and Tilda Swinton.[60] Jarman's willingness to appear as an unidentified, disembodied voice prevents *Blue* from resembling Romantic paeans to omnipotent selfhood. Jarman's film is a complex tapestry of sounds, an aural montage in which private reflection is dialogically linked with matters of unquestionably public import.

This dialogue between the most intimate confessional ruminations and matters of grave public concern again poses the question of the generic status of *Blue*. Can the film be considered "autobiographical", despite the fact that it is also partially a political *cri de cœur* and a stream-of-consciousness meditation on mortality?[61] Wittgenstein's legacy has made us aware of the fact that what Clifford Geertz terms "blurred genres"[62] are now the rule, not the exception. Wittgenstein's own work often seems to be poetry masquerading as philosophy, and Jarman's own films syncretically merge theatre, painting, mock-pageant and performance art. No longer can an autobiographical work trumpet its transparency – its willingness to tell all – with the confidence evinced by Rousseau in his *Les Confessions* (*Confessions*, 1782-89).[63] It matters little whether or not a writer or a filmmaker is willing to confess all; the formal requirements of encapsulating a life within art mitigate against undiluted honesty.[64] Jarman was certainly not reticent about his personal life. Yet, *Blue* has inevitable affinities with far more duplicitous or self-aggrandising confessional works. Like Norman Mailer's *The Armies of the Night* (1968) or Wim Wenders's *Lightning Over Water* (1980), it contains equal amounts of self-revelation and self-obfuscation. *Blue*'s confessional strategy, however, has nothing to do with dishonesty or bogus self-effacement. It is the product of Jarman's desire to express his friends' and colleagues' anguish, as well as his own.

Yet, *Blue* is not exclusively a lamentation for the dead and dying; the film is animated by a militant rage against the dying of the light. Jarman's relentless account of his medical regimen and intermittent suicidal urges are pertinent to an entire community's plight. And Jarman, like Wittgenstein, realises that experiential and political conundrums are usually rooted in linguistic problems. This realisation is sometimes expressed with astringent irony. At one point, the possible side-effects of the AIDS drug, DHPG – a macabre and absurd litany of life-threatening ailments – are enumerated with a mixture of deadpan sardonicism and frank exasperation. The impoverished, depersonalised language of medical discourse illustrates the marginalized status of AIDS patients more forcefully than many sober pamphlets or long-winded panel discussions.

The furiously clotted impasto of Jarman's late paintings springs from a less ironised, modulated rage.[65] These paintings never offer us even the misleading serenity of oceanic blue. The fiery red and flaming yellow splotches of paint evoke images of blood and urine, and are often accompanied by a single accusatory word such as "queer", "sick" or "AIDS". Although the aggressive application of paint bears a superficial resemblance to Jackson Pollock's drip paintings, these are "action paintings"[66] of a decidedly different stripe. In a parallel vein, Jarman's memoir, *At Your Own Risk: A Saint's Testament* (1992), moves inexorably from reminiscences of sexual awakening to impassioned denunciations of the tabloid press's scurrilous treatment of the AIDS crisis.

Jarman's paintings, his memoirs, and *Blue*'s mournful indictment all attempt to represent the fundamentally "unrepresentable" scourge of AIDS. In a manner analogous to poet Paul Celan's evocation of the Holocaust with "a purpose beyond stoic lucidity of vision",[67] Jarman endeavours to suggest the psychic and physical consequences of AIDS – despite the near-impossibility of accurately representing its enormity. The category of the sublime, especially as formulated by Immanuel Kant, remains one of the most influential attempts to explain the function and lure of unrepresentablity for artists and audiences. The French philosopher, Jean-François Lyotard, also known for championing Wittgenstein's work, has spearheaded a revival of interest in the Kantian sublime. Although Kant's masterpiece, *Kritik der Urteilskraft* (*Critique of Judgement*, 1790), is usually seen as the high-watermark of 18th century aesthetic idealism – and Romanticism – his work anticipates some elements of Wittgenstein's stance, since he believed that aesthetic judgments necessarily entail the participation of a linguistic community – "a *sensis communis*".[68] Although Lyotard's equation of modern and, above all, postmodern art with the sublime is marred by a tendency to indulge in sweeping and often politically suspect generalisations, there is an important point of conjuncture between his exegesis of Kant and Jarman's *Blue*. Lyotard hails Kant's citation of the Biblical commandment forbidding the production of graven images as the key to understanding *Critique of Judgement*'s elucidation of sublimity. This prohibition lays the groundwork for the sublime's negative pleasure, engendered by the negative presentation without "figuration or representation".[69] Jarman's own allusion to the Old Testament injunction grapples with the formidable difficulty, but urgent necessity, of formulating an aesthetic response to the virulence of AIDS:

These facts, detached from cause, trapped the Blue Eyed Boy in a system of unreality. Would all these blurred facts that deceive dissolve in his last breath? For accustomed to believing in image, an absolute idea of value, his world had forgotten the command of essence: Thou Shall Not Create Unto Thyself Any Graven Image, although you know the task is to fill the empty page.[70]

Blue's image-track eschews the clutter of figuration, while forsaking modernist art's supposed formal "purity". The compulsion to strip away artifice does not negate the need "to fill the empty page", the desire to fathom the unfathomable.

Whether bracingly flamboyant or rigorously austere, all Jarman's films are prismatic expressions of his own identity. *Wittgenstein* and *Blue* are the most ascetic products of Jarman's fictive self. These films sum up the career of a director who never made concessions to popular taste, but who refused to be relegated to the realm of hermetic "avant-gardism". The final elegiac lines of *Blue* ("Our life will pass like the traces of a cloud...And our lives will run like/Sparks through the stubble/I place a delphinium, Blue, upon your grave)[71] are in the vein of Prospero's farewell speech in *The Tempest*, even if *Blue*'s spare sublimity stands in stark opposition to Jarman's triumphantly florid adaptation of Shakespeare's play. Towards the end of his life, Michel Foucault claimed that "the principal work of art which one has to take care of...is oneself, one's own existence".[72] Derek Jarman's career stands as an exemplary tribute to Foucault's "care of the self" – a concept that paradoxically bridges the gap between dandyism and asceticism. *Wittgenstein* and *Blue* do not reject the early films' refurbished dandyism. They merely chronicle Jarman's attentive cultivation of his self and his art during the dark, dishonest days of the last decade.

* * *

I would like to thank Zeitgeist Films for lending tapes of *Wittgenstein* and *Blue*.

Notes

[1]   See Matei Calinescu, *Five Faces of Modernity: Modernism, Avant-Garde, Decadence, Kitsch, Postmodernism* (Durham, NC: Duke University Press, 1987). The impossibility of reducing Jarman's work to a single rubric points to the tentativeness and, at times, inadequacy of the concepts employed by Calinescu.

[2]   Arthur C Danto, *The Transfiguration of the Commonplace: A Philosophy of Art* (Cambridge, MA; London: Harvard University Press, 1981): 58.

[3]   For a fuller discussion of Jarman's dislike of mainstream British cinema, and his affection for directors such as Pasolini and Powell, see Derek Jarman, *Dancing Ledge*, edited by Shaun Allen (London; New York: Quartet Books, 1984). Jarman's disdain for polished commercial cinema also recalls the artisanship practised in a pre-cinematic era by antinomian British figures, most notably William Blake and William Morris. The late historian E P Thompson's books on Blake and Morris persuasively present the visionary poet and the much-misunderstood Pre-Raphaelite as important precursors of contemporary radical dissenters. Thompson's discussion of Blake's antinomianism – the "mistrust of 'reason', the acceptance of 'energy' and sexuality" – could easily apply to contemporary heretics such as Jarman. See E P Thompson, *Witness Against the Beast: William Blake and the Moral Law* (New York: The New Press, 1993): 20. See also Thompson's *William Morris: Romantic to Revolutionary* (London: Lawrence & Wishart, 1955). See Lawrence Driscoll's essay in this volume for more about Jarman's place in a British dissident tradition.

[4]   For an extensive discussion of *fin de siècle* sexual preoccupations, see Elaine Showalter, *Sexual Anarchy: Gender and Culture at the* Fin de Siècle (New York: Viking, 1990).

[5]   "Overripeness" should not be considered as a pejorative. Richard Gilman recounts how "overripeness" was precisely what Théophile Gautier "found so arresting in ancient societies during their decline". Gilman writes of the so-called "Decadents'" fascination with the "greater imaginative size of the ancient world, its sensual vigor and capacity for extreme pleasures". The Graeco-Roman world was admired for its "violent splendors...life closer to the bone". This type of violent splendour was also prized by Jarman. See Richard Gilman, *Decadence: The Strange Life of an Epithet* (London: Secker & Warburg, 1979): 92-93.

[6]   This quotation is from a brief text included in the published script of *Wittgenstein*. Jarman's terse, epigrammatic style mimics Wittgenstein's own work. See Terry Eagleton and Derek Jarman, *Wittgenstein: The Terry Eagleton Script/The Derek Jarman Film* (London: British Film Institute, 1993): 67.

[7]   The term "gay modernist" is used by Thomas Yingling in "Wittgenstein's Tumour: AIDS and the National Body", *Textual Practice* 8: 1 (1994): 97. Wittgenstein himself certainly would not have been fond of this term.

[8]   See Allan Janik and Stephen Toulmin, *Wittgenstein's Vienna* (New York: Simon and Schuster, 1973): especially 93-102.

[9]   "What we cannot speak about we must pass over in silence" is the famous last sentence of the *Tractatus*. See Ludwig Wittgenstein, *Tractatus Logico-Philosophicus*, translated by D F Pears and B F McGuinness (London: Routledge & Kegan Paul, 1961): 74.

[10]   In an otherwise informative study of Wilde, the critic George Woodcock

makes a facile distinction between Wilde's aestheticism and his commitment to social change. Yet, for both Jarman and Wilde, aestheticism – according to Alan Sinfield, a code word for homosexuality – is inseparable from a larger social and political agenda. See George Woodcock, *Oscar Wilde: The Double Image* (Montreal; New York: Black Rose Books, 1989). See also Alan Sinfield, *The Wilde Century: Effeminacy, Oscar Wilde and the Queer Moment* (London; New York: Cassell, 1994): 84-108.

[11] Oscar Wilde, "The Truth of Masks", in Oscar Wilde, *The Soul of Man under Socialism and Other Essays* (New York: Evanston; London: Harper and Row, 1970): 29.

[12] Albrecht Wellmer, paraphrasing Wittgenstein's discussion of language games. Like Jürgen Habermas, Wellmer combines Anglo-American linguistic philosophy with the neo-Marxist methodology pioneered by the Frankfurt School. See Albrecht Wellmer, *The Persistence of Modernity: Essays on Aesthetics, Ethics, and Postmodernism* (Cambridge, MA: The MIT Press, 1991): 66.

[13] Ludwig Wittgenstein, *Philosophical Investigations*, translated by G E M Anscombe (New York: Macmillan Publishing Company, 1953): 94-97.

[14] Ibid: 6.

[15] Ludwig Wittgenstein, in Cyril Barrett (ed), *Lectures and Conversations on Aesthetics, Psychology & Religious Belief* (Berkeley; Los Angeles: University of California Press, 1970): 1.

[16] See Anthony Kenny's elegant discussion of language games in *Wittgenstein* (Cambridge, MA: Harvard University Press, 1973): 163. The most extensive discussion of Wittgenstein's notion of family resemblance appears in the notes for *Philosophical Investigations*, *The Blue and Brown Books* (New York, London: Harper Colophon, 1965): 17, 81. Marjorie Perloff christens Wittgenstein's work an "assemblage of ironic fables", and likens his provisional, continually fluctuating definition of "language games" to the work of postmodern novelists such as Georges Perec and Lyn Hejinian. Perloff also makes analogies between Wittgenstein's philosophical approach and the more recent work of Stanley Fish and Pierre Bourdieu. See Marjorie Perloff, "From Theory to Grammar: Wittgenstein and the Aesthetic of the Ordinary", *New Literary History* 25: 4 (1994): 899-923.

[17] The implications of this neologism are fleshed out in Jarman's memoir, *At Your Own Risk: A Saint's Testament* (London: Hutchinson, 1992). The significance of what Jarman considers heterosexual society's – "Heterosoc's" – ideological hegemony is filtered through a series of autobiographical ruminations.

[18] George F Custen, *Bio/Pics: How Hollywood Constructed Public History* (New Brunswick, NJ: Rutgers University Press, 1992): 176.

[19] Eagleton and Jarman: 130-132.

[20] In the only reference to Johns of which I am aware, Jarman facetiously

remarks that "Jasper Johns covered the walls of every gallery in the 'free' world with the stars and stripes" – an obvious reference to this painter's pop art appropriation of the American flag. See Jarman (1984): 62. Yet, Peter Wollen links Johns to Andy Warhol, an artist for whom Jarman had considerably more respect. Wollen remarks that, like Warhol, Rauschenberg and Johns were "gay artists who came from art-starved provincial backgrounds", who also offered alternatives to the "straight, macho posturing" of the previous generation. See Peter Wollen, "Notes from the Underground: Andy Warhol", in *Raiding the Icebox: Reflections on Twentieth-Century Culture* (Bloomington and Indianapolis: Indiana University Press, 1993): 159-160.

21   *Chroma: A Book of Colour – June '93* (London: Century, 1994).

22   Jarman, quoted in Roy Grundmann, "History and the Gay Viewfinder: An Interview with Derek Jarman", *Cineaste* 18: 4 (1991): 26.

23   Eve Kosofsky Sedgwick, *Epistemology of the Closet* (Berkeley; Los Angeles: University of California Press, 1993): 75.

24   Bernhard's starkly brilliant novel is in the form of a long monologue delivered by a Wittgenstein-like protagonist named Roithamer, whose main preoccupation is an austere house, referred to as the "Cone", that he is building for his sister. Wittgenstein, himself an amateur architect, did actually design a house (referred to as the *Kundmanngasse*) commissioned by his sister. See Thomas Bernhard, *Correction*, translated by Sophie Wilkins (Chicago: University of Chicago Press, 1978). See also Paul Wijdeveld, *Ludwig Wittgenstein, Architect* (Cambridge, MA: The MIT Press, 1994). Stoppard's comic play, mixing erudition with slapstick, is completely different in tone. See Tom Stoppard, *Jumpers* (New York: Grove Weidenfield, 1972). See also Bruce Duffy's *The World As I Found It* (New York: Ticknor and Fields, 1967), for an intriguing fictionalization of the intertwined lives of Wittgenstein, Moore and Russell.

25   Eagleton and Jarman: 64.

26   Monk's remark appears in an appendix to his biography of Wittgenstein, by far the best life of the philosopher. Monk documents Wittgenstein's homosexuality, but refutes W W Bartley's thesis that "coded remarks" in Wittgenstein's papers confirm a guilty enjoyment of anonymous gay sex in Vienna during 1919-29. See Ray Monk, *Ludwig Wittgenstein: The Duty of Genius* (New York: The Free Press, 1990): 581-586. Wittgenstein's homosexuality also inspired a controversy some years ago in the pages of the journal *Telos*, after Albert William Levi insisted that Wittgenstein's guilt over his homosexuality could be linked to the supposedly "repugnant character" of his ethical thought. For a sampling of this controversy, see Levi's original article, "The Biographical Sources of Wittgenstein's Ethics", *Telos* 38 (winter 1978-79): 63-76, and Allan Janik's reply, "Philosophical Sources of Wittgenstein's Ethics", *Telos* 44 (summer 1980): 131-144.

27   Eagleton and Jarman: 2. MacCabe's remark appears in his preface to the published screenplays.

28 Wittgenstein (1953): 192-196.

29 See Cole Gagne, "Britain's Jarman unveils portrait of Wittgenstein", *Film Journal* 96: 9 (October/November 1993): 18.

30 *Modern Nature: The Journals of Derek Jarman* (London: Century, 1991): 50.

31 Quoted in Denis Donoghue, *Walter Pater: Lover of Strange Souls* (New York: Alfred A Knopf, 1995): 47.

32 Geoffrey Galt Harpham, *The Ascetic Imperative in Culture and Criticism* (Chicago; London: University of Chicago Press, 1988): 20-21.

33 The Cambridge Apostles, founded in 1820, was a group of philosophers who, together with young male acolytes, met to discuss ethical, aesthetic and religious issues. For more information on Moore, Wittgenstein and the Apostles, see Paul Levy, *Moore: G. E. Moore and the Cambridge Apostles* (New York: Holt, Rinehart and Winston, 1979).

34 Michael Holroyd, *Lytton Strachey: The New Biography* (New York: Farrar, Straus & Giroux, 1994): 272-275. Strachey's bisexuality is also discussed in Marjorie Garber, *Vice Versa: Bisexuality and the Eroticism of Everyday Life* (New York: Simon and Schuster, 1995): 105-111.

35 Eagleton and Jarman: 142.

36 Quoted in Monk: 269.

37 A recent article argues the case that *The Measures Taken*'s ostensible Stalinism is irrelevant and a Cold War smear. I am not convinced by this interpretation, and do not think that anti-Stalinism should be equated with anti-leftism. See Peter W Ferran, "New Measures for Brecht in America", *Theater* 25: 2 (1994): 9-23.

38 In Eagleton's view, "[w]here Wittgenstein's philosophy is reactionary is not in its referring of beliefs and discourses to social activity, but in its assumption that such referring constitutes a liberation from the metaphysical". See Terry Eagleton, *Against the Grain: Essays 1975-1985* (London; New York: Verso, 1986): 107.

39 Quoted in Peter Bowen, "In the Company of Saints: Derek Jarman's *Wittgenstein* and Beyond", *Filmmaker* 2: 1 (1993): 19.

40 In a rather unnuanced fashion, Eagleton claims that "[p]olitically speaking, Wittgenstein was for the most part a reactionary remnant of the Austro-Hungarian Empire". Although Wittgenstein was certainly a politically confused individual, Eagleton's conclusion seems slightly glib. See Eagleton and Jarman: 11.

41 Eagleton sardonically concludes that Wittgenstein allows us to possess "the flattering knowledge that we are consequently in on the deepest conceivable mystery". See Terry Eagleton, *The Ideology of the Aesthetic* (Oxford: Basil Blackwell, 1990): 312.

42   Perry Anderson, *English Questions* (New York; London: Verso, 1992): 86.

43   Sadie Plant, *The Most Radical Gesture: The Situationist International in a postmodern age* (London; New York: Routledge, 1992): 89. The Situationist International, which combined elements of anti-Leninist Marxism, anarchism and Surrealism, lasted from 1957 until 1969. The Situationists are perhaps best known for their influential role during the insurrectionary events of May 1968. In addition, one of their leading theorists, Guy Debord, published the still-influential *La Société du spectacle* (*Society of the Spectacle*) in 1967. See also Greil Marcus, *Lipstick Traces: A Secret History of the Twentieth Century* (London: Secker & Warburg, 1989).

44   Eagleton and Jarman: 66.

45   Jarman (1984): 235.

46   Jarman believes that "[t]he *Sonnets* and the *Symposium* are a cultural condom protecting us against the virus of the yellow press. They also relocate the way we view the old photos from...*Physique* magazine." See Jarman (1991): 163-164.

47   Simon Watney, *Practices of Freedom: Selected Writings on HIV/AIDS* (Durham, NC: Duke University Press, 1994): 55.

48   For a spirited denunciation of *Savage Nights*, see Howard Feinstein's review in *Cineaste* (20: 4 [1994]: 50-51). Theatrical, art world, cinematic and televisual responses to AIDS are discussed in Edmund White, "Esthetics and Loss", in *The Burning Library: Writings on Art, Politics and Sexuality 1969-1993* (New York: Alfred A Knopf, 1995): 211-217. Jarman explicitly attacks the rhetoric of "living with AIDS" in *Blue*. Kermit Cole's well-meaning documentary, *Living Proof: HIV and the Pursuit of Happiness* (1993), rather simplistically replicates this rhetoric by featuring exceptionally cheery AIDS survivors.

49   For D N Rodowick, the British structural filmmaker, Peter Gidal, adheres to an "ascetic ideal". Gidal's contempt for narrative is an example of cinematic Puritanism. Compared to his films, even Snow's work seems baroque. See D N Rodowick, *The Crisis of Political Modernism: Criticism and Ideology in Contemporary Film Theory* (Urbana; Chicago: University of Illinois Press, 1988): 126-143.

50   Chris Darke compared Jarman's cinematic modus operandi to "the old Brechtian idea of 'separation of the elements'". See Darke's review in *Sight and Sound* 3: 10 (October 1993): 41.

51   Many enthusiasts of modernist painting consider the self-referential aspect of the art especially distinctive and ground-breaking. Clement Greenberg, for example, identifies modernism with "this self-critical tendency that began with the philosopher Kant". He argues that "[t]he essence of Modernism lies...in the use of the characteristic methods of a discipline to criticize the discipline itself". See Clement Greenberg, "Modernist Painting", in Charles Harrison and Paul Wood (eds), *Art in Theory 1900-1990: An Anthology of Changing Ideas* (Oxford: Basil

Blackwell, 1992): 754-755. Rosalind Krauss, once a disciple of Greenberg, has been severely critical of her former mentor and of his vaunted desire for aesthetic purity. See, for example, Krauss's *The Optical Unconscious* (Cambridge, MA; London: The MIT Press, 1993): 98-107.

[52] Spiritual concerns were frequently emphasised by the artists themselves. Mark Rothko, for example, claimed that "[t]he most important tool the artist fashions through constant practice is faith in his ability to produce miracles when they are needed...Pictures must be miraculous...[and reveal] an unexpected and unprecedented resolution of an eternally familiar need". See Rothko's statement, "The Romantics were Prompted...", in Harrison and Wood (eds): 563-564. Klein was an unorthodox Christian and thought that "through color...little by little" we will "become acquainted with the Immaterial". See "Sorbonne Lecture", in Harrison and Wood (eds): 803-805.

[53] Meyer Schapiro, *Theory and Philosophy of Art: Style, Artist, and Society: Selected Papers, volume 4* (New York: George Braziller, 1994): 207.

[54] Meyer Schapiro, *Modern Art, 19th and 20th Centuries: Selected Papers, volume 2* (New York: George Braziller, 1978): 222.

[55] Wittgenstein (1961): 71.

[56] P Adams Sitney, *Modernist Montage: The Obscurity of Vision In Cinema and Literature* (New York: Columbia University Press, 1990): 2. The critique of the "hegemony of vision" or "anti-occularcentric thought" is the subject of a recent study by Martin Jay, *Downcast Eyes: The Denigration of Vision in Twentieth-Century French Thought* (Berkeley; Los Angeles: University of California Press, 1993).

[57] Annette Michelson describes Dziga Vertov's *Tri pesni Lenina* (*Three Songs of Lenin*, 1934) as "a kinetic icon in the work of mourning". Although Jarman's film practice has little in common with that of Vertov, this phrase is particularly applicable to the concerns of *Blue*. See Annette Michelson, "The Kinetic Icon in the Work of Mourning: Prolegomena to the Analysis of a Textual System", *October* 52 (spring 1990): 17-38.

[58] This is P M S Hacker's interpretation. See his *Insight and Illusion: Wittgenstein on Philosophy and the Metaphysics of Experience* (London; Oxford: Oxford University Press, 1972): 298.

[59] William Gass, *On Being Blue: A Philosophical Inquiry* (Boston: David R Godine, 1978).

[60] For Michel Chion, voice-over commentary, or "textual speech", has the ability "to make visible the images that it evokes through sound – that is, to change the setting, to call up a thing, moment, place, or characters at will". He is at pains to demonstrate that since, in narrative cinema, textual speech has "great power", its use is usually "reserved for certain privileged characters and is only granted for a limited time". It might be interesting to apply Chion's observations to *Blue*'s radically different use of voice-over. See Michel Chion, *Audio-Vision: Sound on Screen*, edited and translated by Claudia Gorbman (New York: Columbia University Press, 1994): 172.

[61] In an essay on gay fiction, Edmund White isolates the "autobiographical urge" as the "site where two codes – the realistic and the spiritual – have crossed". White elaborates on this formulation by maintaining that gay fiction "embodies the continuing documentary realistic ambitions of the realistic novel", but also "participates just as actively in a very different tradition – the confession, which is by its very nature religious and exemplary". Like some of the authors whom White cites – John Rechy, Samuel R Delany and Jean Genet – Jarman's work synthesizes these two modes. See Edmund White, "On Gay Fiction", *London Review of Books* 17: 5 (9 March 1995): 6-9.

[62] See Clifford Geertz, *Local Knowledge* (New York: Basic Books, 1983): 20-35.

[63] Jean Starobinski formulated an influential distinction between Rousseau's "transparency", and his predilection for "obstructing" his own confessional desires. See Jean Starobinksi, *Jean-Jacques Rousseau: Transparency and Obstruction* (Chicago; London: University of Chicago Press, 1988): especially 180-200.

[64] For more on Jarman's use of the life-span as an artistic frame, see Tracy Biga's essay in this volume.

[65] An exhibition catalogue featuring these paintings also contains useful essays by Stuart Morgan, Andrew Renton and Simon Watney. See Derek Jarman, *Queer* (Manchester City Art Galleries in association with Richard Salmon Ltd., 1992).

[66] The art critic Harold Rosenberg coined the term "action painting" to describe the genre created by certain Abstract Expressionist painters. Rosenberg was particularly fond of Jackson Pollock's drip paintings. See Harold Rosenberg, "The American Action Painters", in Harrison and Wood (eds): 581-584.

[67] Charles Taylor, *Sources of the Self: The Making of the Modern Identity* (Cambridge, MA: Harvard University Press, 1989): 485. Taylor, an influential philosopher, argues that certain modernist works can be termed "counter-epiphanies". Taylor maintains that Celan's "resolute turning away from the lived, from a poetry of the self, bespeaks an extreme denuding, a stripping down of language" (486). *Blue* could be termed "counter-epiphanic".

[68] Kant's ideal of a *sensis communis* is discussed in Geoffrey Bennington, *Lyotard: Writing the Event* (New York: Columbia University Press, 1988): 165-169.

[69] Jean-François Lyotard, *The Postmodern Condition: A Report on Knowledge*, translated by Geoff Bennington and Brian Massumi (Minneapolis: University of Minnesota Press, 1984): 78.

[70] Derek Jarman, *Blue: Text of a film by Derek Jarman* (London: Channel 4 Television and BBC Radio 3, 1993): 15.

[71] Ibid: 30.

[72] See Michel Foucault, "What Is Enlightenment?", in Paul Rabinow (ed), *The Foucault Reader* (New York: Pantheon Books, 1984): 41.

Interview with Derek Jarman

Chris Lippard

Interview conducted by telephone, November 1993.

Let me start by asking about what seems to me to be a central paradox in your work. Your films seem to show an intense interest in Englishness – so much so that I think one could make a case for your being, in some ways, the most English of filmmakers – while you are obviously also vastly critical of a repressive and homophobic (what you refer to as "Heterosoc") atmosphere in England. You write in At Your Own Risk *about how England is a true Sodom because of its lack of hospitality. Do you see a tension between being a British filmmaker specifically and the things you are trying to achieve as a filmmaker?*

Not particularly. I suppose that all filmmakers would react to their immediate surroundings, wherever they were. I think that's the natural reaction. I never wanted to move from here: looking at it practically, I've always been quite happy in London. I've never thought I wanted to travel to LA or anywhere else really, because everything that I needed was here. I could do whatever I wanted to do, partly because the scale of the operation is quite small. Compared to what I call normal films, it is very small. There are just a few of us really, myself and a few friends. I feel that would be impossible to carry over, for example, to the States. I don't think it would be possible to have kept that together. It was my great luck, I think, in some ways, that I never really had a success in America, the kind of financial success that would have pushed me into the position of a lot of other filmmakers who have to make a decision whether they work and where. I've avoided that one.

And do you think that would have been a temptation?

No, not a temptation at all. It never went through my mind. But, looking back on it, that chance never happened for me.

Staying with this idea of Englishness for a moment, do you feel that your films are very tied to the English landscape? It seems to me that many of your films appear nostalgic for some kind of a lost landscape.

Yes, that's right. I mean, it could be as simple as the loss of the flower meadows of my childhood. I think that it would be very odd for anyone, as they grow older, not to be conservative, in the sense that I am. I'm not talking politically, of course, but the fact is that you see things disappear which you like and other things appear – which are good, but there is some element of nostalgia.

And that is something which you try to use, for example, in The Last of England *[1987].*

I suspect it is behind *The Last of England*, even if it's not really seen; it's lurking there. I didn't consciously make use of that nostalgia; I have to say I'm a very unconscious filmmaker. I don't have any plans or plots, or anything. I just do more or less what comes off the top of my head, so it was not that I was acting consciously. It is just part and parcel of the business of living here, I suspect. It's not possible for me to avoid some of these things. I don't actually buckle down and say, what am I going to do about this or that or the other.

I imagine that, making films on a relatively small budget, as you have done, the settings become crucial. I remember reading, for example, about your search for the hospital for War Requiem *[1988].*

You're quite right. The settings become absolutely crucial. Sometimes it's almost the first thing you have to get sorted out, because you have to get stuck into one place. For instance, when we made *War Requiem* we made it in two coal cellars which, when you see the film, is hard to believe. They weren't that big either, they were quite small coal cellars. But once we were in there, everything could be done, it was like a little studio. I think that, in a way, it is easier to make studio-based films, with a low budget, simply because you can keep them under some sort of control, but if you start to hit the streets you have problems with, for example, weather, particularly in England. Everything can go haywire. The one thing that I try to do is make certain that the production runs smoothly, because it is ghastly for everyone if they are all out of sync, and some areas start to jostle other areas and make a nuisance of themselves. So setting has been very instrumental. If you look at my films, they all have very simple locations: *Jubilee* [1978] was in my studio and *The Tempest* [1979] in Stoneleigh Abbey.

All the films that were shot on location have a very distinct sense of place, so that when I think of these films I have a picture – of, say, the house of The Angelic Conversation *(1985), or the docks in* The Last of England.

Conversation was really improvised, in the sense that we just took off with the car and the Super 8 camera, and went to places that I'd really liked in my life, like Montacute, and the Dorset coast. It was a way of returning to those places which were quite beautiful and filming [there]. In a sense that film is one where we did take a risk, but then it was in Super 8, so it wasn't a risk *per se*. Because the risk, of course, is in using 35mm. Super 8 is very free and easy. The 35mm work – for me, in any case – is much more plotted out. I think you can see that in the films.

Certainly. Do you think that you have largely exhausted the kind of things that you wanted to do with the Super 8 camera?

Yes, I did that years ago. You can't go any further. You can do it in a different way, but those films went as far as they could go and I became more interested in the formal aspects again, as in *Wittgenstein* and in *Edward II* [1991]; it became more interesting to deal with those problems. It was very useful at the time because it was no bother to get funding, but it was very simple to get the money for them. We got it from Germany, from ZDF, and, quite honestly, without the Super 8 camera I wouldn't have been working. It enabled me to work at a time in which it was quite difficult to get funding.

So, in the latest historical films that you have made, Edward II *and* Wittgenstein *[1993], where you adopt a more conventional narrative, you have also moved into the studio.*

Yes, and they are definitely much more integrated into what I would call traditional film history.

Is it inevitable, when you use that sort of narrative, that you also break from your earlier, looser editing style?

Yes, the whole thing is completely different. You start off one way, and you end that way. Using 35mm, you get these quite formal films – at least when I'm doing them, they tend to be. I'm certain you could loosen it up, but you'd have to have resources and time, which one doesn't have. I mean, the budget is always so small for all the films. I could always say, and I expect it's true, that for any year, if I made a film, it was the cheapest film made in England in that year. There were never the resources for going out and spending time in landscapes.

Clearly, the lack of financial resources is one thing that has influenced the way you have presented historical figures on the screen. Often there seems to be a slippage between a sort of authenticity, which you appeal to in some ways, and a clear disavowal of that in others: putting a motor bike in Caravaggio *[1986], for instance, and a frisbee in* Sebastiane *[1976], and there are many examples in* Edward II. *Is there one thing that you think is the most important in representing historical periods – perhaps the costume or the voice or the décor?*

I was lucky because I was at university doing history and art history. I had a very heavy academic upbringing. It left me free to make all those leaps. You don't actually look at *Caravaggio* and think – unless I deliberately made it funny on the typewriter – "Oh God, this is out of sync, out of kilter". It was just that I had this background which enabled me to dispense with certain concerns. It was a huge advantage. I would see other people attempting to do the same thing but they didn't have enough grounding; they couldn't take the leaps that you needed, say, to set *Edward II* now, or *Caravaggio* in the 1940s. That was partly this academic background. At the time I didn't understand why I was at university, but it actually paid back.

So it enabled you to make those historical linkages and to see how the past comments on the present?

Yes, that's what interests me. I looked at historical films and they always bored me to tears, all of them. They were always so badly designed – at least the English ones were. They looked awful. The costumes were made badly, and you knew perfectly well the 18th century wasn't like that, or the Middle Ages, and so one was *forced* into believing. Of course, I suspect quite a lot of the audience, lacking the knowledge, did go along with things but I'm afraid I had it and I saw through all these films and they didn't work. I wanted to find some sort of bedrock for *Caravaggio* that would work in cinematic terms. That's the reason for updating things.

Do you see yourself as changing your approach as the historical films progress? Does Edward II *represent a different approach, or is it further along the same continuum?*

It is part of a continuum really. Obviously each project enables you to go into slightly different areas, just by the nature of it. But I don't feel that I had a plan through which I was progressing. In fact, I never really believed in progression.

Your recent films have been well received by critics. Writing – very favourably – about Edward II *in* Sight and Sound, Colin MacCabe *suggests that it achieves a more completely successful presentation of the connections between the past and present than your earlier films. Perhaps those connections are a little more direct in that film, although the connections MacCabe draws are more to the age of Elizabeth, and Marlowe, and Walsingham than to Edward's time. Did you see the film as a three-way bridge between medieval, Elizabethan and contemporary England.*

I did. We discussed that quite a lot. Where does this film land, as it were? Is this a medieval film or is it an Elizabethan film, or is it set in the modern times? Christopher [Hobbs] and I designed the film for each of the periods. First of all, we tried it in medieval. We made lots of drawings. And then we tried it in Elizabethan with a little bit of medieval thrown in: it was a sort of an amalgam. Then in the end I was talking to Ken [Butler], who was the assistant director, about this problem and he said "why don't you set it in modern day". We didn't plump for the modern just like that. We went through quite a process before ending up with his suggestion that we should just forget the problem by setting it in modern. As I say, there had been no particular plan to modernise. I've seen so few films that I think are well done historically. There is a great Swedish film called *My Sister, My Love* [*Syskonbädd 1782*, 1966], by [Vilgot] Sjöman, set in the 18th century; it is really one of the best historical films I ever saw. Wonderfully done.

What makes it so good?

I'm not sure. It's the costuming, the way people are actually *living* in the film. It is not just modern actors playing parts; somehow he managed to translate them into that time: their reactions, the way they walk...all from the 18th century. When you see this you realise the potential of actually doing films historically. But I don't think we could have done *Edward II*, for example, like that. We didn't have the resources. I don't know how one would have even begun to cope with the wardrobe. Another imperative in all of this was just the sheer cost. I always said the budget was the aesthetic.

Would you say that Edward II, *or any of your historically set films, primarily gives us greater access to the past, or does a new view of the past illuminate the present?*

I don't really know. Both elements are there, I would have thought. It just seems to me that *Edward II* was such a good modern story. It didn't strike me again as being out of place to be set like that, and I never liked modern dress versions of things. I always thought they were ghastly. But somehow, when you are doing it yourself, it is not so ghastly. I never really liked modern dress in the theatre and here I am making films like that.

The use of the OutRage demos in Edward II *specifically relates that film to the present, commenting on the political situation at that time, rather more directly than in some of the earlier films.*

Absolutely. I knew all those people and it seemed the right moment to put them into a film. It was rent-a-crowd cheaply. Everyone wanted to come for the morning and demonstrate. I got a big crowd of people, very sympathetic people, people who really wanted to do it. That was the difference between them and a small number of others in the film who just went on and on about the union rates, and this and that or the other. They were quibbling over two and sixpence – which they are welcome to, but that attitude didn't make for good working. So, thank God when the OutRage boys came along and just did it, for the love of it. That's one of the reasons I try to avoid the film industry. It's full of that sort of attitude; the kind of films I do, you can't make with that sort of attitude. It's not possible. Those films have got to be made by people because they really want to do them, not because they are being paid to. I always strive to establish a good working environment for myself and the people I am working with. We were actually enjoying ourselves. There is not much point in making a film if it is such grim, hard work that you say at the end of it: "I made a good film but we had a hellish time". I do really believe that one should be able to say "we had a great time and we actually managed to make a successful film". It should be that way round.

Don Boyd, writing an introduction to the script of War Requiem *stresses how much it is your film; that you stamp yourself on it in some way. Indeed, you are very much studied now as a film director, as an auteur. I think your films are very recognisable and I wonder whether you feel that it is you as an individual creator that have something you want to present to people. You also regularly use many of the same people from project to project. Would you say you see the films that you make as mostly cooperative, collaborative ventures?*

I think so, they have become that. I always try to get in a couple of new people. I think it would be a bad idea if we seized up and became a gang of old friends who just kept reconvening. I don't do that. There are always new people in every film. On the other hand, it is always nice to have the same people around because we can discuss issues briefly and forget about them and just get on, which gives you tons of time to think about other problems. Overall, I think it's more collaborative. Although I do get bees in my bonnet from time to time, I don't really operate films from that point of view.

Many of your films, like your books, are sumptuous productions. They have a strong sensuous appeal. In The Last of England *book, for example, you write about making the scenes of dereliction in the film also very beautiful and many viewers would agree that they are.*

Where does this element of your cinema come from?

I have always tried to make things look good. I think that comes from having a visual arts background which most directors don't have. That painted element is very much there in *The Last of England*.

There seems to be a clear tie between the sensuous form of the films and the way the people are shot, and their homoerotic power. One of many examples is the scene in which Ranuccio carefully fixes each coin into his mouth in Caravaggio. *Do you perceive your films as offering, primarily, a sensual experience, rather than an intellectual or even an aesthetic one?*

I hope they do have a sensual power. I don't think they would work as films unless they had that sense – if they were simply intellectual projects – so I'm glad to say it is an important element.

Both in the editing of The Garden *[1990] and in the shooting of several scenes for* Edward II, *you were unable to direct events for health reasons. Would they have been particularly different films if you had been able to maintain control over those elements?*

I don't think so. I feel now that I could just get everyone along and I wouldn't really have to do anything and [the end result] would be one of my films. Strange, but I think that is what would happen. I don't really feel that I've ever been a big controller-director. I just let everything "flow with the glue". There are no big plans which have to be fulfilled, so I don't think that that is important.

Are you generally satisfied with the films you have made?

I look at other films and I think they measure up. The problem is that any film is quite a large enterprise and for it to be consistently good is very complicated. My films have got enough flashes in them, haven't they, to make them work? They seem to be distinguishable from other films.

Very much so. I think your films have a vibrancy which one does not get out of many films.

Yes, there is something going on there. I do think it comes partly from the fact that all the people who work on them like working on them. They enjoy it very much, and I think that this makes a lot of difference to a film.

During the making of a film, do you see yourself making it for any particular audience, as opposed to an audience in general?

No, I've never thought of the audience in my life. This business of who you are making your films for – for whoever comes along. There was a period when you had to be making your films for a specific audience...I always thought it was nonsense. I just made the films and hoped someone would come. Over the years, an audience has grown, as my films have. Each one seems to bring a few more people. It has happened quite organically, there was no plan to [for example] net a group of "arties".

Presumably the wider audience is also an effect of the films being distributed more widely as time has gone by.

Yes, that's helped a lot. I mean, as the years have gone past I have got a better distribution in [many] countries and suddenly I have turned from being "not known at all" to being "known". In Italy, for instance, I do quite well now. They are putting three of the films on Italian television in one night: *The Garden, The Last of England* and *Edward II*. So that's serious media exposure.

What about in Britain? You have talked in the past about some of the earlier films. There was the whole débâcle about Channel 4 not showing Sebastiane. *Now, when the films have been made, are they shown sufficiently in the UK?*

Well, it is still difficult. I could still complain about it. I mean, I couldn't get anyone to put on *Edward II. Blue* [1993] didn't really première. Eventually, we managed to get it on at the MGM in Panton Street for a week. So I must say the distribution of films in Great Britain is terrible. It's the great weak link. You make them and then there's no one there to pick them up, nowhere to put them on.

One thing which has been characteristic of your work for ten years now has been the accompanying books. You have been presenting a parallel, autobiographical text, or the combination of film script or the history of the film project with some sense of a diary, so that your life and the film are told together. Did the idea of having a book with every film just gradually take shape?

Yes. It just became and suddenly I found myself the most autobiographical of artists. It was really strange. I don't think I set out to do that, but in order to explain what I was trying to do, I began the books. What happened was that when we were doing *Caravaggio*, we *weren't* doing it and I hadn't worked for what seemed years, forever. Nicholas [Ward-Jackson], my producer, said "why don't you write down all the problems we're having in making this film". So I started and one thing led to another: there was no way you could isolate the film from life, so life crept into the book and there was *Dancing Ledge*. I spent the best part of one summer writing it and, by the end, it wasn't just a film-book about *Caravaggio*, but a much more general book. And I suppose then, the die was set.

And then, gradually, the films and the books have become more closely tied, so that with Edward II, *for example, it seems, you envisaged the book at the same time as the film. You knew that there would be a chance in the book to do something that went clearly alongside the film, or perhaps went a bit further than the film.*

Yes, it did. It was more punchy than the film in some ways. I think film is a very conservative medium, whereas with writing you can cut through [the obstacles] more easily. You don't have the same wretched funding issues to deal with.

Are there other things that you feel you want to do with film, other questions you feel you have not answered?

No. I've done everything I want to do. Anything I do now is icing. I managed to produce *enough* films and in that way, I'm very lucky.

Derek Jarman: filmography

Compiled by Chris Lippard

The following abbreviations have been used in this filmography:

DJ	Derek Jarman	*ep*	executive producer
ad	art director	*m*	music
bw	black and white	mins	minutes
col	colour	*p*	producer
cost	costumes	*pc*	production company
d	director	*ph*	cinematographer
dist	distributor	*prod des*	production designer
ed	editor	*sc*	scriptwriter

[Unless indicated otherwise, all films are directed by Derek Jarman and produced in Great Britain.]

1970

Studio Bankside 6 mins, Super 8

1971

Miss Gaby 5 mins, Super 8
A Journey to Avebury 10 mins, Super 8

1972

Garden of Luxor 6 mins, Super 8
Andrew Logan Kisses the Glitteratti 8 mins, Super 8
Tarot (aka *The Magician*) with Christopher Hobbs, 10 mins, Super 8

1973

The Art of Mirrors (aka *Sulphur*) 10 mins, Super 8 *cast* Kevin Whitney, Luciana Martinez, Gerald Incandela.

1974

The Devils at the Elgin (aka *Reworking The Devils*) 15 mins, Super 8
Ula's Fete (aka *Ula's Chandelier*) 10 mins, Super 8
Fire Island 5 mins, Super 8
Duggie's Fields 10 mins, Super 8

170

1975

Picnic at Ray's 10 mins, Super 8
Sebastiane Wrap 6 mins, Super 8

1976

Gerald's Film 5 mins, Super 8 *cast* Gerald Incandela.
Sloane Square (aka *A Room of One's Own* / aka *Removal Party*) 12
mins, Super 8. With Guy Ford.

Sebastiane
86 mins col 16mm Latin dialogue, English subtitles
p James Whaley, Howard Malin *pc* Disctac *d* Paul Humfress, DJ *sc* DJ,
James Whaley *Latin translation* Jack Welch *ph* Peter Midddleton
m Brian Eno *ed* Paul Humfress *prod des* DJ *main cast* Leonardo
Treviglio (Sebastian), Barney James (Severus), Neil Kennedy (Max),
Richard Warwick (Justin), Donald Dunham (Claudius), Ken Hicks
(Adrian), Janusz Romanov (Anthony), Steffano Massari (Marius), Daevid
Finbar (Julian), Gerald Incandela (Leopard Boy), Robert Medley
(Emperor Diocletian), Lindsay Kemp and troupe.
dist Megalovision/Cinegate; Axon Video (USA)
video Tartan; Axon Video (USA)

Houston, Texas 10 mins, Super 8

1977

Jordan's Dance 1 minute, Super 8 (later used in *Jubilee*)
Every Woman for Herself and All for Art 1 minute, Super 8 to 16mm

1978

Jubilee
103 mins col 16mm
p Howard Malin, James Whaley *pc* Whaley-Malin Productions for
Megalovision *sc* DJ *ph* Peter Middleton *m* Brian Eno *ed* Nick Barnard,
Tom Priestley *prod des, cost* Christopher Hobbs *main cast* Jenny
Runacre (Bod/Queen Elizabeth I), Little Nell (Crabs), Toyah Willcox
(Mad), Jordan (Amyl Nitrite), Hermine Demoriane (Chaos), Ian
Charleson (Angel), Karl Johnson (Sphinx), Linda Spurrier (Viv), Neil
Kennedy (Max), Orlando (Borgia Ginz), Wayne County (Lounge Lizard),
Richard O'Brien (John Dee), David Haughton (Ariel), Helen Wellington-
Lloyd (Lady-in-Waiting), Adam Ant (Kid), Lindsay Kemp and troupe.
dist Cinegate / *video* Tartan; Mystic Fire (USA)

1979

Broken English (Marianne Faithfull music video featuring three songs:
"Broken English", "Witches' Song", "The Ballad of Lucy Jordan"), 12
mins, Super 8 to 16mm *p* Guy Ford

The Tempest
96 mins col 16mm
ep Don Boyd *p* Guy Ford, Mordecai Schreiber *pc* Boyd's Company *sc* DJ
based on the play by William Shakespeare *ph* Peter Middleton
m Wavemaker (Brian Hodgson, John Lewis) *ed* Lesley Walker, Annette
D'Alton *prod des* Yolanda Sonnabend *ad* Ian Whittaker, Steven Mehea
cost Nicolas Ede *main cast* Heathcote Williams (Prospero), Karl Johnson
(Ariel), Toyah Willcox (Miranda), Peter Bull (Alonso), Richard Warwick
(Antonio), Elisabeth Welch (Goddess), Jack Birkett (Caliban), Ken
Campbell (Gonzalo), David Meyer (Ferdinand), Neil Cunningham
(Sebastian), Christopher Biggins (Stephano), Peter Turner (Trinculo),
Claire Davenport (Sycorax), Kate Temple (young Miranda).
dist Mainline; Zeitgeist Films (USA) / *video* Arthouse Productions

1980

In the Shadow of the Sun (footage shot 1971/72, edited 1973/74, sound
  added 1980. Uses footage from *A Journey to Avebury*, *Tarot*, *Fire Island*
  and *The Devils*) 54 mins, Super 8 *p* James Mackay *pc* Dark Pictures
  m Throbbing Gristle *main cast* Gerald Incandela, Christopher Hobbs,
  Kevin Whitney, Luciano Martinez, Andrew Logan.
  video Visionary Communications

1981

T.G. Psychic Rally in Heaven 8 mins, Super 8 to 16mm *pc* Dark Pictures
  m Throbbing Gristle

1982

Pirate Tape 25 mins, Super 8 to video
Pontormo and the Punks at Santa Croce 10 mins, Super 8

1983

Waiting for Waiting for Godot (from a RADA production of Samuel
  Beckett's play designed by John Maybury), 10 mins, Super 8 and video
B2 Tape/Film 35 mins, Super 8 and video *main cast* Dave Baby, Volker
  Stokes, Judy Blame, Hussain McGaw, James Mackay, Padeluun, Jordan.

1984

The Dream Machine 35 mins, 16mm *d, sc, ph, ed* DJ, Michael Kostiff,
  Cerith Wyn-Evans, John Maybury
Catalan 7 mins, 16mm *pc* TVE (Spanish Television) *prod des* Christopher
  Hobbs *m* Psychic TV
Imagining October 27 mins, Super 8 and 16mm *p* James Mackay *ph* DJ,
  Richard Heslop, Cerith Wyn-Evans, Sally Potter, Carl Johnson *m* David
  Ball, Genesis P.Orridge *ed* DJ, Cerith Wyn-Evans, Richard Heslop, Peter
  Cartwright *main cast* John Watkiss, Peter Doig, Keir Wahid, Toby Mott,
  Steve Thrower, Angus Cook.

1985

The Angelic Conversation
81 mins col Super 8 to 35mm
p James Mackay *pc* BFI/Channel 4 *sc* Shakespeare's sonnets, numbers 27,
29, 30, 43, 53, 55, 56, 57, 61, 90, 94, 104, 126, 148, read by Judi Dench
ph DJ, James Mackay *m* Coil (John Balance, Peter Christopherson)
ed Cerith Wyn-Evans, Peter Cartwright *cast* Paul Reynolds, Phillip
Williamson.
dist BFI / *video* Visionary Communications; Mystic Fire (USA)

1986

Caravaggio
93 mins col 35mm
ep Colin MacCabe *p* Sarah Radclyffe *pc* BFI/Channel 4, Nicholas Ward-
Jackson *ph* Gabriel Beristain *m* Simon Fisher-Turner, Mary Phillips
ed George Akers *prod des* Christopher Hobbs *cost* Sandy Powell *ad* Mike
Buchanan *main cast* Nigel Terry (Michelangelo Caravaggio), Sean Bean
(Ranuccio Thomasoni), Garry Cooper (Davide), Dexter Fletcher (young
Caravaggio), Spencer Leigh (Jerusaleme), Tilda Swinton (Lena), Nigel
Davenport (Giustiniani), Robbie Coltrane (Cardinal Scipione Borghese),
Michael Gough (Cardinal Del Monte), Noam Almaz (boy Caravaggio),
Dawn Archibald (Pipo), Jack Birkett (Pope).
dist BFI / *video* Connoisseur; Cinevista (USA)
award 1986 Berlin Film Festival – Silver Bear

The Queen is Dead (The Smiths music video featuring three songs: "The
  Queen is Dead", "There is a Light that never Goes Out", "Panic"), 14
  mins *p* James Mackay

1987

The Last of England
91 mins col/bw Super 8
p James Mackay, Don Boyd *pc* Anglo International Films. For British
Screen/Channel 4/ZDF *ph* DJ, Christopher Hughes, Cerith Wyn-Evans,
Richard Heslop, Tim Burke *m* Simon Fisher-Turner, Andy Gill, Mayo
Thompson, Albert Dehlen, Barry Adamson, El Tito *ed* Peter Cartwright,
Angus Cook, John Maybury, Sally Yeadon *prod des* Christopher Hobbs
cost Sandy Powell *main cast* Spring, Gerrard McCarthur, John Phillips,
Gay Gaynor, Matthew Hawkins, Tilda Swinton, Spencer Leigh, (voice of)
Nigel Terry.
dist Blue Dolphin / *video* Blue Dolphin; Mystic Fire (USA)
award LA Films Critics' Award for best independent/experimental film,
1988.

Louise (segment from *Aria*, total length 89 mins, to accompany
  Charpentier's "Depuis le jour") 5 mins, col/bw, Super 8 and 35mm
  pc Boyd's Co. Film Productions. For Lightyear Entertainment, Virgin
  Vision *p* Don Boyd *ph* Mike Southon, Christopher Hughes *ed* Peter
  Cartwright, Angus Cook *prod des* Christopher Hobbs *cost* Sandy Powell

173

cast Amy Johnson (Old Lady), Tilda Swinton (Young Girl), Spencer Leigh (Young Man).

1988

L'Ispirazione 3 mins, 35mm *p* James Mackay *m* Sylvano Bussotti *ed* John Maybury, Peter Cartwright *cast* Tilda Swinton, Spencer Leigh.

War Requiem
86 mins col/bw Super 8 and 35mm
ep John Kelleher *p* Don Boyd *pc* Anglo International Films. For the BBC/ Liberty Film Sales *ph* Richard Greatrex *m* "War Requiem" by Benjamin Britten, performed by the London Symphony Orchestra, with poems by Wilfred Owen *ed* Richard Elgood *prod des* Lucy Morahan *cost* Linda Alderson *main cast* Nathaniel Parker (Wilfred Owen), Tilda Swinton (Nurse), Laurence Olivier (Old Soldier), Patricia Hayes (Mother), Rohan McCullough (Enemy Mother), Nigel Terry (Abraham), Owen Teale (Unknown Soldier), Sean Bean (German Soldier), Alex Jennings (Blinded Soldier), Claire Davenport (Charge Sister/Britannia), Spencer Leigh (1st Soldier), Milo Bell (2nd Soldier), Richard Stirling (3rd Soldier), Kim Kindersley (4th Soldier), Stuart Turton (5th Soldier).
video Polygram; Mystic Fire (USA)

1989

Pet Shop Boys Tour Film 40 mins (back-projection footage to accompany eight songs)

1990

The Garden
92 mins col 35mm
p James Mackay *pc* Basilisk, in association with Channel 4/British Screen/ ZDF/Uplink *ph* Christopher Hughes *assistant ph* David Lewis, James Mackay, Nick Searle, Steve Farrer, Richard Heslop, DJ *m* Simon Fisher-Turner *ed* Peter Cartwright *prod des* Derek Brown, Christopher Hobbs *cost* Annie Symons *main cast* Tilda Swinton (Madonna), Johnny Mills, Kevin Collins (lovers), Pete Lee-Wilson (Devil), Spencer Leigh (Mary Magdalene/Adam), Jody Graber (young boy), Roger Cook (Christ), Jessica Martin (Singer), Philip MacDonald (Joseph/Jesus), Dawn Archibald (Nature Spirit), Michael Gough (voice-overs).
dist Artificial Eye / *video* Artificial Eye; Fox Lorber Video (USA)

1991

Edward II
91 mins col 35mm
ep Sarah Radclyffe, Simon Curtis *p* Steve Clark-Hall, Antony Root
pc Edward II Limited. Working Title for British Screen/BBC Films *sc* DJ, Stephen McBride, Ken Butler *based on the play by* Christopher Marlowe *ph* Ian Wilson *m* Simon Fisher-Turner *ed* George Akers
prod des Christopher Hobbs *cost* Sandy Powell *ad* Rick Eyres *cast* Steven

Waddington (Edward II), Kevin Collins (Lightborn), Tilda Swinton (Isabella), Andrew Tiernan (Piers Gaveston), John Lynch (Spencer), Dudley Sutton (Winchester), Jerome Flynn (Kent), Jody Graber (Prince Edward), Nigel Terry (Mortimer), Roger Hammond (Bishop), Allan Corduner (Poet), Annie Lennox (Singer)
dist The Sales Company

1993

Wittgenstein
75 mins col 35mm and 16mm
ep Ben Gibson, Takashi Asai *p* Tariq Ali *pc* Channel 4/BFI in association with Uplink. A Bandung Production *sc* DJ, Terry Eagleton, Ken Butler *ph* James Welland *m* Jan Latham-Koenig *ed* Budge Tremlett *cost* Sandy Powell *ad* Annie Lapaz *main cast* Karl Johnson (Ludwig Wittgenstein), Michael Gough (Bertrand Russell), Tilda Swinton (Ottoline Morrell), John Quentin (Maynard Keynes), Kevin Collins (Johnny), Clancy Chassay (young Ludwig Wittgenstein), Jill Balcon (Leopoldine Wittgenstein), Sally Dexter (Hermine Wittgenstein), Gina Marsh (Gretyl Wittgenstein), Vanya del Borgo (Helene Wittgenstein), Ben Scantlebury (Hans Wittgenstein), Howard Sooley (Kurt Wittgenstein), David Radzinowicz (Rudolf Wittgenstein), Jan Latham-Koenig (Paul Wittgenstein).
dist BFI; Zeitgeist Films (USA) / *video* Connoisseur; Kino Video (USA)

Blue
76 mins col 35mm
p James Mackay, Takashi Asai *pc* Basilisk Communications/Uplink production for Channel 4, in association with the Arts Council of Great Britian/Opal/BBC Radio 3 *sc* DJ *m* Simon Fisher-Turner *voices* John Quentin, Nigel Terry, DJ, Tilda Swinton.
dist Basilisk Communications; Zeitgeist Films (USA
video Artificial Eye; Kino Video (USA)
award Michael Powell Prize, 1993 Edinburgh Film Festival.

1994

Glitterbug 52 mins, Super 8 *p* James Mackay *pc* Basilisk Communications/BBC, by association with Opal and Dangerous To Know *m* Brian Eno *ed* Andy Crabb
dist/video Dangerous To Know

* * *

Jarman directed many music videos in addition to those (included above) compiled into "films" for Marianne Faithfull, The Smiths and The Pet Shop Boys. As well as additional work for these bands, he worked with Psychic Television, Bryan Ferry, Wang Chung, Lords of the New Church, Marc Almond, Orange Juice, Easterhouse, Bob Geldof and Annie Lennox.

Jarman worked as set designer on Ken Russell's *The Devils* (1970) and *Savage Messiah* (1972). In 1986 he appeared briefly in two films as an actor, playing Pasolini in Julian Cole's *Ostia*, and Patrick Procktor in Stephen Frears's *Prick Up Your Ears*. In 1993 he acted in two short films: Alexis Bisticas's *The Clearing* and Ken McMullen's *There We Are John*.

Derek Jarman: selected bibliography

Compiled by Chris Lippard

PRIMARY BIBLIOGRAPHY

A: Texts by Jarman

At Your Own Risk: A Saint's Testament (London: Hutchinson, 1992).

Blue: Text of a film by Derek Jarman (London: Channel 4 Television and BBC Radio 3, 1993).

Chroma: A Book of Colour – June '93 (London: Century, 1994; Woodstock, NY: Overlook Press, 1995).

Dancing Ledge (London; New York: Quartet Books, 1984). [Reprinted, with a new preface by Jarman, 1991.]

Derek Jarman's Caravaggio: The Complete Film Script and Commentaries by Derek Jarman (London: Thames and Hudson, 1986).

derek jarman's garden, with photographs by Howard Sooley (London: Thames and Hudson, 1995).

The Last of England, edited by David L Hirst (London: Constable, 1987) [reissued in paperback in 1996 as *Kicking the Pricks*].

Modern Nature: The Journals of Derek Jarman (London: Century, 1991; Woodstock, NY: Overlook Press, 1994).

Queer Edward II (London: British Film Institute, 1991).

Up In The Air: Collected Film Scripts (London: Vintage, 1996).

War Requiem (London; Boston: Faber, 1989) [screenplay].

Wittgenstein. The Terry Eagleton Script. The Derek Jarman Film (London: British Film Institute, 1993) [with material by Eagleton and Ken Butler, preface by Colin MacCabe, and foreword by Tariq Ali].

A Finger in the Fishes Mouth (Bettiscombe, Dorset: Bettiscombe Press, 1972) [poetry].

"Freedom Fighter for a Vision of Truth", *The Sunday Times* 17 January 1988: C9 [a response to "Through a Lens Darkly", Norman Stone's attack on the contemporary British cinema, including *The Last of England*, in the previous week's paper (10 January): C1-2].

Get the Rubber Habit! The Sisters of Perpetual Indulgence, photography by Denis Doran, with a foreword by Derek Jarman (London: Blase, 1994) [Jarman contributes a very brief introduction to a collection of postcards from the Sisters of Perpetual Indulgence advocating safe, fun sex and AIDS awareness, and is pictured in several of the postcards as "Saint Derek of Dungeness of the Order of Celluloid Knights"].

"Queer Questions", *Sight and Sound* 2: 5 (September 1992): 34-35 [Jarman's is one of four responses by filmmakers – the others by Pratibha Parmar, Isaac Julien and Constantine Giannaris – to B. Ruby Rich's article, "New Queer Cinema", on the preceding pages].

"Saintly passion", *New Statesman & Society* 2: 80 (15 December 1989): 10-12 [four opinions of Nigel Wingrove's *Visions of Ecstasy*, a film about Saint Teresa. Jarman's short piece is taken from his submission to the British Board of Film Classification. The other pieces are by Wingrove, Fay Weldon and Marina Warner].

"2nd Opinion", *Time Out* 750 (3-9 January 1985): 6 [Jarman begs to differ with David Puttnam's idea of what British Film Year should promote].

Wilms, Anno. *Lindsay Kemp & Company*, photographs by Anno Wilms, preface by Derek Jarman (London: GMP Publishers, 1987).

B: Catalogues of art exhibitions

Today and Tomorrow, catalogue of exhibition by Derek Jarman (London: Richard Salmon, 1991).

The Exhibition of Derek Jarman's "Luminous Darkness", catalogue of exhibition by Derek Jarman (Tokyo: Uplink, 1991) [very few copies printed].

Queer, catalogue of exhibition by Derek Jarman (Manchester: Manchester City Art Galleries, in association with Richard Salmon Ltd., 1992) [includes brief reviews by Norman Rosenthal, Stuart Morgan, Simon Watney and Andrew Renton].

Evil Queen, catalogue of exhibition by Derek Jarman (Manchester: Whitworth Gallery, in association with Richard Salmon Ltd., 1994) [Jarman's last seventeen paintings. Includes a reprint of Ken Butler's "All the Rage" piece listed below].

Derek Jarman: A Portrait: Artist, Film-maker, Designer (London: Barbican Art Gallery and the Hatton Gallery, in association with Thames and Hudson, 1996).

C: Published interviews

"Britannia on Trial", with Michael O'Pray. *Monthly Film Bulletin* 53: 627 (April 1986): 100-101.

"Cinema: Talking to Derek Jarman", with Timothy Hyman. *London Magazine* 20: 7 (October 1980): 70-75.

"Derek Jarman", with Michael Petry. *Arts Review* 41 (27 January 1989): 55 [Jarman comments on an exhibition of his paintings].

"Derek Jarman: The Final Interview", with Richard Morrison. *Art and Understanding* 3: 1 (April 1994): 17-22.

"Fade to Blue", with Gerard Raymond. *Genre* 19 (June 1994): 44-47.

Hacker, Jonathan and David Price. *Take Ten: Contemporary British Film Directors* (Oxford: Clarendon Press, 1991): 248-260 [preceded by an essay on Jarman's films by the authors].

"History and the Gay Viewfinder: An Interview with Derek Jarman", with Roy Grundmann. *Cineaste* 18: 4 (1991): 24-27.

"History is Punk", with Philip Oakes. *The Sunday Times* 19 February 1978: 35 [Jarman discusses *Jubilee*].

"Home Movie Man", with Simon Watney. *Marxism Today* October 1987: 40-41.

"Interview with Derek Jarman". *Film Directions* 2: 8 (1979): 14-15.

"*Jubilee*", with Keith Howes. *Gay News* 23 February 1979.

"Left to his Own Devices", with Don Watson. *City Limits* 405 (6-13 July 1989): 12-13 [discusses Jarman's filmed backdrop for The Pet Shop Boys].

"A Modern kind of Hero", with Lynn Barber. *The Independent on Sunday* 4 August 1991: 2-5.

"A Natural Obsesssion", with Nicholas de Jongh. *The Guardian* 17 April 1986: 13 [discussion is focused on *Caravaggio*].

"News from Home: Super-8, video and home movies: Derek Jarman discusses 'real' film-making with Michael O'Pray", *Monthly Film Bulletin* 51: 605 (June 1984): 189-190.

"On *Imaging October*, Dr. Dee and Other Matters: An Interview with Derek Jarman", with Simon Field and Michael O'Pray. *Afterimage* (London) 12 (autumn 1985): 40-58 [part of a special Jarman issue, entitled "Derek Jarman ...Of Angels & Apocalypse"].

"Painting the Big Screen", with Maureen Cleave. *Observer Magazine* 22 February 1987: 18 [discussion focuses on *The Last of England*].

"Please God, send me to Hell", with Robert Chalmers. *Sunday Correspondent* 18 November 1990: 36-37.

"Positive Direction", with Minty Clinch. *The Observer Magazine* 13 October 1991: 62-63 [discussion focuses on *The Garden* and *Edward II*].

"Positive Thinking", with Anthony Clare. *The Listener* 124: 3178 (16 August 1990): 7-10 [transcription of Jarman's interview with Clare on "In the Psychiatrist's Chair", first broadcast on BBC Radio 4 on 15 August 1990].

"Renaissance Man", with Martin Sutton. *Stills* 26 (April 1986): 11.

"Super 8 Artist", with Stuart Dollin. *Movie Maker* 18: 7 (July 1984): 41-43.

"This Jarman Man", with Anne-Maree Hewitt. *Cinema Papers* 65 (September 1987): 12-14.

"Vision of a Nightmare", with Don MacPherson. *Screen International* 182 (24-31 March 1979): 19 [discussion focuses on *The Tempest*].

"Where Angels Tread", with Mark Finch. *City Limits* 18-24 October 1985: 17-18.

"Witt's End", with Tony Rayns. *Time Out* 1179 (24-30 March 1993): 60.

Jarman interviews Lindsay Kemp in "Kemp Follower". *Time Out* 754 (31 January-6 February 1985): 14-16.

SECONDARY BIBLIOGRAPHY

A: Articles in journals and magazines

Aasarød, Pauline. "Derek Jarman: Perspektiver på 'No-Budget' filmproduksjon", *Z* 46 (1993): 26-27 [in Norwegian].

"An Artist in the Cinema", *Continental Film and Video Review* 28: 7 (May 1981): 52 [brief survey of Jarman's career up to *In the Shadow of the Sun*].

Ball, Edward. "I, Camera", *Village Voice* 36: 5 (29 January 1991): 54.

Bennett, Catherine. "Lesson of the Gay Guru", *The Guardian* 9 April 1992: 27.

Butler, Ken. "All the Rage", *Vogue* [London] December 1993: 157-160.

Comino, Jo. "Passion to Purge", *City Limits* 17-23 February 1984: 16-17.

Cooper, Dennis. "The Queer King: Derek Jarman and the New Gay Film", *LA Weekly* 10 April 1992: 22.

"Derek Jarman ...Of Angels & Apocalypse", *Afterimage* (London) 12 (autumn 1985) [special Jarman issue, which includes the following: "The

Troublesome Cases", by Simon Field (3-5); "Derek Jarman's Cinema: Eros and Thanatos", by Michael O'Pray (6-15); "A Filmography" (16-21); "P.P.P. in the Garden of Earthly Delights/Nijinsky's Last Dance. Two Projects", by Derek Jarman (22-29); "Innocence and Experience", by Mark Nash (30-35); "Painting the Apocalypse", by John Roberts (36-39); "On *Imaging October*, Dr. Dee and Other Matters: An Interview with Derek Jarman", with Simon Field and Michael O'Pray (40-58); "Submitting to Sodomy: Propositions and Rhetorical Questions about an English Film-maker", by Tony Rayns (60-65)].

Dieckmann, Katherine. "Dancing Among the Ruins", *Village Voice* 33: 4 (24 January 1989): 59-60.

Driscoll, Lawrence. "Burroughs/Jarman: Anamorphosis, Homosexuality and the Metanarratives of Restraint", *The Spectator [Los Angeles]* 10: 2 (spring 1990): 78-95.

Field, Simon. "The Garden of Earthly Delights", *The Face* 21 January 1993: 62.

Frick, Thomas. "Fragments of History, Tinted Blue", *LA Weekly* 13-19 May 1994: 27-28.

Gill, John. "Longing for Paradise: Documentary content in the work of Derek Jarman", *Dox* 7 (autumn 1995): 44-47.

Horrigan, William. "Of Angels and Apocalypse" (Minneapolis: Walker Art Center, 1986) [pamphlet published to coincide with a tour of *Sebastiane*, *Jubilee*, *The Tempest* and *Caravaggio* around US art centres, 1986-87].

Kennedy, Harlan. "The Two Gardens of Derek Jarman", *Film Comment* 29: 6 (November/December 1993): 28-31, 33-35.

Lipman, Andy. "Currents: Learning to Dream", *City Limits* 170 (4-10 January 1985): 45 [reviews Jarman's criticisms of British Film Year and of James Park's book, *Learning to Dream*].

Nowlan, Bob. "Reflections: Jarman's life and work", *Against the Current* May/June 1995: 32-36.

O'Pray, Michael. "If you want to make films", *Sight and Sound* [supplement] 4: 7 (July 1994): 20-22.

——————————. "The Art of Mirrors – Derek Jarman", *Monthly Film Bulletin* 58: 684 (January 1991): 28 [biofilmography].

Rayns, Tony. "Private Viewing", *Time Out* 702 (2-8 February 1984): 31.

Rothwell, Kenneth S. "Jarman vs Branagh", *Sight and Sound* 1: 9 (January 1992): 63.

Searle, Adrian. "London: Derek Jarman", *Artforum* 26: 7 (March 1988): 154-155 [review of an exhibition of Jarman's paintings at the Richard

Salmon Gallery in London].

Sewell, Dennis. "Not the Last of Jarman", *Spectator [London]* 260: 8339 (7 May 1988): 17-18.

Woods, Chris. "Derek Jarman Breaks the Rules", *Advocate* 593 (31 December 1991): 64-66.

B: Chapters or sections on Jarman and his work in books

Dyer, Richard. *Now you see it: Studies on lesbian and gay film* (London; New York: Routledge, 1990): 168-169 [discusses *Sebastiane*].

Lippard, Chris and Guy Johnson. "Private Practice, Public Health: The Politics of Sickness and the Films of Derek Jarman", in Lester Friedman (ed), *Fires Were Started: British Cinema and Thatcherism* (Minneapolis: University of Minnesota Press, 1993): 278-293.

MacCabe, Colin. "A Post National European Cinema: A Consideration of Derek Jarman's *The Tempest* and *Edward II*", in Duncan Petrie (ed), *Screening Europe: Image and Identity in Contemporary European Cinema* (London: British Film Institute, 1992): 9-18.

MacKay, James. "Low-budget British Production: A Producer's Account", in Duncan Petrie (ed), *New Questions of British Cinema* (London: British Film Institute, 1992): 52-64.

Murray, Timothy. "Dirtier Still? Wistful gazing and homographic hieroglyphs in Jarman's *Caravaggio*", in *Like a Film: Ideological fantasy on screen, camera and canvas* (London; New York: Routledge, 1993): 124-171.

Walker, Alexander. "Young Prospero" and "Punk and Circumstance", in *National Heroes: British Cinema in the Seventies and Eighties* (London: Harrap, 1985): 228-239.

Wollen, Peter. "The Last New Wave: Modernism in the British Films of the Thatcher Era", in Lester Friedman (ed), *Fires Were Started: British Cinema and Thatcherism* (Minneapolis: University of Minnesota Press, 1993): 35-51.

C: Discussion of Jarman and his work within other or broader topics in journals and books

Dixon, Wheeler Winston. "*The Long Day Closes*: An Interview with Terence Davies", in Wheeler Winston Dixon (ed), *Re-viewing British Cinema, 1900-1992: Essays and Interviews* (Albany: State University of New York Press, 1994): 249-259.

Fuller, Graham. "Battle for Britain: The Empire Strikes Back", *Film Comment* 24: 4 (July/August 1988): 62-68 [a response to "Through a Lens Darkly", Norman Stone's attack on the British cinema, including *The Last of England*, in *The Sunday Times* 10 January 1988].

Kennedy, Harlan. "The Brits Have Gone Nuts", *Film Comment* 21: 4 (July/August 1985): 51-55.

O'Pray, Michael. "The B movie phenomenon: British cinema today", *Aperture* 113 (winter 1988): 68-71 [focus is on Jarman and Peter Wollen].

Petrie, Duncan J. *Creativity and Constraint in the British Film Industry* (London: Macmillan; New York: St Martin's Press, 1991).

Reed, Jeremy. "Whatever happened to Poets?", *New Statesman & Society* 8: 335 (13 January 1995): 40-41 [includes Reed's poem, "For Derek Jarman"].

Rich, B. Ruby et al. "New Queer Cinema", *Sight and Sound* 2: 5 (September 1992): 30-39.

Satuloff, Bob. "I Just Called to Say I Hate You", *Christopher Street* 14: 18 (16 March 1992): 3-5.

Saynor, James. "Tilda Swinton", *Interview* 22: 4 (April 1992): 104-107.

Stone, Norman. "Through a Lens Darkly", *The Sunday Times* 10 January 1988: C1-2.

D: Selected reviews

(i) Films

Glitterbug

Kermode, Mark and Peter Dean. "*Glitterbug*", *Sight and Sound* 4: 4 (April 1994): 59.

Romney, Jonathan. "Business and pleasure", *New Statesman & Society* 7: 292 (4 March 1994): 34-35.

Rooney, David. "*Glitterbug*", *Variety* 355: 1 (2 May 1994): 91.

Blue

Brown, Georgia. "*Blue* written and directed by Derek Jarman", *Village Voice* 38: 42 (19 October 1993): 56.

Burston, Paul. "Blue Yonder", *Time Out* 1200 (18-25 August 1993): 20-21.

Dargis, Manohla. "Even cinema gets the blues", *Interview* 23: 12 (December 1993): 54.

Darke, Chris. "*Blue*", *Sight and Sound* 3: 10 (October 1993): 40-41.

Dean, Peter. "*Blue*", *Sight and Sound* 4: 1 (January 1994): 62.

Del-Re, Gianmarco. "La trilogia di al grado zero dell'imagine", *Cineforum* 33: 6 (June 1993): 47-48 [in Italian].

Hirshey, Gerri. "The Philadelphia Story", *GQ* 64: 1 (January 1994): 24 [surveys the treatment of AIDS in films].

Holden, Stephen. "A Movie Where all Motion is Metaphorical", *The New York Times* 143 (2 October 1993): C16 [an excerpt from this review is reprinted in issue 143 (8 April 1994): C13(L)].

Klawans, Stuart. "Films: *Blue* directed by Derek Jarman/*Wittgenstein* directed by Derek Jarman", *Nation* 257: 10 (4 October 1993): 364-366.

Lombardo, Patrizia. "Cruellement bleu–*Blue* directed by Derek Jarman", *Critical Quarterly* 36: 1 (spring 1994): 131-135.

McCarthy, Todd. "*Blue*", *Variety* 352: 7 (27 September 1993): 38.

Romney, Jonathan. "Living colour slowly fades", *New Statesman & Society* 6: 269 (10 September 1993): 35-36.

Shulman, Ken. "When Creation fills a Deathly Silence", *The New York Times* 143 (3 October 1993): H13+.

Smith, Paul Julian. "*Blue* and the outer limits", *Sight and Sound* 3: 10 (October 1993): 18-19.

Thomas, Michael Anthony. "Derek Jarman's *Blue*", *Art and Understanding* 3: 1 (April 1994): 30.

Walters, Barry. "Mood indigo: *Blue* by Derek Jarman", *Advocate* 653 (19 April 1994): 72-73 [reviews the soundtrack].

Wittgenstein

Bowen, Peter. "In the Company of Saints: Derek Jarman's *Wittgenstein* and Beyond", *Filmmaker* 2: 1 (autumn 1993): 18-19.

Cohen, Jessica. "Movies: reviews, previews, our views: *Wittgenstein*. Directed by Derek Jarman", *Interview* 23: 9 (September 1993): 56.

Darke, Chris. "*Wittgenstein*", *Sight and Sound* 3: 4 (April 1993): 63.

Elley, Derek. "*Wittgenstein*", *Variety* 350: 3 (15 February 1993): 86.

Gagne, Cole. "Britain's Jarman unveils portrait of Wittgenstein", *Film Journal* 96: 9 (October/November 1993): 18.

Hammond, Wally. "*Wittgenstein*", *Time Out* 1179 (24-30 March 1993): 61.

"The importance of being Ludwig", *Economist* 327: 7807 (17 April 1993): 88.

Indiana, Gary. "Philosopher in the Bedroom: *Wittgenstein* directed by Derek Jarman/*Household Saints* directed by Nancy Savoca", *Village Voice* 38: 38 (21 September 1993): 60.

Kauffmann, Stanley. "A pilgrimage", *The New Republic* 209: 15 (11

October 1993): 38-39.

Letts, Vanessa. "All green to me", *Spectator [London]* 270: 8595 (3 April 1993): 36, 38.

Maslin, Janet. "*Wittgenstein*", *The New York Times* 143 (18 September 1993): 12(N).

Monk, Ray. "Between earth and ice", *Times Literary Supplement* 4694 (19 March 1993): 16.

O'Pray, Michael. "Philosophical extras", *Sight and Sound* 3: 4 (April 1993): 24-25.

Romney, Jonathan. "Baroque and role-reversal", *New Statesman & Society* 6: 243 (12 March 1993): 34-35.

——————. "When film goes awol", *New Statesmen & Society* 6: 245 (26 March 1993): 32-33.

Seligman, Craig. "Fanciful fiction: *Wittgenstein* directed by Derek Jarman", *Advocate* 636 (24 August 1993): 71.

Suntinger, Diethard. "'Die Welt ist alles, was der Fall is'. Zu Jarmans 'Wittgenstein'", *Blimp* 25 (autumn 1993): 28-32 [in German].

Edward II

Bronski, Michael. "Raging Correctly: *Edward II* directed by Derek Jarman", *Gay Community News* 19: 37-38 (19 April 1992): 16-17.

Comuzio, Ermano. "*Eduardo II*", *Cineforum* 31: 12 (December 1991): 66-68 [in Italian].

Ehrenstein, David. "Jarman's *Edward II* cuts to the Heart of the Gay Movie Revolution: *Edward II* directed by Derek Jarman", *Advocate* 600 (7 April 1992): 79.

Feay, Suzy. "Crimes of Fashion", *Time Out* 1104 (16-23 October 1991): 16-17, 63.

Frascella, Lawrence. "Reviews–*Edward II* directed by Derek Jarman", *Us* 171 (April 1992): 86.

Gagne, Cole. "*Edward II*", *Film Journal* 95: 3 (April 1992): 38-39.

Hoberman, J. "Prisoners of Sex–*Edward II* directed by Derek Jarman/ *Raise the Red Lantern* directed by Zhang Yimou", *Village Voice* 37: 12 (24 March 1992): 57, 70.

Holden, Stephen. "Historical *Edward II* and Gay issues Today", *The New York Times* 141 (20 March 1992): C16.

Horger, J. "Derek Jarman's Film Adaptation of Marlowe's *Edward II*",

Shakespeare Bulletin 11: 4 (autumn 1993): 37-40.

Kennedy, Harlan. "An Affectionate Beast", *Film Comment* 27: 6 (November/December 1991): 42-44.

Kermode, Mark. "*Edward II*", *Sight and Sound* 1: 12 (April 1992): 66 [review upon the film's video release].

MacCabe, Colin. "Throne of blood", *Sight and Sound* 1: 6 (October 1991): 12-14.

Martini, Emanuela. "The 1991 Venice Film Festival: Elizabethan Rage", *Cineforum* 31: 10 (October 1991): 10-12 [in Italian].

O'Pray, Michael. "Damning desire", *Sight and Sound* 1: 6 (October 1991): 8-11 [includes many of Jarman's comments on specific shots, costumes and lighting decisions].

O'Toole, Lawrence. "Movies", *Entertainment Weekly* 148 (11 December 1992): 77.

Prasch, Thomas. "*Edward II*", *American Historical Review* 98: 4 (October 1993): 1164-1166.

Richard, Frédéric. "*Edward II*", *Positif* 382 (December 1992): 58 [in French].

Romney, Jonathan. "*Edward II*", *Sight and Sound* 1: 7 (November 1991): 41-42.

Rozen, Leah. "Picks and Pans–*Edward II* directed by Derek Jarman and starring Steven Waddington and Andrew Tiernan", *People Weekly* 37: 13 (6 April 1992): 22.

Spufford, Francis. "Blank Verse and Body Fluids", *Times Literary Supplement* 4624 (15 November 1991): 19.

Stratton, David. "*Edward II*", *Variety* 344 (16 September 1991): 90.

Talvacchia, Bette. "Historical Phallicy: Derek Jarman's *Edward II*", *Oxford Art Journal* 16: 1 (1993): 112-128.

Travers, Peter. "Movies-*Edward II* directed by Derek Jarman", *Rolling Stone* 627 (2 April 1992): 41-42.

Waugh, Harriet. "Not a pretty story", *Spectator [London]* 267: 8519 (19 October 1991): 48-49.

Williamson, Bruce. "Movies–*Edward II* directed by Derek Jarman", *Playboy* 39: 5 (May 1992): 20.

The Garden

Devo. "*The Garden*", *Variety* 340: 13 (8 October 1990): 61.

"The Garden of Earthly Delights", with Jonathan Romney. *City Limits* 3-10 January 1991: 12-14 [Romney reviews *The Garden* and discusses the film with Jarman].

Hoberman, J. "A Sentimental Journey–*The Garden* written and directed by Derek Jarman", *Village Voice* 36: 4 (22 January 1991): 51.

Maslin, Janet. "Derek Jarman's *Garden* offers vision of decay", *The New York Times* 140 (17 January 1991): C16.

O'Pray, Michael. "*The Garden*", *Monthly Film Bulletin* 58: 684 (January 1991): 15-16.

Schwartzberg, Shlomo. "*The Garden*", *Screen International* 775 (22-28 September 1990): 18.

Sexton, David. "Jesus of Dungeness–*The Garden* directed by Derek Jarman", *Times Literary Supplement* 4580 (11 January 1991): 10.

Timofeevsky, Aleksandr. "The bitter end", *Sight and Sound* 1: 6 (October 1991): 32 [discusses *The Garden* at the Moscow Film Festival].

War Requiem

Adam. "*War Requiem*", *Variety* 333: 11 (4 January 1989): 73.

Canby, Vincent. "Britten's War Requiem to Images by Derek Jarman", *The New York Times* 139 (20 January 1990): C10.

Ferdinand. "Jarman's silent movie", *Sight and Sound* 58: 1 (winter 1988-89): 40-41.

Keates, Jonathan. "The art of war: *War Requiem*", *Sight and Sound* 58: 2 (spring 1989): 133-134.

Kerner, Leighton. "Look Back in Anger", *Village Voice* 35: 5 (30 January 1990): 70.

Petley, Julian. "*War Requiem*", *Monthly Film Bulletin* 56: 661 (February 1989): 60-61.

Porter, Peter. "*War Requiem*", *Times Literary Supplement* 4488 (7 April 1989): 368.

Powell, Dilys. "Maggie's Passion", *Punch* 296: 7721 (6 January 1989): 54.

The Last of England

Adam. "*The Last of England*", *Variety* 328: 5 (26 August 1987): 18.

Greene, Kent. "*The Last of England*", *Cineaste* 18: 4 (1991): 59-60.

Harvey, Stephen. "*The Last of England*", *Film Comment* 24: 6 (November/December 1988): 60.

Hoberman, J. "Twilight Zone: The Movies", *Village Voice* 34: 3 (17 January 1989): 61.

Jenkins, Steve. "*The Last of England*", *Monthly Film Bulletin* 54: 645 (October 1987): 307-308.

Marriott, John. "*The Last of England*", *Films and Filming* 397 (October 1987): 37.

'QSF'. "*The Last of England*", *Screen International* 612 (8-15 August 1987): 26.

Williamson, Judith. "Pictures of pictures: *The Last of England*", *New Statesman* 114: 2952 (23 October 1987): 26.

The Queen is Dead

Hebdige, Dick. "The Sick Rose ('The Queen is Dead' (1986))", in "Digging for Britain: An excavation in seven parts" [in Dominic Strinati and Stephen Wagg (eds), *Come On Down?: Popular media culture in post-war Britain* (London; New York: Routledge, 1992): 336-377].

Stringer, Julian. "Serendipity into Style *The Queen Is Dead*", *Millennium Film Journal* 27 (winter 1993-94): 3-14.

Caravaggio

Baxter, Brian. "*Caravaggio*", *Films and Filming* 379 (April 1986): 33-34.

Finch, Mark. "*Caravaggio*", *Monthly Film Bulletin* 53: 627 (April 1986): 99-100.

Fuller, Graham. "On location: *Caravaggio*", *Stills* 21 (October 1985): 27, 29 [production report].

Goodman, Walter. "A Portrait of the Artist", *The New York Times* 135 (29 August 1986): C15.

Haenlein, Charlotte. "*Caravaggio*", *Du* 7 (1986): 82-83 [in German].

"Low-Life *Caravaggio*", *History Today* 36 (May 1986): 3-4.

Mars-Jones, Adam. "More Shadow than Light", *New Statesman* 111: 2874 (25 April 1986): 29.

Masoni, Tullio. "*Caravaggio*", *Cineforum* 27: 267 (September 1987): 76-80 [in Italian].

Masson, Alain. "*Caravaggio*", *Positif* 325 (March 1988): 79 [in French].

Newport, David. "Life and loves of a renaissance artist designed for a mainstream audience", *Screen International* 519 (19-26 October 1985): 393-394 [production report].

Prendergast, Mark. "*Caravaggio*: The Making of a Dream", *Films and Filming* 376 (January 1986): 27-30.

Pym, John. *Film on Four, 1982/1991: A survey* (London: British Film Institute, 1992): 63-64.

Rayns, Tony. "Unnatural Lighting", *American Film* 11: 10 (September 1986): 44-47, 59-61.

Schutte, Wolfram. "The Cave", *Artforum* 24 (summer 1986): 13.

Stanbrook, Alan. "Cutting the painter", *Stills* 26 (April 1986): 42.

Stratton, David. "*Caravaggio*", *Variety* 322: 5 (26 February 1986): 16.

Suntinger, Diethard. "Medusas Haupt", *Blimp* 19 (spring 1992): 26-28 [in German].

Taylor, John Russell. "Love among the waxworks: *Caravaggio*", *Sight and Sound* 55: 2 (spring 1986): 136-137.

Tillman, Lynne. "Love Story", *Art in America* 75 (January 1987): 21-23.

Woodward, Richard B. "*Caravaggio*: the movie", *Art News* 85 (November 1986): 11-12.

The Angelic Conversation

Green, William. "*The Angelic Conversation*", *Sight and Sound* 1: 9 (January 1992): 61 [review upon the film's video release].

Hitch. "Angelic Conversations", *Variety* 318: 10 (3 April 1985): 21.

Jenkins, Steve. "*The Angelic Conversation*", *Monthly Film Bulletin* 52: 619 (August 1985): 241-242.

Stein, Elliott. "The Gay Film Festival: Desperately Seeking Sodom", *Village Voice* 31: 3 (21 January 1986): 57.

Imagining October

Kennedy, Harlan. "*The Dream Machine/Imagining October*", *Film Comment* 21: 6 (November/December 1985): 76.

The Tempest

Auty, Chris. "*The Tempest*", *Time Out* 524 (2-8 May 1980): 49 [a brief review].

Auty, Martyn. "*The Tempest*", *Monthly Film Bulletin* 47: 555 (April 1980): 78-79.

Bilbow, Marjorie. "*The Tempest*", *Screen International* 244 (7-14 June 1980): 15.

Holderness, Graham. "Shakespeare Rewound", *Shakespeare Survey* 45 (1992): 63-74 [reviews *The Tempest* alongside other adaptations of Shakespeare to film].

Kennedy, Harlan. "Prospero's Flicks", *Film Comment* 28: 1 (January/ February 1992): 45-49 [compares Jarman's film with *Prospero's Books* and *Forbidden Planet* as versions of Shakespeare's play].

Perry, Simon. "*The Tempest*", *Variety* 296: 6 (12 September 1979): 20.

Rayns, Tony. "News: Rich and Strange", *Time Out* 475 (25-31 May 1979): 36.

Sutherland, Allan T. "Britain at Edinburgh", *Sight and Sound* 49: 1 (winter 1979-80): 14-16.

"Taking a new look at the Bard", *Screen International* 217 (24 November-1 December 1979): 12.

Zarkin, Robert. "*The Tempest*", *Films and Filming* 26: 9 (June 1980): 28.

Jubilee

Coli. "*Jubilee*", *Variety* 289: 13 (1 February 1978): 24.

Gow, Gordon. "*Jubilee*", *Films and Filming* 24: 7 (April 1978): 40.

Kermode, Mark and Peter Dean. "*Jubilee* directed by Derek Jarman", *Sight and Sound* 5: 4 (April 1995): 62 [a brief review].

Meek, Scott. "*Jubilee*", *Monthly Film Bulletin* 45: 531 (April 1978): 66.

Ramasse, François. "*Jubilee*", *Positif* 208/209 (July/August 1978): 89-90 [in French].

Rayns, Tony. "Queendom Come", *Time Out* 412 (24 February-2 March 1978): 11.

Sebastiane

"Boys and Arrows", *Films and Filming* 23: 2 (1976): 46-50.

Elley, Derek. "*Sebastiane*", *Films and Filming* 23: 4 (January 1977): 44.

Kermode, Mark and Peter Dean. "*Sebastiane*", *Sight and Sound* 5: 4 (April 1995): 59 [a brief review upon the film's video re-release].

Malcolm, Derek. "*Sebastiane*", *The Guardian* 21 December 1976 [also includes a survey of Jarman's work for Ken Russell].

Mosk. "Locarno Festival Reviews: *Sebastian*", *Variety* 284: 3 (25 August 1976): 22.

Rayns, Tony. "*Sebastiane*", *Monthly Film Bulletin* 43: 514 (November

1976): 235-236.

Rayns, Tony. "Unblocked Talents", *Time Out* 346 (5-11 November 1976): 12-13.

Sanderson, Mark. "*Sebastiane*", *Time Out* 1079 (24-30 April 1991): 150 [tackles issues of television censorship].

Wilson, David. "Festivals '76: Locarno", *Sight and Sound* 45: 4 (autumn 1976): 241.

(ii) Books

At Your Own Risk: A Saint's Testament

Athey, Ron. "Saint, Martyr, Queer: The Activist testaments of Derek Jarman", *LA Weekly* 6-12 August 1992: 35-36.

Fletcher, Martin. "Bombs of bitterness: *At Your Own Risk: A Saint's Testament* by Derek Jarman", *New Statesman & Society* 5: 202 (15 May 1992): 38.

Woods, Gregory. "A Distinctly Jolly Martyr–*At Your Own Risk: A Saint's Testament* by Derek Jarman", *Times Literary Supplement* 4656 (26 June 1992): 32.

Blue

hooks, bell. "Bookforum: *Blue* by Derek Jarman", *Artforum* 33: 3 (November 1994): SS10.

Steinberg, Sybil. "Fiction–*Blue* by Derek Jarman", *Publishers' Weekly* 241: 22 (30 May 1994): 36.

Chroma

Buck, Louisa. "Bright sparks", *New Statesman & Society* 7: 289 (11 February 1994): 38-39.

Camhi, Leslie. "Brief Encounters: *Chroma* by Derek Jarman", *Village Voice* 40: 15 (11 April 1995): SS5-SS6.

"True Colors", *Economist* 330: 7852 (26 February 1994): 92.

Dancing Ledge

Chua, Lawrence. "Bookforum: *Dancing Ledge* by Derek Jarman/*Modern Nature* by Derek Jarman", *Artforum* 32: 4 (December 1993): 67-68.

Clark, John. "Shelf life: *Dancing Ledge* by Derek Jarman", *Premiere* 6: 12 (August 1993): 36.

Ehrenstein, David. "*Dancing Ledge*", *Film Quarterly* 39: 1 (autumn 1985): 57-58.

O'Pray, Michael. "Lines and Ledges", *Undercut* 12 (summer 1984): 57-58.

Yacowar, Maurice. "*Dancing Ledge* by Derek Jarman and edited by Shaun Allen", *Choice* 31: 4 (December 1993): 612.

Modern Nature

Fletcher, Martin. "Shining On–*Modern Nature*: The Journals of Derek Jarman", *New Statesman & Society* 4: 164 (16 August 1991): 37-38.

Pickles, Stephen. "*Modern Nature*–The Journals of Derek Jarman", *Times Literary Supplement* 4614 (6 September 1991): 19.

Rothke, Joy. "Books for your shelves – *Modern Nature* by Derek Jarman", *10 Percent* 2: 7 (March 1994): 10.

Thomson, David. "The British Invasion", *The New Republic* 210: 17 (25 April 1994): 39-41.

Queer Edward II

Frith, Simon. "Art of the book of the film–*Prospero's Books* by Peter Greenaway/*Queer Edward II* by Derek Jarman/*Diary of a Young Soul Rebel*", by Issac Julien and Colin MacCabe, *Sight and Sound* 1: 8 (December 1991): 32.

Welt, Bernard. "Jarman Meets Marlowe: *Queer Edward II* by Derek Jarman", *Lambda Book Report* 3: 4 (May 1992): 29-30.

Wittgenstein

Luckhardt, C G. "*Wittgenstein: The Terry Eagleton Script, the Derek Jarman Film*", *Choice* 31: 6 (January 1994): 948-49.

McGinn, Colin. "Soul on Fire", *The New Republic* 210: 25 (20 June 1994): 34-39.

E: Obituaries

"British filmmaker known for his visually-stunning cinematography and depictions of gay life", *Facts on File* 54: 2778 (24 February 1994): 132.

Brown, Georgia. "Gardening Angel – Derek Jarman, 1942-1994 featuring 19 films directed by Derek Jarman", *Village Voice* 39: 13 (29 March 1994): 51 [previews a forthcoming retrospective of Jarman's work in New York].

Cook, Roger. "Derek Jarman", *Art Monthly* 174 (March 1994): 34.

"Derek Jarman", *The Times* 21 February 1994: 17 [also includes a brief tribute by John Russell Taylor].

"Derek Jarman, 52, outspoken British film maker", *The New York Times*

143: 49614 (21 February 1994): C7/D8.

Hobbs, Christopher. "In memory of Derek Jarman", *Sight and Sound* 4: 4 (April 1994): 7.

Królikowska-Avis, Elżbieta. "Derek Jarman", *Kino* 28: 4 (April 1994): 38-39 [in Polish].

Lyons, James. "A Dream for Derek", *Village Voice* 39: 15 (12 April 1994): 60.

MacCabe, Colin. "Derek Jarman", *The Independent* 21 February 1994: 14 [also includes brief tributes by Don Boyd and Simon Garfield, a survey of friends' and colleagues' reactions compiled by Stephen Ward, and a front-page article, "Gay champion dies on eve of Vote", placing Jarman's death alongside the parliamentary debate on the age of consent].

——————. "Derek Jarman-Obituary", *Critical Quarterly* 36: 1 (spring 1994): iv-ix [a reprint of *The Independent* obituary].

Middleton, Peter. "Middleton Remembers Jarman", *Eyepiece* 17: 1 (February/March 1996): 8-11.

Natale, Richard. "Derek Jarman", *Variety* 354: 4 (28 February 1994): 74.

Robinson, David. "A subversive master of art", *The Guardian* 21 February 1994: G2, 4-6 [also includes Derek Malcolm's brief tribute, "Visions from a War with hypocrisy"].

Taubin, Amy. "Am I blue?", *Village Voice* 39: 10 (8 March 1994): 58-59.

Thomas, Kevin. "Jarman: Artist, Activist and Iconoclast", *Los Angeles Times* 24 February 1994: C3.

Walker, Alexander. "A Prospero whose magic bewitched a generation", *Evening Standard* 24 February 1994: 14.

Watney, Simon. "Derek Jarman 1942-94: A political death", *Artforum* 32: 9 (May 1994): 84-85 ff.

[For a dissenting view, highly critical of Jarman's work and life, printed in one of the tabloids that Jarman so much despised, see Christopher Tookey, "How can they turn this Man into a Saint?", *Daily Mail* 23 February 1994: 8.]

Index

Abstract Expressionism 160n66
Accattone 45
Adam Ant 76
Afterimage (magazine) 1
Agony and the Ecstasy, The 121
AIDS
4, 5, 7, 41, 50, 51, 53, 57, 59, 77, 99, 118, 126-130, 133n25, 147-152, 154n7, 158n48
All Quiet On the Western Front 95, 100
Amis, Martin 81n55
Anderson, Lindsay 135
Anderson, Perry 69, 76, 145
Angelic Conversation, The 1, 3, 13, 20, 22, 24, 35, 41, 53, 56, 58, 73, 75, 76, 80n35, 100, 106, 120, 121, 148, 162
Anger, Kenneth 23, 32, 86, 136
"Anthem for Doomed Youth" (poem) 95
Araki, Gregg 38
Archibald, Dawn 28n29
Aria 13, 90, 91
Aristotle 145
Armies of the Night, The 151
Art of Mirrors, The 117
Ashton, Sir Frederick 2
Astaire, Fred 23
"At a Cavalry near the Ancre" (poem) 98
At Your Own Risk 1, 13, 15, 16, 29n42, 41, 152, 155n17, 161
Bakeless, John 132n15
Balet, Mark 2
Barrett, Cyril 155n15
Bartley, W W 156n26
Battleship Potemkin **see** *Bronenosets Potemkin*

Baudelaire, Charles 1
BBC **see** British Broadcasting Corporation
BBFC **see** British Board of Film Censors
Beckett, Samuel 141
Beecham, Sir Thomas 89
Bemerkungen über die Farben (Remarks on Colour) 150
Bennington, Geoffrey 160n68
Beowulf (poem) 74
Betjeman, Sir John 75
BFI **see** British Film Institute
Bible 18, 44, 152
Biga, Tracy 6-8, 160n64
bio-pics 4, 89, 138-140
Black Narcissus 89
Black Panther movement 41
Blake, William 65-68, 72, 74, 78, 154n3
Blanchot, Maurice 150
Blood of a Poet, The **see** *Le Sang d'un poète*
Bloomsbury group 54, 67, 143
Blue 1, 4, 6, 8, 9, 25, 26, 53, 57, 59, 77, 79n18, 135, 136, 138, 147-153, 168
Blue and Brown Books, The 155n16
Blue: Text of a film by Derek Jarman 13
Boethius, Anicius Manlius Severinus 112, 116n12
Bonnes, Les (The Maids) (play) 38
Boorman, John 84
Bourdieu, Pierre 155n16
Bowen, Peter 157n39
Bowers, Faubion 101n14
Boyd, Don 85, 90, 166
Brakhage, Stan 136

Branigan, Edward 24
Braudy, Leo 115n1, 115n2, 115n4
Brecht, Bertolt
141, 144, 157n37, 158n50
Bredbeck, Gregory 111
Brideshead Revisited 36
British Board of Film Censors
(BBFC) 70
British Broadcasting Corporation
(BBC)
5, 85, 89, 132n14, 133n24, 148, 149
British Film Institute (BFI) 11n22, 35
Britten, Benjamin
5, 7, 54, 58, 73, 85, 86, 91-100
Britten-Pears Foundation 85, 86
Broken English 13
*Bronenosets Potemkin (Battleship
Potemkin)* 39, 57
Brooke, Rupert 77, 78
Brooks, Peter 12, 26, 27n2
Brown, Ford Madox 4
Bryant, Anita 128
"Bugles Sang" (poem) 96
Butler, Ken 9n4, 24, 165
Caesar, Gaius Julius 113
Calinescu, Matei 135
Cambridge Apostles 143
"Canticle II: Abraham and Isaac" 97
Caravaggio
1, 2, 4, 13, 23, 32, 35, 41, 42, 44-47,
50, 56-58, 73, 106, 138, 140, 163,
164, 167, 168
Caravaggio, Michelangelo Merisi da
3, 4, 23, 34, 41-52, 54, 59, 68, 73,
97, 140
"Care and Control" (exhibition)
11n19
Carey, George 122
Carpenter, Humphrey 102n29
Celan, Paul 152
Channel 4 Television
6, 8, 10n11, 57, 168
Chant d'amour, Un 37, 54, 61n14
Chariots of Fire 36, 57, 78
Charleson, Ian 57
Chassay, Clancy 8, 17
Chaucer, Geoffrey 75
Chion, Michel 159n60
Christie, Ian 90, 101n16
Chroma 1, 30n47, 63n59, 140, 150

Churchill, Sir Winston Leonard
Spencer 71
Clause 28 (Local Government Act,
1987-88)
57, 67, 72, 79n17, 124, 126
Cocteau, Jean
7, 32, 34, 39, 54-57, 59, 97, 136
Cohen, Marshall
115n1, 115n2, 115n4
Coil 3, 80n35, 100, 121
Cold War 157n37
Cole, Kermit 158n48
Coleridge, Samuel Taylor 66
Collard, Cyril 148
Collins, Keith
10n13, 10n15, 18, 114, 123
Confessions, Les (Confessions) 151
Conrad, Joseph 68
Conservative Party 7, 69, 124
Consolation of Philosophy, The **see**
De Consolatione Philosophiae
Constable, John 68
Cook, Roger 18
Corner, John 82n73
Correction **see** *Korrektur*
County, Wayne 106
Coventry Arts Committee 92, 93
Coventry Cathedral 93
Critique of Judgement **see** *Kritik
der Urteilskraft*
Cromwell, Oliver 71
Cukor, George 60n2
Culhane, John 101n15
Custen, George F 155n18
Dada 54, 147
Dallas 69
"Dance of the Sugar Plum Fairy,
The" 125
Dancing Ledge
13, 16, 35, 85, 87, 140, 147, 168
Dante's Inferno 89
Danto, Arthur C 154n2
Darke, Chris 158n50
David, [Jacques] Louis 4
Davies, Terence 36
Day-Lewis, Daniel 85
Dayan, Daniel 29n46
*De Consolatione Philosophiae (The
Consolation of Philosophy)*
116n12

de Lauretis, Teresa 105
Dean, James 69
Death of the Past, The 68
Debord, Guy 158n43
Dee, John
    3, 21, 56, 76, 84, 106, 117
Delany, Samuel R 160n61
Demme, Jonathan 148
Dench, Judi 4, 20, 121
"Depuis le jour" (aria) 91
Derek Jarman's Caravaggio
    13, 29n42, 168
derek jarman's garden 5
Devils, The 2, 56, 58
DHPG (drug) 151
Dieckmann, Katherine
    100n2, 102n24
Discipline and Punish: The Birth of
    the Prison see *Surveiller et*
    punir: Naissance de la prison
Discorso (Discourses) 111
Disney, Walt 7, 88
Donen, Stanley 56
Donne, John 5
Donoghue, Denis 157n31
Doty, Alexander 60n2
Dr Ehrlich's Magic Bullet 139
Dreyer, Carl Theodor 56
Driscoll, Lawrence
    7, 10n10, 130n5, 154n3
Duchamp, Marcel 147
Duffy, Bruce 156n24
Dyer, Richard 37, 38, 63n48
Eagleton, Terry
    6, 144-146, 154n6, 155n19, 156n25,
    156n27, 157n35, 157n40, 157n41,
    158n44
Easdale, Brian 89
Edens, Roger 6
Edipo Re (Oedipus Rex) 44
Edward II
    5-8, 9n2, 13, 15, 19-21, 23, 30n47,
    32, 35, 39, 51, 53, 54, 56-58, 85,
    106, 109, 111, 114, 115, 118, 122,
    124, 127, 129, 133n24, 135, 137,
    138, 147, 148, 163-165, 167-169
Eisenstein, Sergej
    7, 25, 32, 36, 39, 46, 56-59, 87, 88
Elizabeth I
    3, 18, 21, 56, 71, 76, 84, 106, 107

Elizabeth II 3, 21, 71, 84, 106
"End, The" (poem) 97, 98
Enfants terribles, Les 54, 55
English Civil War 71
"Entombment of Christ, The"
    (painting) 42
"Every Time We Say Goodbye"
    (song) 6, 23
Evil Queen (exhibition) 1, 9n4
"Execution of John the Baptist,
    The" (painting) 48
Factory 58
Faithfull, Marianne 58, 91
Falklands War 53
Fantasia 7, 88, 90
Fascism 44, 52, 62n28, 69, 77
Fassbinder, Rainer Werner
    38, 39, 46, 51, 54, 61n11
Feinstein, Howard 158n48
Ferran, Peter W 157n37
Ferry, Bryan 91
Field, Simon 27n4, 29n41, 65, 82n79
Finch, David 82n72
Fischer-Dieskau, Dietrich 93
Fish, Stanley 155n16
Forster, E M 67
Foucault, Michel
    36-38, 43, 53, 61n14, 153
Frampton, Hollis 148
Frankfurt School 155n12
Frears, Stephen 9, 36, 46, 79n21
Freud, Sigmund 28n27
Friedman, Lester
    82n76, 102n36, 131n9, 131n10
Funeral Rites see *Pompes funèbres*
Funny Face 18, 23, 56
Fuss, Diana 133n25
"Futility" (poem) 97
Gable, Robin 83n92
Gabriel, Teshome 34
Gagne, Cole 157n29
Gandhi, Mohandâs Karamchand 93
Garber, Marjorie 157n34
Garden, The
    1, 5, 6, 13, 18, 20, 23, 24, 28,
    30n47, 35, 41, 51, 56-58, 66, 75,
    120, 132n20, 133n24, 137, 147, 167,
    168
"Garden of Love, The" (poem) 66
Gardener's World 5

Gardner, David   7, 8, 131n8
Gass, William   150
Gate Cinema, London   3
Gautier, Théophile   154n5
Geertz, Clifford   11n20, 151
Genet, Jean
  7, 32, 34-41, 51-54, 59, 140, 160n61
Genre (journal)   11n22
George V   97
Gibson, Ben   11n22
Gidal, Peter   158n49
Gilbert and George   74, 83n94
Gilman, Richard   154n5
Girard, René   20
Gissing, George   136
Glitterbug
         6, 13, 25, 58, 63n58, 78, 148
Godard, Jean-Luc   22
Goethe, Johann Wolfgang von   150
"Going, Going" (poem)   75
Goldberg, Jonathan   103
Gomez, Joseph A   7, 101n18
Gospel According to St Matthew, The
  see *Il Vangelo secondo Matteo*
Graber, Jody   124, 133n24
Gramsci, Antonio   131n7
Grant, Duncan   143
Greater London Council   73
Greenaway, Peter   9, 59
Greenberg, Clement   158n51
Greenblatt, Stephen   103
Grundmann, Roy   156n22
Guardian, The   11n22, 128
Gunning, Tom   105
Habermas, Jürgen   155n12
Hacker, Jonathan   10n9, 101n6
Hacker, P M S   159n58
Hackney Hospital   11n19
Hall, Marguerite Radclyffe   67
Hall, Stuart   119, 131n7
Halliwell, Kenneth   47
Harpham, Geoffrey Galt   143
Harrison, Charles
            158n51, 159n52, 160n66
Harvey, Sylvia   82n73
Hawkes, David   7, 80n38, 131n10
Haynes, Todd   38
Healey, Denis   70, 71
Hebdige, Dick   78n1, 80n33

Hegel, Georg Wilhelm Friedrich
                             138, 146
Hejinian, Lyn   155n16
Hellman, Lillian   62n27
Hepburn, Audrey   23
Herder, Johann   87
Heseltine, Michael   114
"Heterosoc"
     7, 15, 16, 21, 117-134, 138, 161
Higdon, David Leon   79n19
Hirst, David   73, 75
Hitchcock, Alfred   60n2
HIV (human immunodeficiency
  virus)
  1, 4, 7, 17, 50, 57, 58, 77, 99, 127,
                             133n25
Hoare, Quintin   131n7
Hobbs, Christopher   4, 123, 165
Hoberman, J   109
Hobsbawm, Eric   78
Hockney, David   2, 68
Hollywood
     56, 60n2, 103, 104, 107, 109, 114,
                        121, 138, 139
Holocaust   152
Holroyd, Michael   157n34
Holst, Gustav   90
Hope and Glory   84
Howards End   67
Hurd, Douglas   71
Hutchinson, Lord   71
Hutton, Betty   146, 147
Hyman, Timothy   90
Imagining October
                 13, 32, 57, 58, 66
IMF **see** International Monetary
  Fund
In the Shadow of the Sun
                         13, 54, 117
Independent, The (newspaper)
            10n15, 11n21, 11n22
International Monetary Fund (IMF)
                              80n32
Irish Republican Army (IRA)   53
Isaacs, Jeremy   9, 9n5, 10n6
*Isadora Duncan: The Biggest
  Dancer in the World*   89
Ivan grozny (Ivan the Terrible)
                          56, 87, 88
Jacques, Martin   131n7

Jagger, Charles Sargeant 94
James, Barney 19
James I and the Politics of
Literature 103
Janik, Allan 136, 156n26
Jarman, Elizabeth [Betty] (mother)
16, 17, 71
Jarman, Lance (father)
2, 5, 7, 15-17, 42, 65, 66, 77, 78n5,
125
Jay, Martin 159n56
Jeffery-Poulter, Stephen 132n21
Jennings, Humphrey 75
"Jerusalem" (poem) 78
Johns, Jasper 140
Johnson, Guy
82n76, 83n95, 102n36, 131n9
Johnson, Karl 76
Jordan 117
Jordan, Neil 36
Joyce, James 68
Jubilee
1, 3, 7, 13, 18, 21, 24, 53, 56-58,
69-71, 76, 79n9, 84, 106, 107, 117,
130n2, 136, 138, 146, 148, 162
Julien, Isaac 36
Jumpers (play) 141
Kalin, Tom 38
Kant, Immanuel 138, 152, 158n51
Kaplan, E Ann 105
Keats, John 95
Kennedy, Michael 93, 98
Kenny, Anthony 155n16
Keynes, Geoffrey 78n1, 79n8, 79n9
Keynes, John Maynard 143, 144
King's College, London 15
Kirschbaum, Leo 132n15
Klein, Yves 149, 150
Know What I Mean?
10n11, 11n23, 71
Korrektur (Correction) 141
Krauss, Rosalind 159n51
Kritik der Urteilskraft (Critique of
Judgement) 152
Kuchar Brothers 148
Kureishi, Hanif 36
Labour Party 69, 76, 118
Lacan, Jacques 28n27, 29n40
Larkin, Philip 65, 75

Last of England, The (book)
3, 13, 166
Last of England, The (film)
4, 5, 8, 13, 17, 24, 32, 35, 53, 56-58,
68, 73-76, 82n85, 86, 120, 137, 162,
166, 167, 168
Late Show, The 9, 9n5, 10n6, 10n12
Leigh, Mike 36
Leigh, Spencer 68, 74, 82n85
Lemaire, Anika 29n40
Leninism 144, 146
Lennox, Annie 6, 23
Leonardo da Vinci 121
lesbianism 31, 61n14, 126, 133n27
Lessing, Gotthold 87
Levi, Albert William 156n26
Levy, Paul 157n33
Lewis, Cecil Day 78n3
Lewis, Matthew 55
Life of Emile Zola, The 139
Lightning Over Water 151
Lippard, Chris
82n75, 82n76, 82n77, 83n95,
102n36, 131n9
Living End, The 38
Living Proof: HIV and the Pursuit
of Happiness 158n48
Local Government Act (1987-88)
79n17, 124
"London" (poem) 66
Loos, Adolf 136
Lopokova, Lydia 143
"Love's Wine" (poem) 1
Lumley, Bob 131n7
Lyotard, Jean-François 152
MacCabe, Colin
10n15, 11n22, 28n39, 141, 164
McCarthyism 62n27
McFayean, Melanie 133n24
McKellen, Ian 53, 57, 130n6
McKibbin, Ross 83n96
McLaren, Malcolm 70
McLennan, Gregor 131n7
Machiavelli, Niccolò 109, 111-114
Maids, The (play) *Les Bonnes*
Mailer, Norman 151
Mallarmé, Stéphane 150
Maltin, Leonard 101n15
"Man With the Blue Guitar, The"
(painting) 150

Marat, Jean Paul 4
Marcus, Greil 158n43
Marlowe, Christopher
6, 19, 46, 54, 106, 109-111, 113,
114, 122-124, 147, 164
Marxism
73, 77, 119, 146, 155n12, 158n43
*Massnahme, Die (The Measures
Taken)* (play) 144
Massood, Paula 130
Mast, Gerald 115n1, 115n2, 115n4
Mayne, Judith 105
Measures Taken, The (play) **see**
Die Massnahme
Meyer, David 108
Michelangelo (Michelagnioli di
Lodovico Buonarroti) 47, 121
Michelson, Annette 159n57
Mills, Johnny 18
Milner, Anthony 97, 98
Milton, John 74
Miranda, Carmen 146
Mishima, Yukio 40
Modern Nature
5, 13, 15, 16, 29n42, 42, 142, 147
modernism
38, 52, 68, 73, 76, 135, 136, 138,
140, 141, 145, 149, 150, 153,
158n51, 160n67
Money 81n55
Monitor 89
Monk, Ray 6, 141, 157n36
Monopoly (game) 70
Montacute House 75, 163
Moore, George Edward
140, 143, 144, 156n24
Morgan, Stuart 160n65
Morris, William 67, 74, 75, 154n3
Morrison, Richard 85
MTV 86, 90
Mulvey, Laura 104, 105, 115
Murnau, F W 46
Music Lovers, The 89
Music, Music, Music (project) 90
My Sister, My Love **see** *Syskonbädd
1782*
Mysterium 88
Nairn, Tom 67
Nash, John 81n68
National Film Theatre (NFT) 73

Nazism 62n27, 93, 141
Neve, Christopher 81n56, 81n68
"New Historicism" 103
Newman, Barnet 149
"Next War, The" (poem) 96
NFT **see** National Film Theatre
Night with Derek, A
8, 10n11, 11n23
Noscoe, Robin 14
Nowell-Smith, Geoffrey 131n7
Nuits fauves, Les (Savage Nights)
148
"Nutcracker Suite, The" 88
O'Brien, Richard 117
October **see** *Oktyabr'*
Oedipus Rex **see** *Edipo Re*
Offenbach, Jacques 89
O'Hagan, Sean 76
Oktyabr' (October) 57
Olivier, Laurence 85, 94
Omnibus 89
*On Being Blue: A Philosophical
Inquiry* 150
OPEC **see** Organization of
Petroleum Exporting Companies
Opium 55
O'Pray, Michael
29n39, 29n41, 100n1, 101n8, 101n9,
102n24
Organization of Petroleum
Exporting Companies (OPEC)
80n32
Orphée (Orpheus) 54, 56, 57
Orton, Joe 45-47, 79n21, 141
Ottaway, Hugh 93
OutRage
6, 8, 57, 59, 130, 133n27, 165, 166
Owen, Wilfred
5, 7, 54, 65, 77, 85, 86, 92-100
Palmer, Christopher 102n33, 102n35
Palmer, Samuel 68
"Parable of the Old Man and the
Young, The" (poem) 97
Parker, Nathaniel 85
Pasolini, Pier Paolo
7, 32, 34, 36, 41-47, 49, 51-53, 59,
61n11, 77, 136
Pasolini, Susanna 62n29
*Passion de Jeanne d'Arc, La (The
Passion of Joan of Arc)* 56

Pater, Walter 142
Patniak, Gayatri 130
"Pearl" (poem) 70
Pears, Sir Peter 85, 86, 93
Penley, Constance 115n3
Perec, Georges 155n16
Perloff, Marjorie 155n16
Pet Shop Boys 91
Philadelphia 148
Philosophical Investigations
137, 138, 140, 142, 143, 145
Physique (magazine) 147
Picasso, Pablo 89, 150
Piero della Francesca 99
"Piers Plowman" (poem) 70
Pitkin, Hanna Fenichel 113
Planets, The 90
Plant, Sadie 146
Plato 138, 147
Plumb, J H 68
Pocock, J G A 116n12
Poem of Ecstasy 88
Poison 38
Pollock, (Paul) Jackson 152
Pompes funèbres (Funeral Rites) 38
pop art 68, 69, 156n20
Pope, Angela 148
Porter, Cole 6
Porton, Richard 8
postmodernism
4, 106, 107, 135, 141, 152
Potter, Sally 36, 57
Pound, Ezra 77
Powell, Michael 7, 8, 88-90, 136
Pressburger, Emeric 89
Price, David 10n9, 101n6
Prick Up Your Ears 46, 79n21
principe, Il (The Prince) 111, 112
Procktor, Patrick 2, 68
"Profane Love" (painting) 4, 68
Prospect Cottage, Dungeness
5, 35, 55, 57, 75, 77
Proust, Marcel 150
punk
3, 53, 58, 69, 70, 106-108, 117, 138, 146
Puttnam, David 36
QE2 53
Queen is Dead, The 4, 13, 91
Queer (exhibition) 1

Queer Edward II
6, 13, 19, 24, 29, 29n42, 53, 109, 114, 132n16, 169
Quentin, John 26, 151
Querelle 38, 39, 51, 54
Querelle de Brest 38, 54
Quinn-Meyler, Martin
7, 8, 9n2, 80n38
Rabinow, Paul 160n72
ragazzi, The 42, 44
"Raising of Lazarus, The" (painting)
97
Rake's Progress, The (opera) 2
Rauschenberg, Robert 156n20
Rear Window (organisation) 11n19
Rechy, John 160n61
Red Shoes, The 89
Reed, Oliver 2
Reisz, Karel 135
Remarks on Colour see
Bemerkungen über die Farben
Renaissance
3, 7, 8, 40, 44, 50, 54, 86, 90, 103-116, 121, 122, 138, 147
Renaissance Self-fashioning 103
Renton, Andrew 160n65
"Resurrection" (painting) 99
Richardson, Tony 135
Rickels, Laurence A 28n27
Ricotta, La (episode in *RoGoPaG*)
45
Rimsky-Korsakov, Nikolai 88
Rodowick, D N 158n49
Roeg, Nicolas 90
Romanticism
38, 66-68, 89, 135, 151, 152
Rosenberg, Harold 160n66
Rosenthal, Norman 2
Rothko, Mark 149, 150
Rousseau, Jean Jacques 151
Rowse, A L 132n15
Royal Academy of Art 2
Royal Ballet 2
"Rule Britannia" 106, 117
Ruskin, John 65, 67
Russell, Bertrand
64n60, 84, 144, 145, 156n24
Russell, Ken 2, 3, 7, 56, 58, 88-90
Sade, Donatien Alphonse François,
Comte de (Marquis) 52

Saint Genet   37

Salò, o le centiventi giornate di Sodoma (Salò, or the 120 Days of Sodom)   52

Sang d'un poète, Le (The Blood of a Poet)   54, 97

Sartre, Jean-Paul   37, 39

Savage, Jon   80n36

Savage Messiah   2, 58

Savage Nights see *Les Nuits fauves*

Schapiro, Meyer   149, 150

Scriabin, Alexander   87, 88

Sebastiane
2-4, 9, 13, 18, 20, 23, 24, 32, 40, 41, 50, 56, 58, 117, 120, 130n2, 138, 142, 164, 168

Sedgwick, Eve Kosofsky   141

Shakespeare, William
4, 20, 22, 23, 53, 58, 65, 67, 73, 80n35, 85, 87, 100, 103, 106-109, 121, 132n15, 147, 153

Showalter, Elaine   154n4

"Sick Rose, The" (poem)   72

Sight and Sound   164

Sinfield, Alan
7, 66, 67, 70-72, 79n11, 79n13, 79n14, 79n20, 80n29, 80n30, 80n31, 80n43, 80n45, 155n10

Sitney, P Adams   150

Situationism   146

Sjöman, Vilgot   165

Skal, David   134n30, 134n31

Slade School of Art, London
2, 15, 68

Smith, Ann-Marie   79n17

Smith, Jack   148

Smith, Paul Julian   34

Smiths, The   4, 58, 91

Snow, Michael   148, 158n49

Socialism   62n27, 64n60

Société du spectacle, La (Society of the Spectacle)   158n43

"Soldier, The" (poem)   78

Sonnets (Shakespeare)
4, 20, 58, 72, 73, 80n35, 100, 121, 147

Soul of Man under Socialism, The   137

Spartacus   121

Spence, Jo   11n19

Spencer, Stanley   81n56

Spinoza, Baruch de   145

Spring   68, 69

Spufford, Francis   134n29

Stalinism   144, 145

Stamp, Terence   62n28

Starobinski, Jean   160n63

Stein, Gertrude   150

Stein, Jack M   101n12, 101n13

Stevens, Wallace   150

Stoneleigh Abbey   75, 162

Stonewall   131n6

Stoppard, Tom   141

"Stormy Weather" (song)
3, 23, 56, 86, 109

Strachey, (Giles) Lytton   143

"Strange Meeting" (poem)   94, 99

Stravinsky, Igor   2

Strinati, Dominic   78n1

Stringer, Julian   102n25

"Sun Rising, The" (poem)   5

Super 8 films
1-3, 5, 6, 13, 22, 56, 63n58, 86, 87, 95, 96, 100, 101n8, 117, 130, 130n2, 163

Surrealism   146, 158n43

Surveiller et punir: Naissance de la prison (Discipline and Punish: The Birth of the Prison) 36, 37, 53

Sutherland, Graham   89

Sutton, Dudley   122

Sweet As You Are   148

Swift, Jonathan   82n85

Swinton, Tilda
24, 26, 74, 94, 98, 122, 132n20, 151

Swoon   38

Swords, Sarah   28n29

Symposium   147

Syskonbädd 1782 (My Sister, My Love)   165

Tales of Hoffmann, The   89

Talvacchia, Bette   28n39, 29n43

Tatchell, Peter   8, 118

Taylor, Charles   160n67

Tchaikovsky, Piotr Ilyich   89, 125

Teale, Owen   85

Telos (journal)   156n26

Tempest, The
1, 3, 7, 8, 13, 17, 23, 53, 56, 58, 73, 75, 85-87, 90, 106, 107, 109, 136, 138, 148, 153, 162
Temple, Julien 36
Teorema (Theorem) 62n28
Terry, Nigel 26, 97, 111, 122, 151
Thatcher, Margaret
4, 7, 35, 36, 53, 58, 69-73, 76, 77, 84, 118, 124, 131n7, 131n10, 147, 148
Theorem see *Teorema*
Theory of Colours see *Zur Farbenlehre*
"Think Pink" (song) 6, 18, 23, 56
Thomas, Dylan 89
Thompson, E P 154n3
Three Songs of Lenin see *Tri pesni Lenina*
Thwaite, Anthony 82n70
Tiernan, Andrew 122
Time Machine, The 68
Tolstoy, Count Leo Nikolayevich 145
Tommy 90
Toulmin, Stephen 136
Tractatus Logico-Philosophicus 136, 139, 143
Treviglio, Leonardo 19
Tri pesni Lenina (Three Songs of Lenin) 159n57
Triumph des Willens (Triumph of the Will) 90
Trotsky, Leon 144, 146
Turner, Joseph Mallord William 68, 74
Turner, Simon Fisher 151
Two of Us, The 133n24
University of London 2
Vangelo secondo Matteo, Il (The Gospel According to St Matthew) 44, 45
Vertov, Dziga 159n57
Vishnevskaya, Galina 93
vita violenta, Una 45
Waddington, Steven 122, 132n20
Wagg, Stephen 78n1
Wagner, Jon 29n40
Wagner, (Wilhelm) Richard 87, 88
Walsingham, Sir Francis 164

"Wanderer, The" (poem) 80n35
War Requiem (book) 13
War Requiem (film)
4, 7, 13, 23, 35, 51, 54, 58, 84-102, 162, 166
War Requiem (mass) 5, 73, 84-102
Ward-Jackson, Nicholas 168
Warhol, Andy 68, 86, 156n20
Watney, Simon
67, 75, 133n25, 148, 160n65
Welch, Elisabeth 3, 56, 86, 109
Wellmer, Albrecht 155n12
Wells, H G 68
Wenders, Wim 151
White, Edmund 158n48, 160n61
Wijdeveld, Paul 156n24
Wilde, Oscar 51, 67, 136, 137, 141
Willcox, Toyah 108
Willemen, Paul 63n48
Williams, Heathcote 3
Williams, Raymond
81n54, 83n92, 131n7
Wittgenstein
5, 6, 8, 13, 17, 18, 24, 25, 32, 51, 53, 58, 64n60, 133n24, 135, 136, 138-143, 146, 148, 150, 153, 163
Wittgenstein, Ludwig Josef Johann
6, 8, 12, 17, 54, 135-147, 149-152
Wizard of Oz, The 10n11, 87
Wolfenden Report (1957) 118
Wollen, Peter 57, 131n10, 156n20
Wood, Paul
158n51, 159n52, 160n66
Wood, Robin 63n48
Woodcock, George 155n10
Woolf, Virginia 67
Wordsworth, Dorothy 66
Wordsworth, William 67
World War I 88, 93, 99, 100
World War II 92, 93
Worth, Fabienne 105
Yingling, Thomas 60n4, 154n7
ZDF see Zweites Deutsches Fernsehen
Zeitgeist Films 153
Zur Farbenlehre (Theory of Colours) 150
Zweites Deutsches Fernsehen (ZDF) 163

Notes on contributors

Tracy Biga teaches film and theory in the Los Angeles area. She has contributed to various journals, including *Film Quarterly* and *Studies in Popular Culture*, and was a 1994-95 Mellon Fellow in Arts Criticism at the California Institute of the Arts. She is currently working on a book-length study of the films of Peter Greenaway.

Lawrence Driscoll is an artist and writer living in Los Angeles. He teaches cultural studies at the University of Southern California.

David Gardner is currently completing a doctorate on film and gay criminals at the University of California, Los Angeles.

Joseph A Gomez is a Professor of English and Director of Film Studies at North Carolina State University. He is the author of *Ken Russell: The Adaptor as Creator* (1976) and *Peter Watkins* (1979), as well as of articles published in *Film Quarterly*, *Literature/Film Quarterly*, *Film Criticism*, *The Velvet Light Trap* and other journals.

David Hawkes teaches English at Lehigh University in Pennsylvania. His first book, *Ideology*, was published in 1996.

Chris Lippard teaches English and film at the University of Utah. He contributed an essay on Jarman's work to *Fires Were Started: British Cinema and Thatcherism* (1993), and is currently working on a study of class and medical issues in the television of Dennis Potter.

Richard Porton is on the editorial board of *Cineaste*, and has contributed to various journals including *Persistence of Vision*, *Film Quarterly*, *Iris* and *Millennium Film Journal*. He is currently completing a dissertation on the relationship between film and anarchism at New York University.

Martin Quinn-Meyler is currently completing his doctorate in cultural anthropology at the New School for Social Research, and teaches popular culture studies at Parson's School of Design. His current research examines the influence of contemporary American film on the formation of queer subcultures in urban Italy.